The Emergence of China

ANCIENT CHINA IN CONTEXT

Ancient China in Context

立政篇

The Emergence of China

From Confucius to the Empire

E Bruce Brooks

A Taeko Brooks

Warring States Project

University of Massachusetts at Amherst

2015

The Emergence of China

ISBN 978-1-936166-35-0 *cloth,* 75-6 *paper,* 95-4 *ebook*

Copyright © 2015 by E Bruce Brooks and A Taeko Brooks
All rights reserved

LCCN 2015930277

The cover illustration is a detail from a photograph by "Nuria" of some of the terracotta soldiers from the tomb of the First Emperor of the Chín Dynasty; used by permission . Illustrations within the book are from fragments of the Hàn Stone Classics, engraved between 175 and 183 from an original by Tsàı Yūng 蔡邕 (133-192) and here adapted from reproductions in 馬衡, 漢石經集存 (1957), and from other inscriptions or photographs of ancient objects.

PRINTED IN THE UNITED STATES OF AMERICA

To

Frederick W "Fritz" Mote

2 June 1922 – 10 February 2005

Preface

If one had to summarize the history of China in two words, what would the two words be? Our answer is: "It changes."

China's classical period has two phases. Following the 0771 collapse of Jōu, the former feudatories of Jōu, now merely a collection of palace states, fought each other during the three centuries traditionally called "Spring and Autumn."[1] In the following "Warring States" period, the 05c to the late 03c, the larger of them remade themselves into bureaucratic resource states, shifted from elite chariot forces to mass infantry armies, and at last fought their war to a finish.[2] The result, achieved in 0221, was a unified state under the rule of ruthless Chín. This state, or Empire, we may for the first time properly call "China."[3]

This Warring States transition is one of the major events in world history. It is little known outside Sinology, and it is misrepresented *within* Sinology by the legends which were being woven around it even as it happened – new tracts put out as ancient texts, new wisdom attributed to ancient sages – all to confer an ancient pedigree on the new ideas which the effort of the time required.

It has been suggested that our studies of the date and nature of the classical texts could be drawn on to make the Warring States transition more available to modern readers. The present book is the result. Ancient China is much less amply documented than, say, ancient Greece. From that modest material, only a small sample can be included here. We offer the book nevertheless, as a set of readings that is philosophically more diverse than usual, with a commentary giving our best sense of their context and importance. For the historically minded reader, we have sometimes hinted at wider perspectives by noticing parallel situations in ancient and modern times.

The current world is not our subject, but worlds are best understood in terms of the past out of which they come. There may thus be contemporary relevance in a book like this one, which aims to present classical China in its own voice: as nearly as possible, within the limits of present knowledge and present space, "as it really was."

---

[1]The name derives from the Chūn/Chyōu 春秋, the court chronicle of Confucius's state of Lǔ. As preserved, it covers the years from 0722 to an uncanny event in 0481.

[2]Specialists disagree on where "Warring States" begins. We find 0479 (the death of Confucius) convenient, but elements of the Warring States transition are already visible decades earlier: Confucius himself was a key transitional figure. Our chapters are subdivided by BC centuries, which match the realities moderately well. For the lack of a comparable transformation in classical Greece, see Brooks and Lombardi **Peace**.

[3]We use the term "Sinitic" for the Chinese peoples before the Empire. It will appear in the following pages that non-Sinitic states and peoples also made a contribution.

Conventions. Keyword citations are expanded in the Works Cited section at the end of the book. "0312" is "312 BC," a universal convention that works also in French and German, as the well-intentioned "BCE" does not; "04th century" may be abbreviated as "04c" and so on. "Circa" dates (such as c0348) are best-guess positions within a system of relative dates. Chinese words are spelled in the Common Alphabetic system, which has been designed to be less misleading for beginners than other systems; it has the further advantage that it is compatible with the universally used Hepburn system for Japanese. It follows the formula "consonants as in English, vowels as in Italian," plus these conventions for vowels with no fixed English spelling: -æ as in "cat," -v [compare the linguist's inverted ʌ] as in "gut," -r as in "fur," -z as in "adz," -yw (after l or n, simply -w) for "umlaut u." Tones are hīgh, rísing, lǒw, fàlling. A table comparing CA and two other systems is given at p239. Pronunciations are modern standard Chinese, but initial ng- has been restored to distinguish the states Wèı 衛 and Ngwèı 魏, both now pronounced "Wèı." Note also the early *state* of Hán 韓 (rising tone, as in a question) and the later Hàn 漢 *Dynasty* (falling tone, as in an exclamation).

Acknowledgements. We are grateful to Don and Loretta Gibbs and to the Mercer Trust for financial assistance along the way, and for initial technical help to our colleagues at the University of Massachusetts Press. Several teachers and students reported on classroom trials of early drafts of the book: Sigrid Schmalzer (University of Massachusetts at Amherst); Paul Ropp, Mike Andres, Greg Houghton, and Matt Valko (Clark); and Stephen C Angle (Wesleyan). Others, here thanked collectively, also made helpful suggestions. The final responsibility for our conclusions remains our own.

Dedication. For all its obvious differences, several of our consultants did pick up a certain resemblance between this book and F W Mote's standard Intellectual Foundations of China. Fritz knew we meant to write a book like this, and he approved. He thought well of our researches on the classical texts, and felt that one day our work, such as it might prove to be, would replace his. He was a very generous man. This book is dedicated to him.

E Bruce Brooks
A Taeko Brooks

14 September 2014

Contents

Introduction

This Introduction supplements the Preface by giving information about the intent and arrangement of the book, and noting some difficulties with which any student of the Chinese classical period must somehow cope.

Audience. In books like this, there is a temptation to make the facts few and the translations easy. This we have resisted, by somewhat respecting the actual complexity of the period (the rival viewpoints were more than three), and by leaving intact some of its courtesies (one addresses a ruler in the third person). We have also shunned "relevance:" the ancient texts were not talking to us, they were arguing with each other. In these ways, we have sought to preserve the pastness of the past, rather than adjust it to the predilections of the present. We entirely agree with the colleague who announces on the first day of class, "This course is not about you; it's about China."

Schools. The arguments of rival viewpoints make up much of the classical literature (we have little information about political events as such). Many texts are advocacy tracts, put out by groups or "schools," in the sense of "schools of thought." Major schools were: (1) the Legalists or theorists of state, the ones who really made the Empire; (2) the Confucians, who derived from the warrior class but later focused on ritual, renounced war, and lost influence; (3) the socially lower Micians, followers of Mwò Dí or Mwòdž ("Master Mwò"), who at first opposed war; and (4) the Dàuists, who taught a technique of breath control and inner cultivation, but also made a contribution to political theory. As with modern political parties, each "school" included a range of viewpoints, and those viewpoints could change over time, in response to new conditions.

For clarity, we introduce each new source text with a box containing basic information, and identify each translation with its source text. Translated passages are numbered within a chapter (**4:5** is the 5th passage in Chapter 4) for easy cross-reference. An index to translated passages begins on page 247.

States. The Jōu Dynasty fell in 0771. Its kings relocated to a small central domain; its former fiefs emerged as rival states. The chief ones (see the map on page 21) were Chín in the west, in the old Jōu domain; Chí in the east, with Yēn north of it and Confucius's Lǔ south of it; and Jìn in the center; Jìn later split into Jàu, Hán, and Ngwèi. Southern Chǔ was the chief non-Sinitic state. Some key dates in the history of the period are given on page 237.

Society. The texts have a narrow social range. They come from the upper strata of society: those taking part *in* the government or recommending policy *to* the government. They are propagandist rather than documentary in nature. And before we can even read them in chronological order, to see what issues they reflect or what changes they imply, the texts themselves must be dated.

Dating the Texts is not a simple proposition. Many "texts" are the files of an advocacy group, and include tracts written at different times. Some groups had a long life: the Gwǎndž Legalists began in the 04c and were still writing in the 02c. In this culture, ancient precedent was valued, and texts claimed to be earlier than they were: the Gwǎndž is named for an 07c statesman, Gwǎn Jùng, who lived long before the Gwǎndž text had begun to be written. To older texts, new material was often added, to create ancient credentials for modern ideas.

The work of sorting out this confusion has barely begun. The traditional view of the period (embodied in the Dzwǒ Jwàn, itself a Warring States text, and the Hàn Dynasty texts Jàn-gwó Tsv̀ and Shř Jì) is still reflected in books which readers of this book will encounter. What to believe? The answer is a question of method. Scattered among our eight chapters are glances into the workshop, under the rubric **Methodological Moment**, which will give an idea of the kind of arguments philologists and historians use. These we recommend. For clarity, the end of each Moment is marked by a spacer:

————————•••••————————

Chapters. Chapter 1 is introductory: the situation that preceded the Warring States proper. Chapter 8 gives the final outcome: the unified Chín Empire.

In between, in Chapters 2-7, comes China's high classical age, the Warring States period, seen from six aspects, each in its own chronologically arranged chapter. Together, they give a multi-faceted sense of the state modernization process, the background fact against which everything else takes its place. For the convenience of those readers who, whether as a school assignment or out of a special interest, are following one chapter without the preceding one, some persons and events are first-identified more than once. Otherwise, see the Subject Index. Footnotes suggesting further reading may be ignored as desired. At the back of the book are aids for getting an overview of the material: major events, a text chronology, a romanization table, and lists of works cited, passages translated, and subjects treated. We do not give Chinese text for translated passages (see the other books in this series), but characters are useful. To memorize those we do give, write them; to write them, see Bjorksten.

At The End, readers will have met some of the texts which represent the classical period, as part of the heritage of China and the global modern world. The selections include many literary and philosophical favorites, but also excerpts from the military and statecraft writings, which best show how the states grew strong and the wars were won. It is, we feel, against that realistic background, at once harsh and pedestrian, that the more philosophical pieces can best tell their part of the story.

Here, then, is China – a distant and in many ways an unfamiliar China, glimpsed in the process of becoming the China that we know.

The Emergence of China

1. Antiquity

This is a story of world conquest.

The world in question was the Yellow River valley; the home of the Sinitic peoples.[1] Through war and cultural assimilation, that world gradually expanded to the Yángdž River, the homeland of another distinctive culture.[2] Both rivers flow eastward to the sea, and the coastal peoples constituted a third culture.[3] The unification process would eventually include all of them.

1. Shāng and Jōu

China's classical age is a long period of political fragmentation, from the fall of Jōu in 0771 to the reunification under Chín in 0221. Before Jōu, the classical thinkers were aware of two earlier unified dynasties: Syà and Shāng.

Syà

Syà 夏 is something of a mystery. Information about it from later tradition consists chiefly of two names: (1) its virtuous first ruler Yǔ 禹, who is reported to have drained away the great floodwaters and carved out the river valleys, and (2) its monstrously depraved last ruler Jyé 傑, who lost the approval of Heaven.

---

[1] We regularly use "Sinitic" in preference to "Chinese." The latter word derives from the state of Chín 秦, and does not strictly apply until the Chín unification of 0221.

[2] The non-Sinitic languages of this area include Kadai (Thai), Myáu-Yáu (now "Hmong-Mien"), and Austro-Asiatic (Vietnamese). See Ramsey **Languages**.

[3] For a detailed study of this distinctive early culture, see Luo **Coastal**.

Methodological Moment. The hero who accomplishes a superhuman task, such as draining floodwaters, is a theme (topos) found in many traditions; the Bad Last Ruler is a favorite *Chinese* topos. When all we hear about a dynasty is topoi good or bad, we may reasonably suspect the historicity of that dynasty.[4]

------------··•··------------

Shāng

Shāng 商 is best known to us through the "oracle bone" inscriptions discovered in the late 19c. A bone or shell is heated, and the resulting cracks are interpreted as a short-term prediction, in answer to a question of this kind: Will that campaign prosper? Will this sacrifice be accepted? Will rain fall?[5]

The kings to whom Shāng sacrificed can be reconstructed from these texts. First come 6 predynastic rulers, then 28 kings proper, from Tāng 湯 the founder (sacrificial name Dà Yī 大乙)[6] to Jòu 紂 (Dì Syīn 帝辛), later mythologized as a Bad Last Ruler. Shāng kings mentioned in classical-period writings include:

1. Tāng 湯	(Dà Yī 大乙)	
12.	(Dzǔ Yī 祖乙)	
18.	(Pán Gvng 盤庚)	
21.	(Wǔ Dīng 武丁)	reigned c01200-01181[7]
23.	(Dzǔ Jyǎ 祖甲)	c01170-01151
27.	(Dì Yī 帝乙)	c01090-01071
28. Jòu 紂	(Dì Syīn 帝辛)	c01070-01041

The remembered predynastic *rulers* imply a predynastic *period*, but what previous power Shāng at one point conquered, the bone texts do not tell us.

Several western techniques appeared via Central Eurasia. Bronze appeared early; the chariot later.[8] Shāng chariot burials are also Indo-European in style.[9] Writing, possibly inspired by Near Eastern models, also appears at this time.[10]

---

[4]So also, after examining the archaeological evidence, Thorp **China** 61. *Something* preceded Shāng, but that the Chinese political myths applied to it is doubtful.

[5]The answer is inscribed on the same bone. See further Keightley **Landscape**.

[6]The second elements in these names are from a cycle of ten day names. These were combined with a second series of twelve to produce a cycle of 60 days; see #**1:1** below.

[7]Estimated from average reign lengths (Keightley **Sources** 171-176 and 228).

[8]Chariots appeared in India in c01600, in early Shāng (Drews **Coming** 62f), but in China in *late* Shāng (Thorp **China** 171). This was not the expansion of a winning culture, but the exit of an obsolete one: Near Eastern chariot warfare had been refuted in c01200 by a new javelin technique (Drews **End** 174f). The Western origin of the chariot is obvious: the Sinitic word for "horse" (mǎ 馬) is Indo-European (compare Old High German "marah," English "mare." For chariot terms, see Lubotsky **Tocharian**.

[9]Beckwith **Empires** 12f and 43-45.

[10]That is, not earlier than Wǔ Dīng (Keightley **Sources** 139 and 97 n23).

The inscriptions on the Shāng oracle bones are concerned with weather and the harvest, but they do not tell us about other aspects of land tenure or resource management.[11] There is no evidence for law codes or legal procedures.[12]

Shāng warfare used a non-chariot "mass" (jùng 眾)[13] along with the newly introduced chariot. Campaigns could be long. Many were against enemies in the northwest (such as the Gwěi-fāng 鬼方 "Demon region") and the southeast (such as the Rýn-fāng 人方 "Man region"). The Shāng enemies in the north and west also possessed the war chariot; Shāng did not have a complete monopoly. Indeed, the last Shāng kings *lost* territory in the northwest;[14] at the same time, they were exhausted by the effort of continuing military action in the southeast. Shāng was eventually conquered by the Jōu, one of the northwestern peoples.

Jōu

The conqueror of Shāng was Wǔ-wáng 武王 or King Wǔ. Like the Shāng, the **Jōu** 周 also recognized predynastic rulers, the most important of whom was Wǔ-wáng's father, Wýn-wáng 文王 or King Wýn. The epithets Wýn "civil" and Wǔ "military" became a standard opposition in classical political theory, which held that Wýn-wáng by his virtue had gained the approval of Heaven, and that Wǔ-wáng had merely realized that approval by his actual conquest.[15]

After the conquest, in c01040, most land was assigned as fiefs to relatives of the Jōu King and others who had aided the conquest, or were willing to collaborate afterward.[16] Their loyalty was doubtful, and control was a problem: the Jōu homeland lay in the west, whereas the newly conquered territory was in the east. The city of Chýng Jōu 成周 was established on the Lwò River,[17] in the middle Yellow River plain, to coordinate security operations in the east. From that center, eight "Yīn" armies could be summoned to deal with unrest in the former Yīn (or Shāng) territory.[18] Six "western" armies were similarly administered from the Jōu capital in the west.[19]

---

[11] An important early Shāng economic transition is argued in Liu **State**.

[12] David N Keightley, personal communication, 2009.

[13] Of not more than 100 men. David N Keightley, personal communication, 2010.

[14] Keightley **Shang** 288f.

[15] This is the "Mandate of Heaven" (Tyēn-mìng 天命) theory. In Jōu, the phrase meant a charge from the Jōu ancestors. Later ages conceived of a supradynastic Heaven presiding over transitions in general. The roles of Wýn-wáng and Wǔ-wáng in the actual Jōu conquest would undergo a profound change in 04c theory; see #**3:11-12.**

[16] For two enfiefment documents, see Shaughnessy **Sources** 318f.

[17] Near to modern Lwò-yáng 洛陽; the name probably means "City 城 of Jōu."

[18] It is militarily unlikely that these were Shāng troops serving the Jōu conquerors.

[19] Creel **Origins** 305f. It is economically unlikely that these were "standing armies."

Long after the first distribution of conquered land, a Jōu warrior might win recognition for military exploits, as we see from inscriptions like this one . . .

. . . which records a gift presented by Mù-wáng, the fifth Jōu King, to the warrior Chyóu Wèi 裘衛. The ceremony went as follows:

> **1:1** (Chyóu Wèi Gwěi, c0960). It was the King's 27th year, third month, after the full moon, on [the cyclical day] wù/syw 戊戌 (#35).[20] [The King] was at Jōu, and took his place in the great hall. Nán-bwó came in on the right. Chyóu Wèi entered the main gate and stood in the center of the court, facing north.[21] The King called the Palace Astrologer[22] to present to Wèi purple knee covers, a red jade ring, and a [harness] bell.[23] Wèi bowed and touched his head to the ground; he ventured in response to praise the Son of Heaven's[24] great munificence. He then made for his accomplished ancestor and his father this precious gwěi vessel. May his sons' sons and grandsons' grandsons forever treasure and use it.[25]

That is, his service to Jōu has enriched his own ancestral observances.

---

[20]We will translate future "cyclical day" dates simply by the number in the cycle.

[21]On these formal occasions, the ruler always faced south.

[22]The nèi-shř 內史, here "palace astrologer," had charge of omens and portents, including lucky days; it thus fell to him to keep records of these presentations.

[23]Gifts on these occasions are of military character; Shaughnessy **Sources** 82f.

[24]The king is the "Son of Heaven" because his ancestors, the former kings, are now spirits in Heaven, whence they can send aid and blessings if they are fed by sacrifices.

[25]In sacrificing to the spirit of Wèi's father.

Land. A gift to a warrior might include land, in which case the warrior joined the ranks of the older vassals or local lords. In return for land, the local lord with his own circle of warriors owed military service to Jōu.[26]

State Structure. Another inscription records the bestowing on Chyóu Wèi of the position of sż-mǎ 司馬 or "marshal," the one responsible for horses and presumably other resources of war. The existence of named offices marks Jōu as having taken some steps toward bureaucracy. Shāng, before it, had had some named offices, such as sż-chvng 司城, the one responsible for fortifications.

War. About Shāng we cannot be sure, but the Jōu chariot warrior had lifelong training in the difficult arts of driving a two-horse war chariot and shooting from it with the powerful compound bow of the period. Such warriors could be assembled at need to form a campaign force. The chariot horse needed long nurture and preparation; an 014c Ancient Near Eastern manual spells out a 7-month regimen for training a war horse.[27] Land was needed too: 10 acres of good grain land were required to feed the basic team of two horses.[28] Chariots were accompanied in battle by a complement of foot soldiers, perhaps on average ten per chariot; the only Jōu inscription to specify chariot numbers mentions 100 chariots (and 1,000 foot troops) under a subcommander.[29] A great vassal's whole force might have consisted of 300 chariots plus their infantry. The total force available at Chvng Jōu would then have been eight armies of that size, which could be called together when a military emergency arose.

Economy. The basic economy was agricultural. Cowry shells served as money for certain local purposes. Long-distance acquisition of materials such as copper for bronze casting was probably in the form of tribute rendered by the King's vassals, or by gift-exchange with the less formally dominated territories. For trade as we know it in later times, there is no firm evidence.

Law. There were no law codes or standard legal procedures in Jōu times. Inscriptions tell us that the Jōu King adjudicated land disputes among his vassals; this is unsurprising since he had bestowed the land in the first place.[30] In his own domain, the Jōu King punished his subjects (by death or mutilation) as he saw fit. The vassals, within *their* domains, probably did the same.

---

[26]This land-for-service feature is typical of feudal situations. For the pattern, see Beckwith **Empires** 13-18, Stephenson **Feudalism** 2-8, Reynolds **Europe** 164). The troubles with the term "feudalism" come from taking mediaeval France as standard, or making "feudal" a stage in a fixed developmental sequence (see rather Strayer **Idea**).

[27]For the 014c manual of Kikkuli, see Drews **Coming** 90f. The chariot itself, and chariot warfare, are much better documented in their homeland, the Ancient Near East.

[28]Piggott **Horse** 27.

[29]Creel **Origins** 276.

[30]See Skosey **Legal**, but ignore those conclusions that are based on Shū documents.

Feudal Tenure. Conferral of land in the Jōu system was to a person, and technically lapsed at the death of that person. His son would typically inherit, but a formal renewal was customary. In Lǔ, whose ties to Jōu were close (it had been the fief of the esteemed regent Jōu-gūng), that formality was observed even after the end of Jōu power in 0771. In the court chronicle of Lǔ:

> **Chūn/Chyōu** 春秋 "Spring and Autumn" (CC). A Lǔ court chronicle covering the span 0722-0481; the only extensive contemporary source for Lǔ and other states in that period. Translated by Legge.

there are three relevant entries. Here are two of them:

> **1:2** (CC 3/1:6, 0693). The King sent Rúng Shú to confer the Mandate of [the late] Hwán-gūng 桓公命.

Hwán-gūng died in 0694, and was then given the sacrificial name "Hwán." Now, a year later, his mandate from Jōu to rule Lǔ is transferred to his son.[31]

> **1:3** (CC 6/1:5, 0626). The King under Heaven sent the Elder Máu to confer the princely Mandate 公命.

The eighth Lǔ Prince was also recognized by Jōu. The others were in some way (such as being the son of a concubine) not technically entitled to inherit.[32]

The Jōu King was stronger than any of his local lords, and could call on one for aid against another. He could thus *dominate* an area that he was not strong enough to *conquer*. This is the key to many indirect-sovereignty arrangements. Eventually, one Jōu King (Yōu-wáng 幽王) was no longer strong enough to play that role. In 0771, his capital was attacked by a non-Sinitic tribe, and no vassal came to his aid. His successor Píng-wáng moved in 0770 to the eastern capital Chv́ng Jōu, where he and his powerless successors reigned in a merely ceremonial way, until the Jōu line of Kings was finally extinguished in 0249.

Spring and Autumn

This period, from 0770 to the death of Confucius in 0479,[33] is the background for the Warring States. It was a sovereignty vacuum: the Jōu feudal system without an effective head. A multi-state system, but one which, unlike the classical Greek states, had a defining memory of an earlier political unity.[34]

---

[31] We follow the convention of referring to rulers by their posthumous names, but note that these names were assigned at burial, and were not known previously.

[32] For details of this process in Spring and Autumn Lǔ, see Brooks **Enfiefment**.

[33] Some scholars date the end of Spring and Autumn (and the beginning of Warring States) as late as 0403, a fact which causes needless but now unavoidable confusion.

[34] Contrast the merely cultural "Hellenism" of the Greek states; see Finley **Greeks**. For several acephalous situations of different origin, see Reynolds **Europe** 221f.

Chín occupied the old Jōu homeland, with Jōu itself displaced to its eastern capital in the middle Yellow River area. The most powerful Spring and Autumn states were Jìn in the center, Chí in the east (Confucius' Lǔ, a second-rank state, was on the other side of the Tài-shān mountains), and non-Sinitic Chǔ (in early Spring and Autumn, called Jīng) in the south.

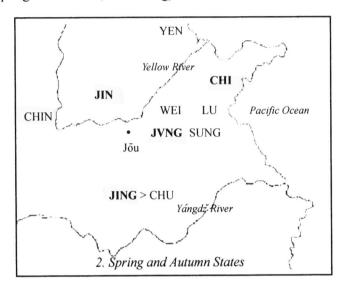

2. *Spring and Autumn States*

Rulership was hereditary.[35] Sacrifices to the ruler's ancestors were thought to secure protection for the state, but only a descendant could offer them. Succession disputes thus centered around sons or brothers of the ruler. When Chí Hwán-gūng[36] died in 0643, two of his sons contended for the succession, one with military support from Sùng, and another backed by Lǔ. The Sùng force defeated a Chí force acting for the candidate who was supported by Lǔ. A rescue operation by Lǔ failed to dislodge the Sùng candidate, who did become the next ruler; he was posthumously known as Chí Syàu-gūng. This led to a certain diplomatic coolness between Chí under Syàu-gūng and Lǔ.

The State was personal; there was no major function that the ruler did not himself perform. Military and diplomatic tasks might be delegated, but only to a kinsman or a noble, and only for the duration of that campaign or mission. There were few named functions and no permanent delegation of responsibility, such as had existed in Shāng and Jōu. Sùng (the successor to Shāng) and the Jōu domain alone preserved such official titles, inherited from earlier times.

---

[35] And in the male line. The female rulers who took their states with them when they married, thus complicating European history, have no counterpart in classical China.

[36] Ruler titles in descending order are gūng 公 "Prince," hóu 侯 "Lord," bwó 伯 "Elder," dž 子 "Master," and nán 男 "Leader." A general term is jywn 君 "ruler."

Examples are dzǎı 宰 "steward," attested for Jōu in 0722, 0708, 0651, and 0630 (when he served as a diplomat), and in Sùng, sz̄-chv́ng 司城 (which is found in Shāng bone inscriptions) and sz̄-mǎ 司馬 (found also in Jōu bronze inscriptions). The Lǔ chronicler probably learned these titles from diplomatic contacts, and the rest of the official structures of Jōu and Sùng are hidden from us. In Lǔ, where our information is fuller, no permanently delegated functions are mentioned, though some are likely. The chronicle keeper himself, who also looked after the calendar, was probably one, though naturally his title is not given in the chronicle itself; later ages called it shř 史 "astrologer."[37]

One functional title which does appear in the second half of Spring and Autumn is diplomatic in nature: the syíng-rv́n 行人, literally "journeyman," which we will translate as "envoy." It first appears in the Lǔ chronicle in 0562 (an envoy from Jv̀ng, seized by Chǔ); then in 0555 (from Wèı, seized by Jìn), 0534 (from Chv́n, seized and killed by Chǔ), 0504 (from Sùng, seized by Jìn), and 0503 (from Wèı, seized by Chí, which then went on to invade Wèı). Envoys from Lǔ, who are named but not called syíng-rv́n, were seized in 0575 (by Jìn) and 0529 (again by Jìn). Finally in 0519 we have the function title:

1:4 (CC 10/23:3, 0519). A man of Jìn 晉人 seized *our envoy* Shúsūn Shv̀.

It seems the term syíng-rv́n was first used in Lǔ between 0529 and 0519, or a generation after Lǔ records its use by other states. A named function need not imply that the function was permanently delegated. It seems that Sùng and the Jōu remnant (the former Jōu and Shāng dynasties) were *residually* bureaucratic, and the others were at most, and only toward the end of Spring and Autumn, *incipiently* bureaucratic, with Lǔ lagging behind the rest.

Social Structure. A son of a ruler who did not succeed that ruler could form a collateral lineage, and such lineages could become powerful. The classic case is the Three Hwán Clans, founded by sons of Lǔ Hwán-gūng, and from their birth order called Jùngsūn 仲孫 or "Second," Shúsūn 叔孫 "Younger," and Jìsūn 季孫 "Youngest." They were given land in strategic locations on the borders, and later fortified them, becoming almost rival states within Lǔ. They came to exercise most military and diplomatic functions; the great drama of Lǔ politics in the 06th century was the effort to reclaim power from the Three Clans. A failed attempt of this kind probably led to Jāu-gūng's exile in 0517. These challenges apart, the doings of the ruler and his family bulk less large in the late Lǔ chronicle than previously. The initial reluctance of the keepers of the Lǔ chronicle to record names of non-noble persons from other states (they appear in the record as 晉人 "a man [an officer] of Jìn," as in the above entry) gradually waned, and non-noble persons were increasingly mentioned by name.

---

[37]The sense "historian" arose only in the 04c. Astrologers did keep *omen* records, and the Chūn/Chyōu chronicle itself may be seen as a developed form of omen record.

The Supernatural. Much space in the Lǔ chronicle is given to things about which supernatural guidance might have been sought. As in Shāng times, these included sacrifices and intended military campaigns, but now also meetings, which might end with a covenant solemnized by an oath. As in Shāng, supernatural displeasure was thought to be indicated by uncanny occurrences, including eclipses, which are presumably recorded in the CC for that reason. Eclipses, and natural disasters such as floods, received in Lǔ what we can only call a primitive response:

1:5 (CC 3/25:3, 0669). 6th month, day #8, new moon. Sun had something eating it.[38] Drummed and made sacrifices at the altar of the soil.

1:6 (CC 3/25:5, 0669). Autumn. Great floods. Drummed and made sacrifices at the altar of the soil and at the gates.

1:7 (CC 3/30:5, 0664). 8th month, day #20, new moon. Sun had something eating it. Drummed and made sacrifices at the altar of the soil.

1:8 (CC 6/15:5, 0612). 6th month, day #38, new moon. Sun had something eating it. Drummed and made sacrifices at the altar of the soil.

The drumming and the sacrifices were evidently meant to ward off disasters, or further disasters, which might otherwise follow. Weird events such as birds flying backward or nesting out of season were also considered to be ominous. The omens recorded in the Chūn/Chyōu are indeed often followed by disasters: the birds flying backward (in 0644) by deaths in the Lǔ ruler's family; the birds nesting unseasonably by the exile of the Lǔ ruler Jāu-gūng (in 0517). Jāu-gūng found his "nest" not in his own capital, but far away on the border with Chí.

These state superstitions are much like those recorded by Shāng diviners; they are still recognizable in the duties of the Hàn "Grand Astrologer."[39] They amounted to a cult of appeasement, centering on the ruler's ancestors, and having no points of contact with the beliefs of the people (which centered on tutelary deities of the field, or the gods of the gate and house). Nor did the ancestral observances of the elite have points in common *with each other:* ancestors are specific to a lineage, and only a member of that lineage could sacrifice to them.[40] The many supernatural observances in early China were thus not a common religion. They tended to divide, and not to unite. Only in the late 04c was a more inclusive ground of belief discovered. Its basis was no supernatural entity, but Sinitic culture, and the state as embodying that culture. The religion of China, when it finally emerged, was precisely China.

---

[38]日有食之. This conventional idiom is usually and correctly translated as "the sun was eclipsed," but in these cases, the literal sense of being "eaten" is relevant.

[39]The Hàn title is Tài-shř 太史. For Shāng, see Keightley **Landscape** 118f.

[40]Whereas any Greek visiting the oracle at Delphi (and even some non-Greeks, such as Gyges of Lydia or Midas of Phrygia) could and did sacrifice or dedicate to Apollo, and this fact was openly acknowledged as a source of Greek cultural unity.

War was waged by an elite chariot force, which in the chronicle is called shr̄ 師, "the host." The force available to the strongest states was about 600 chariots at the beginning of the period, and about 1000 chariots by the end.[41] The warriors themselves hoped to win personal honor in battle,[42] but there were few battles: most military actions were unopposed raids. They were ordered by the ruler not for military glory, but for political advantage. This cost-accounting view of war included a concern to minimize casualties (the replacement rate for hereditary warriors was slow) and to maximize gains, whether territorial or political. Concern for tactical frugality led to an emphasis on rapid movement: striking before the other side had time to call together a defensive force.

Much that is otherwise puzzling about Spring and Autumn warfare is explained by the small size of the forces. When dispersed, the warriors on their landholdings were self-supporting, and gave some local protection. At need, they could be assembled into a strike force. That potential force honed its skills in musters and group hunts, which are recorded in the CC in 0706 and (under a different name) in 0534, 0531, 0520, 0497, and 0496. Once it was assembled, the host could move rapidly because of its small size; its forage needs were readily met by local gathering, and the force could travel light.[43]

Even a small force entering another state's territory had local superiority until the invaded state could assemble a counterforce. Small states in this way could sometimes make territorial gains at the expense of larger neighbors. But once a force had left on campaign, the home state was largely unprotected; there was no second army. The ways to relieve a besieged city were thus two: attack the besiegers or threaten their home state, thus forcing their withdrawal. Both these methods were used throughout the period.

Láng. Some Lǔ rulers were pretty good at their primary job of leading the host. In 0714, Lǔ had walled Láng 郎, a town within the Sùng zone of interest. In 0684, forces from Chí and Sùng camped at Láng. But before they could combine for an attack, Jwāng-gūng, commanding the Lǔ force, attacked and defeated the Chí force, the more dangerous of the two, at Shv̀ng-chyōu, just north of Láng. There were no further challenges to the Lǔ occupation of Láng.

Enemies. The Sinitic states had each other as their primary enemies. There were also the non-Sinitic states and tribes. The smaller ones were gradually eliminated; the larger ones like Chǔ (or their ruling elites) were culturally assimilated. By the end of Spring and Autumn, it was thus possible to envision the world as a Sinitic center surrounded by a hostile non-Sinitic periphery. This is how things were seen in Warring States times, and for long afterward.

---

[41]For the argument, which is indirect, see Brooks **Numbers**.

[42]For the warrior psychology see Brooks **Defeat**.

[43]See further Brooks **Capacity**.

The Economy remained agricultural. There is no hint in the court chronicle of any interest in trade. The Lǔ court was concerned for the harvest and for threats to the harvest, such as locusts and droughts. Forest was steadily cleared for cultivation. Yield was increased by planting two crops a year in the same field (first implied in an entry of 0687) and by introducing new and efficient crops such as the soybean (first mentioned in 0505).

The basic wealth of the Spring and Autumn states was thus in grain, and grain was stored by the state as a hedge against famine. On two occasions, grain was transferred between states for famine relief:

1:9 (CC 3/28:5, 0666). Great lack of wheat and grain. Dzāngsūn Chv́n asked permission to buy (dí 糴) from Chí.

1:10 (CC 11/5:2, 0505). Summer. Sent (gwēi 歸) millet to Tsài.

These interstate transactions show that states had considerable storage capacity, as well as substantial transport capacity, for food supplies.

Law. There was no organization above the state, save the weak Jōu Kings. There were no law codes. No judicial functions were exercised by the states, save for a ruler's imposing the traditional punishments. Those of high rank were not exempt from punishment; rather, they were especially vulnerable. Here are two examples. In 0632, Lǔ was supporting a pro-Chǔ faction in Wèi:

1:11 (CC 5/28:1-2, 0632).
• 28th year, spring: The Lord of Jìn made an incursion into Tsáu. The Lord of Jìn attacked Wèi.
• Gūngdž Mǎı 買 was to guard Wèi. He did not in the end succeed in guarding it 不卒戍. Executed him 刺之.

Mǎı was a son of Jwāng-gūng, and thus a brother of the current Lǔ ruler. That intimate relationship did not save him when it came to military responsibility.

Later that year, Chǔ killed the general who lost the battle of Chv́ng-pú:

1:12 (CC 5/28:5-6, 0632).
• Summer, 4th month, day jǐ/sż (#6). The Lord of Jìn and the armies of Chí, Sùng, and Chín fought with a man of Chǔ at Chv́ng-pú. The host of Chǔ was defeated.
• Chǔ killed its senior officer Dv́-chv́n.[44]

The Locus of Guilt. In the second entry, it is "Chǔ" that kills the failed army leader. Sometimes the head of state is said to act personally:

1:13 (CC 9/26:6, 0547). Autumn. The Prince of Sùng killed his heir Dzwó.

---

[44]The "man" leading the army in the previous entry is this same Chǔ noble Dv́-chv́n, whose noble status did not protect him.

Later lore has it that the heir was plotting to kill his father. As a mere intention, this was personal: there had been no crime *against the state*. But the damage done by the unsuccessful Chǔ military leader *was* to the state, and the state is recorded as killing him. It seems that these CC entries are reflecting a perceived difference in the nature of the offense. That difference suggests that there were moments when the ruler was not *entirely* identical with the state.[45]

If death was the penalty for defeat in battle, what happened if the *ruler* led the defeated host? The answer is: Nothing. CC entries for such defeats are in the passive voice, thus, grammatically, the leader did not need to be named.[46] No ruler was ever put to death after leading an unsuccessful military campaign. But for the failures of other high persons, military tradition prescribed death.

Methodological Moment. Consider dàu 盜 (usually "robber") in the CC:

1:14 (CC 11/8:16, 0502). A robber 盜 stole the precious jade and the great bow.

1:15 (CC 11/9:3, 0501). Recovered the precious jade and the great bow.

The miscreant was undoubtedly known to the court. He is called a robber, which in this case seems accurate. But other CC entries using that word . . .

1:16 (CC 9/10:8, 0563). Winter. A dàu killed Gūngdž Fēi, Gūngdž Fā, and Gūngsūn Chv̀ of Chv́n.

1:17 (CC 10/20:3, 0522). Autumn. A dàu killed Jŕ, the elder brother of the Lord of Wèi.

1:18 (CC 12/4:1, 0491). 4th Year, Spring, 2nd month, day #47. A dàu killed Shv̄n, the Lord of Tsài.

1:19 (CC 12/13:11, 0482). A dàu killed Syà Kōu-fŭ of Chv́n.

. . . imply not robbery, but political assassination. Then probably the person who took the Lǔ state regalia in #**1:14** was also involved in a plot concerning the rulership of Lǔ. The translation "robber," which is normal in other contexts, does not fit here. The sense of the term in CC is something nearer to "thug."

Dàu in the CC is a descriptor replacing a personal name. It occurs only in the last four reigns covered by the CC. This is also the range of the functional term sýing-rv́n 行人 "envoy" in the CC. Together, they suggest a trend toward functional terminology: names for government tasks or government problems.

In such details, the tendency of ancient thinking can sometimes be detected.

—————————··•··—————————

[45]For other intricacies of Spring and Autumn word usage as reflected in the Lǔ chronicle, see Defoort **Words** and Brooks **Distancing**.

[46]See Brooks **Defeat**.

Law Between States did not exist.[47] Obligations between rulers were in the form of covenants (mvng 盟), solemnized by oaths and typically about joint military action. Longer term agreements were personal. They might be renewed at the death of one party, but no agreement obligated the state. And no authority *above* the state, save the gods if any, existed to punish violations of covenant.

We now take up the two most famous Spring and Autumn rulers, who had key roles in northern resistance to the threat of southern and non-Sinitic Chŭ. The beginning and the end of that threat together define the middle period of Spring and Autumn history.

CHI HWAN-GUNG

Chí Hwán-gūng 齊桓公 (r 0684-0643) was the first Spring and Autumn ruler to exercise leadership among the northern states, in response to the aggressions of Jīng 荊 (later called Chŭ 楚), the non-Sinitic state in the south. The chief focus of contention was Jvng 鄭, located near the Jōu domain. South of Jvng was Chŭ, with level land, suitable for chariots, between them.

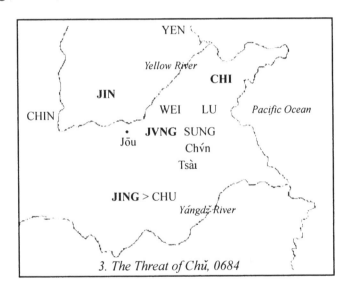

3. *The Threat of Chŭ, 0684*

Chŭ moved first against Tsài; it defeated Tsài in 0684 and carried the Tsài ruler back to Chŭ.[48] Chŭ again took its forces into the capital of Tsài in 0680. The right flank of Chŭ was now presumably secured for an advance on Jvng.

---

[47]The League of Nations was founded in part on misconceptions about the system of the Spring and Autumn states; it failed (Brooks **Hegemon**). For actual interstate relations in an ancient Near Eastern multi-state system, see Westbrook **International**.

[48]CC 3/10:5. This is the first mention of Jīng (later called Chŭ) in the CC.

The Túng-Mv́ng 同盟. Jv̀ng had invaded Sùng in the autumn of 0679. In response, Chí and Wèi joined Sùng in attacking Jv̀ng in summer 0678. Then:

1:20 (CC 3/16:2-4, 0678).

• Summer. A man of Sùng, a man of Chí, and a man of Wèi attacked Jv̀ng.

• Autumn. Jīng attacked Jv̀ng.

• Winter, 12th month. Met with the Lord of Chí, the Prince of Sùng, the Lord of Chv́n, the Lord of Wèi, the Elder of Jv̀ng, the Leader of Syw̌, the Elder of Hwá, and the Master of Tv́ng. Made a joint covenant at Yōu.

The commentaries are at a loss to say how a túng-mv́ng 同盟 "joint covenant" differs from a regular mv́ng 盟 "covenant." The map suggests that it was a mutual security agreement, expressing concern by the states east of Jv̀ng (including Chv́n, north of recently violated Tsài) about Chǔ. The túng-mv́ng thus marked a new diplomatic initiative.[49] It had no immediate deterrent effect:

1:21 (CC 3/17:1, 0677). Spring. A man of Chí seized Jǎn of Jv̀ng.

Jǎn was presumably a pro-Chǔ officer of Jv̀ng. He presently escaped from Chí, and in 0676 came as a refugee to Lǔ. There is no record of any response by Chí. It turns out that Chí and Lǔ had a more important matter before them. This was:

The Extermination of the Rúng. Rúng 戎 or "Braves" is the Chūn/Chyōu term for the non-Sinitic peoples of the east. Lǔ, the fief of Jōu-gūng, had originally been close to the Jōu eastern capital, but was relocated east of Sùng to outflank any rebellions of the Shāng people who had been settled there. This was non-Sinitic territory, and resistance to Sinitic overlordship continued in Spring and Autumn. Yǐn-gūng (r 0722-0712), the first Lǔ ruler covered by the chronicle, had treated the Rúng peaceably, even ignoring the awkward incident of their capturing a Jōu envoy on his return from a visit to Lǔ:[50]

1:22 (CC 1/2:1, 0721). 2nd year, spring. The Prince met with the Rúng at Chyén.

1:23 (CC 1/2:4, 0721). Autumn, 8th month, day #17. The Prince and the Rúng covenanted at Táng.

1:24 (CC 1/7:6-7, 0716).

• Winter. The Heavenly King[51] sent the Lord of Fán on a friendly visit.

• The Rúng attacked the Lord of Fán at Chǔ-chyōu and took him back.

---

[49]For the details of what is briefly summarized below, see Brooks **League**.

[50]Since the envoy had completed his mission to Lǔ, the abduction may have been regarded as an offense against Jōu, rather than a breach of the peace with Lǔ.

[51]Tyēn-wáng 天王 "King under the authority of Heaven" is the standard CC phrase. Tyēn-dž 天子 "the Son of Heaven" is found on Jōu bronzes, and in the later theoretical literature, but except for what look like two later scribal slips, not in the CC.

Whether the Lord was killed or later released, the record does not tell us. Either way, the incident must have been something of an embarrassment to Lǔ.

Lǔ Hwán-gūng (r 0711-0694), who often traveled to other states to defuse tensions, went to Rúng territory in his second year to renew the covenant:

1:25 (CC 2/2:8-9, 0710).
- The Prince and the Rúng covenanted at Táng.
- Winter. The Prince returned from Táng.

Peace with the Rúng thus held during these first two reigns.

Twenty years passed quietly under Jwāng-gūng (r 0693-0654), and now we have reached the year 0676, when the Chí prisoner found refuge in Lǔ. It was in this year that Lǔ and Chí adopted an extermination policy against the Rúng:

1:26 (CC 3/18:2, 0676). Summer. The Prince pursued the Rúng as far as west of the Jì River.[52]

1:27 (CC 3/20:4, 0674). Winter. An officer of Chí attacked the Rúng.

Unlike Chǔ, the Rúng had not adopted the Sinitic state or the Sinitic style of chariot warfare. They were thus doomed to extinction by the Sinitic states.

In spring 0671, an envoy came from Jīng (still officially so called) to Lǔ on a mission of friendly inquiry. So did envoys from several small states. All the while, Chí and Lǔ continued to exchange ceremonial visits. No further actions were taken by either against the Rúng. Then, in 0670, the ruler of Tsáu died, and the Rúng began to interfere in the resulting succession struggle:

1:28 (CC 3/24:2, 0670). [Spring]. Buried Jwāng-gūng of Tsáu.

1:29 (CC 3/24:8-10, 0670).
- Winter. The Rúng made an incursion into Tsáu.
- Jì 羈 of Tsáu left that state and fled to Chv́n.
- Chì 赤 returned to Tsáu.

It seems that the intended heir of Tsáu fled under pressure from the Rúng, and that another son, Chì, sponsored by the Rúng, became the next ruler of Tsáu.

1:30 (CC 3/26:1-3, 0668).
- 26th year, spring. The Prince attacked the Rúng.
- Summer. The Prince returned from attacking the Rúng.
- Tsáu killed one of their nobles.

So the situation in Tsáu was resolved by an internal execution, possibly under pressure from Lǔ, of the ruler who had earlier been sponsored by the Rúng.[53]

---

[52]The Jì 濟 River, part of which separated Lǔ and Chí 齊, also ran through Tsáu.

[53]The name of the next Tsáu ruler which we know from the CC was not Jì, or Chì, but Bān 班 (CC 5/7:5, 0653). Tsáu ruler names and dates in such later lists as Shr̆ Jì (SJ) 14 and 35 diverge from this CC evidence, and thus are probably defective.

In 0667, many of the previous túng-mv́ng signatories, as though sensing a revival of the threat from Chǔ, renewed their mutual security covenant:

1:31 (CC 3/27:2, 0667). Summer, 6th month. The Prince met with the Lord of Chí, the Prince of Sùng, the Lord of Chv́n, and the ruler of Jv̀ng. Made a joint covenant 同盟 at Yōu.

Late that winter, the rulers of Chí and Lǔ met at Chv́ng-pú, a place in Wèi which 35 years later would be the site of an epochal battle. This was to put pressure on Wèi, which had joined in the previous covenant, but not in this one. Next spring, Chí applied more direct pressure by making an incursion into Wèi. A battle resulted, and the Wèi force suffered a defeat. And sure enough, Chǔ resumed its incursions into the north that autumn, at its preferred location:

1:32 (CC 3/28:3-4, 0666).

• Autumn. Jīng attacked Jv̀ng.

• The Prince met with a man of Chí and a man of Sùng. Went to the relief of Jv̀ng.

The attention of Chí and Lǔ now turned again to the Rúng. The only Rúng left in the east lived either in the Tài-shān, the mountains between Chí and Lǔ, or at a location further north. The northern Rúng were exclusively a Chí concern, but Lǔ cared about the Tài-shān, and a prior understanding was needed. It was reached at a meeting on neutral territory: a river lying between Chí and Lǔ:

1:33 (CC 3/30:6-7, 0664).

• Winter. The Prince and the Lord of Chí met on the Lǔ side of the Jì.

• An officer of Chí attacked the mountain Rúng.

1:34 (CC 3/31:4, 0663). 6th month. The Lord of Chí came to present spoils from the Rúng.

Lǔ Jwāng-gūng died in 0662. Chí covenanted with his successor, Mǐn-gūng, who came to the throne aged eight, and died in his second year of reign, 0660. The first year of the new Prince, Syī-gūng, was marked by another Chǔ attack on Jv̀ng.[54] Syī-gūng met with Chí, Sùng, Jv̀ng, Tsáu, and Jū the next month, but no covenant resulted; it seems that interest in this form of security measure had lapsed. In fact, there would be no túng-mv́ng covenants during the rest of Chí Hwán-gūng's reign. Chǔ aggression continued, but other methods were used to counter it. The first one to be tried was a joint military demonstration.

The Incursion Into Chǔ was Chí Hwán-gūng's masterpiece. In the autumn of 0657, Chí and Sùng met with representatives from two states on the Chǔ border, Jyāng 江 and Hwáng 黃, which had complained of Chǔ aggression. Nothing was done. That winter, Chǔ again attacked Jv̀ng, penetrating yet again into what the northern states considered to be their territory.

---

[54]It is from this point on that the CC chronicle uses the name Chǔ.

This brought things to a head, and produced the following response:

1:35 (CC 5/4:1-3, 0656).

• 4th year, spring, the Royal 1st month. The Prince met with the Lord of Chí, the Prince of Sùng, the Lord of Chv́n, the Lord of Wèi, the Elder of Jv̀ng, the Leader of Syw̌, and the Elder of Tsáu, and made an incursion into Tsài. The Tsài [forces] having dispersed, they proceeded to attack Chǔ, halting at Syíng.

• Summer. Syīn-chv́n, the Leader of Syw̌, died.

• Chyw̄ Wán of Chǔ came to make a covenant amid the host; a covenant was made at Shàu-líng.

Chǔ had perhaps the largest army of the period, and with that army it had attacked Jv̀ng without a need for allies. No one northern state was strong enough to retaliate. What Chí Hwán-gūng had done, on this one occasion, was to assemble a large enough force to confront Chǔ in its homeland.

The covenant made in 0656 did not hold for long. In 0655, Chǔ conquered and absorbed Syén 弦, a tiny Chǔ border state; its ruler fled to the larger border state Hwáng 黃. Syw̌ 許, one of the 0656 allies, was besieged by Chǔ in 0654. Chí and several other states abandoned an attack on Jv̀ng to raise that siege.

Chí and others now tried a new approach to the problem of Chǔ and Jv̀ng:

1:36 (CC 5/9:2, 0651). Summer. The Prince met with the [Royal] Steward Prince of Jōu, the Lord of Chí, the Master of Sùng, the Lord of Wèi, the Elder of Jv̀ng, the Leader of Syw̌, and the Elder of Tsáu at Kwéi-chyōu.

1:37 (CC 5/9:4, 0651). Ninth month, day #5. The several Lords made a covenant at Kwéi-chyōu.

These comprised the major eastern states, in the presence of a delegate from the King. For the rest of Chí Hwán-gūng's life, Chǔ confined its attacks to states adjoining it. Those which had taken part in the 0651 covenant were left alone.

In that relative lull, the matter of the Rúng was once again taken in hand:

1:38 (CC 5/10:4, 0650). Summer. The Lord of Chí and the Leader of Syw̌ attacked the Northern Rúng.

Thus vanished from history the Rúng peoples of the eastern Sinitic world.[55]

Hwán-gūng died in 0643. He was a strong leader. His "joint covenant" idea, though soon dropped, had articulated the concept of a larger northern unity. His intimidation campaign into Chǔ, made possible by putting together a sufficient multi-state force, did not have lasting consequences, but it showed the value of collaboration. His inclusion of royal authority in the covenant of 0651 showed what might be done with militarily weak but still ceremonially powerful Jōu. All this was good. It was presently to be done better by Jìn Wv́n-gūng.

---

[55]For the fate of other branches of the Rúng peoples, see below, #1:43-46.

Methodological Moment. It was later thought that Gwǎn Jùng 管仲, a supposed merchant, had reorganized Chí to support a mass infantry army, making it stronger than other states, and that Jōu had recognized Hwán-gūng as a Hegemon: the enforcer of order among the states. Can we test this claim?

We might reflect: If Chí had such military superiority, it could act alone in some military matters, and dominate weaker states. But the facts do not match. In Hwán-gūng's reign, Chí used allies in 18 out of 27 military actions (67%). And its 9 independent actions were trifling: 3 statelets extinguished; 3 attacks on the Rúng; 1 relief of Syíng when attacked by the Dí 狄 people; 1 incident where Chí officers in occupied Swèı were killed by the populace; 1 victory in battle against middling Wèı. This is not the record of a great military power.

And if Hwán-gūng *had* made Chí a great power, the effect should have survived him, giving Chí a permanent edge over its neighbors. So again we ask: Was Chí after Hwán-gūng consistently superior to those neighbors? Again, no. Chí 6 times unsuccessfully attacked small Jyw̌, and 18 times unsuccessfully attacked middling Lǔ. If this is strength, what would weakness look like?

Here is one year's Lǔ record, from ten years after Chí Hwán-gūng's death:

1:39 (CC 5/26:1-8, 0634).

• 26th year, spring, the Royal first month, day #56. The Prince met with the Master of Jyw̌ and Níng Sù of Wèı. Covenanted at Syàng.

• A man of Chí made an incursion into our western border. The Prince pursued the Chí host as far as Syī, but could not overtake it.

• Summer. A man of Chí attacked our northern border.

• A man of Wèı attacked Chí.

• Gūngdž Swèı went to Chǔ to beg a host.

• Autumn. A man of Chǔ extinguished Kwéı and took the Master of Kwéı back with him.

• Winter. A man of Chǔ attacked Sùng and besieged Mín.

• The Prince, in command of a Chǔ host, attacked Chí and took Gǔ.

• The Prince returned from the attack on Chí.

Whether with his own host or one borrowed from an ally, the Prince of Lǔ here proves to be more than a match for Chí. This is the long answer to our original question. The short answer is to ask: If Chí *had* carried out a comprehensive restructuring, giving it a strong state and an infantry army in the mid 07c, why did the Chí statecraft and military experts of the 05c and 04c (as we shall see) go to the trouble of inventing these things all over again?

Conclusion: We have here a clear example of the Warring States tendency to project new developments back into earlier times, and, still more important, to give a new interpretation to what was still remembered of earlier events.

———————•••••———————

JIN WVN-GUNG

Jìn Wv́n-gūng 晉文公 (r 0635-0628) was the other great hero of Spring and Autumn. His years of wandering in exile before finally gaining the throne of Jìn would later generate legends. As with Chí Hwán-gūng, his great exploit was achieved against Chǔ, but this time on northern ground, when a Chǔ incursion set up a battle which the north, by sufficient exertions, could actually win.

We have already read several CC entries from 0632. Here are several more. It seems that the conflict centered around rival ruling factions in Wèi:

1:40 (CC 5/28:1-6, 0632).

• 28th year, spring. The Lord of Jìn invaded Tsáu. The Lord of Jìn invaded Wèi. Gūngdž Mǎi was to guard Wèi. He did not in the end succeed in guarding it. Executed him.

• A man of Chǔ came to the rescue of Wèi.

• 3rd month, day #43. The Lord of Jìn entered Tsáu, seized the Elder of Tsáu, and gave him to a man of Sùng.

• Summer, 4th month, day #6. The Lord of Jìn, the host of Chí, the host of Sùng, and the host of Chín fought with a man of Chǔ at Chv́ng-pú. The Chǔ host was disgracefully defeated.

• Chǔ killed its noble Dv́-chv́n.

• The Lord of Wèi left and fled to Chǔ.

Chv́ng-pú. The northern states were individually inferior to Chǔ, whose force probably numbered about 600 chariots. But between the arrival of Chǔ (2nd month) and the battle (4th month), Jìn had brought a force from Chín to join with Chí and Sùng, making perhaps 700 chariots. (Lǔ was on the other side; an ally of Chǔ). Chǔ's defeat was decisive.[56] The Chǔ leader, Dv́-chv́n, was executed on his return. Chǔ made no further military effort for eight years, and then only against the small border state Hwáng. It took time to rebuild a shattered army from the resources available under the elite-warrior system.

Jìn, as the coordinator of victory, was now the major power in the north, and Wv́n-gūng moved at once to secure general assent to that situation:

1:41 (CC 5/28:8-10, 0632).

• 5th month, day #50. The Prince met with the Lord of Jìn, the Lord of Chí, the Prince of Sùng, the Lord of Tsài, the Elder of Jv̀ng, the Master of Wèi, and the Master of Jyw̌. Covenanted at Jyèn-tǔ.

• The Lord of Chv́n went to the meeting.

• The Prince paid court at the place where the King was.

• 6th month. Jv̀ng, the Lord of Wèi, returned to his state from Chǔ. Yw̌æn Syw̌æn of Wèi left and fled to Jìn.

---

[56]The graves of many Chǔ soldiers have been found; see Brooks **Numbers**.

The King is in the vicinity. The Prince of Lǔ visits him separately. At the big meeting, Wv́n-gūng is the chief figure; one senses that the King's presence has been compelled by Jìn, to validate Wv́n-gūng as Hegemon of the North. Meanwhile, the Chǔ candidate for the Wèi rulership had returned to Wèi.

1:42 (CC 5/28:15-18, 0632).

• Winter. The Prince met with the Lord of Jìn, the Lord of Chí, the Prince of Sùng, the Lord of Tsài, the Elder of Jv̀ng, the Master of Chv́n, the Master of Jyw̌, the Master of Jū, and a man of Chín, at Wv̄n.

• The Heavenly King held a hunt at Hv́-yáng.

• Day #9. The Prince paid court at where the King was.

• A man of Jìn seized the Lord of Wèi, and took him to the capital. Ywǽn Sywæ̌n of Wèi returned from Jìn to Wèi.

The last charade. A meeting is held without the King. The King holds a public occasion, but the Prince of Lǔ visits him separately, on a different day. The Lord of Jìn proceeds to act as the enforcer of order by taking the Chǔ candidate from Wèi and delivering him to the King, as though for punishment. The Jìn candidate is installed in Wèi.[57] Behind the phony stage manipulations, the domination of Jìn is clear. It marked a new era in Spring and Autumn history.

Yáu. Wv́n-gūng's last years saw several attacks by northern tribes on Wèi, which moved its capital in 0629. Wv́n-gūng died in 0627. His death changed the strategic picture, and Chín promptly crossed Jìn territory to attack Jv̀ng. With the aid of Rúng allies, Jìn defeated the Chín army on its way back home:

1:43 (CC 5/33:1, 3-4, 0627).

• 33rd year, spring, the Royal 2nd month. A Chín force entered Hwá.

• Summer, 4th month, day #18. A man of Jìn with the Jyāng Rúng defeated Chín at Yáu.

• Day #30. Buried Wv́n-gūng of Jìn.

Jìn had always been on good terms with the Rúng. During his wanderings, Wv́n-gūng had been sheltered by the Rúng,[58] who gave wives to him and his chief follower, and the Rúng had remained allies of Jìn during his reign.[59]

The next two rulers of Jìn were Syāng-gūng (r 0627-0621) and Líng-gūng (r 0620-0607), who came to the throne as a minor. Líng-gūng's reign began violently. In 0618, Chǔ attacked Jv̀ng. In 0617, Chín entered Jìn territory. There were further attacks by Chǔ, and in 0615, a battle between Chín and Jìn forces. The situation was perilous for Jìn, powerful though it still was.

---

[57]We will take up the orthodox interpretation of this "hegemony" in Chapter 4.

[58]In the Dzwǒ Jwàn called the Dí 狄, just as all eastern peoples are called Yí 夷. This "Four Direction" ethnographic schematism belongs to a later time.

[59]For an imagined episode from this Jìn/Rúng military relationship, see #**6:20**.

Again the Túng-Mv́ng. At this time, Chí Hwán-gūng's idea of a security agreement, the túng-mv́ng 同盟, was revived, but at first for narrow purposes. An officer of Jìn, Jàu Dùn, acting for the Jìn ruler (who was still a minor), presided over a covenant in 0613 which included neither Chín nor Chí, and had in view a Jìn interest in interfering with the succession in Jū 邾. The next two túng-mv́ng were similarly local in scope; any implied "solidarity" was simply an acceptance of Jìn interest by the small states near it. Only in 0586, as a response to Chǔ pressure on Jv̀ng, did the túng-mv́ng covenants resume a collective security function. Nine such covenants were made in the next two decades. Attacks were not made on Chǔ itself, but on states like Jv̀ng or Chv́n, which had been compelled by Chǔ pressure to *switch allegiance* to Chǔ.[60]

The End of the Rúng. The central and western Rúng came under attack at the end of the 07th century. The last mentions of the Rúng in the CC are:

1:44 (CC 7/3:3, 0606). The Master of Chǔ attacked the Lù-hún Rúng.

1:45 (CC 8/1:6, 0590). Autumn. The Royal host was disgracefully defeated by the Máu Rúng.

1:46 (CC 10/17:4, 0525). 8th month. Syv́n Wú of Jìn led a host and exterminated the Lù-hún Rúng.

And with their extermination, Sinicization moved forward one more step.

Wú 吳. The end of Chǔ aggression came not from any northern action (a túng-mv́ng covenant in 0548 was not followed up militarily), but from the east. The non-Sinitic coastal power Wú, which had first appeared in the CC in 0584, was attacked by Chǔ as early as 0570. The ruler of Chǔ led another attack on Wú in 0549. In 0548, the ruler of Wú died in attacking the gate of Cháu, a town on the Wú/Chǔ border. This required a response from Chǔ, and in 0546 Chǔ met with northern Jìn, Chí, Lǔ, Jv̀ng, Wèı, and Tsáu, plus border states Syw̌, Chv́n, and Tsàı. A covenant, in effect a peace treaty, followed. This event marks another great division in Spring and Autumn history. The axis of conflict had shifted from north/south to east/west.[61]

Such was the large geostrategy of the times. But there are other dimensions. What was life like for a typical aspiring late Spring and Autumn warrior?

Confucius' Father, whose name was Hv́ 紇, was born in the 6th month of 0592.[62] His grandfather, Kǔng Fáng-shú of Sùng, had offended the Sùng noble Hwà Ywǽn and fled to Lǔ in 0607. But Hwà Ywǽn remained influential in Sùng, and perhaps for that reason, the Kǔngs did not greatly prosper in Lǔ.

---

[60]For details on this series of covenants, see Brooks **League**.

[61]Chǔ was right to recognize a serious new antagonist. In 0506, Wú defeated a Chǔ land force, and went on to enter Yǐng, the capital of Chǔ.

[62]For the reconstruction of this and associated dates, see Brooks **Analects** 263-268.

Hv́, the grandson, took the drastic step of abandoning the surname Kǔng,[63] moving to Dzōu 鄒, south of the capital, and seeking his separate fortune as a nonlanded warrior in the service of Lǔ. His chance came in 0563, in this way:

1:47 (CC 9/10:1-2, 0563).

　　• 10th year, spring. The Prince joined the Lord of Jìn, the Prince of Sùng, the Lord of Wèi, the Elder of Tsáu, the Master of Jyw̌, the Master of Jū, the Master of Tv́ng, the Elder of Sywē, the Elder of Chǐ 杞, the Master of Little Jū, and Gwāng, the Heir Apparent of Chí, in meeting with Wú at Jā.

　　• Summer, 5th month, day #31. Went on to extinguish Bī-yáng.[64]

Between these two entries, much has obviously taken place, which it is not the purpose of the CC to record. A later text . . .

Dzwǒ Jwàn 左傳 (DJ). A commentary on the Chūn/Chyōu, written during the 04c (see Brooks **Heaven**). At first it focused on ritual; later layers propose several different theories of morality and government. Attributing DJ stories not to the 04c, but to the period they purport to describe, is a major source of modern confusion. Translated by Legge.

. . . fills in the story with what, in this case, is probably Kǔng family tradition.

One contingent of the allied forces was led by a noble of the Mv̀ngsūn clan. Serving under him were Chín Jǐn-fǔ, probably of exile stock as the clan name "Chín" implies, and "Hv́ of Dzōu," who as we know was also of exile stock.

The direct attack on the city walls having failed, a ruse was attempted:

1:48 (DJ 9/10:2, excerpts, c0355). Chín Jǐn-fǔ, in the service of the Mv̀ng family, hauled up a heavy cart as though he were a servant. The men of Bī-yáng opened the gate, and the officers of the allies stormed it. The hanging gate was released, but Hv́ of Dzōu lifted it up again, allowing the attacking party to escape . . .

Chín Jǐn-fǔ then distinguished himself by an *almost* successful exploit:

The inhabitants let down a strip of cloth, and Jǐn-fǔ climbed up it. When he was almost at the top, they cut it. After he had fallen, they let down another. In all, he made the ascent three times, after which the inhabitants desisted. He withdrew, and wearing the cut-off pieces of cloth as a sash, he showed them around the army for the next three days . . .

These were remarkable feats, but of different kinds. The solitary prowess of Chín Jǐn-fǔ led to no military result; Dzōu Hv́'s exploit saved his companions in the assault party from certain death. This was of advantage to the attackers.

---

[63]His son would later resume the Kǔng surname, by which he is known to posterity.
[64]Bī-yáng was south of Lǔ, in the zone of possible Chǔ influence.

Bī-yáng was finally taken in an assault by the whole force. Hv́'s exploit came to the notice of the Shú clan,[65] and with that sponsorship, Hv́ gained a place among the landed warriors of Lǔ. Here is the old Jōu pattern: rewarding prowess with land, and expecting further prowess in return for the land.

His opportunity to display that prowess came soon. In an attempt to break the military stalemate that was setting in by the mid 06c, Chí tried a novel double attack. In autumn 0556, Chí assembled *two* forces. One, led by the Chí ruler, besieged Táu, northwest of the Lǔ capital, while a second, led by a Chí noble, besieged Fáng, *east* of the capital. This was a serious threat. It failed due to the repulse of the attack on Fáng, and this owed something to the enterprise of Hv́, plus two members of the Dzāng clan, whose seat was at Fáng:

> **1:49** (DJ 9/17:3, excerpt, c0370). In autumn, The Lord of Chí attacked our northern border, and surrounded Táu; Gāu Hòu surrounded Dzāng Hv́ in Fáng. A force from Yáng-gwān went to meet the head of the Dzāng clan at Lwˇ-sūng. Shú Hv́ of Dzōu, Dzāng Chóu, and Dzāng Jyǎ in command of 300 armored men attacked the Chí force at night, escorted him thither, and returned. The Chí host left the place.

The confidence of the Shú clan and the Lǔ ruler had been well bestowed. Such was the landed warrior system. Up to this point, it was working well.

Lull and Resumption. Spring and Autumn warfare was indecisive. Tiny states vanished, but no large state destroyed another. An equilibrium obtained. If military unification was to be achieved, a new effort would be required.

That effort was a revolutionary reshaping of states and armies. At first there was a lull. After the peace of 0546, in the time of Lǔ Jāu-gūng (r 0541-0510), the tempo of CC military events dropped from 0.28 to 0.17 per year. The states were thinking.[66] The Chí double attack of 0556 was not the answer; something else was needed. When the rate rose again to 0.28 per year, under Dìng-gūng (r 0509-0495), war had changed: there were fewer allies in a typical campaign, and many actions were internal: sieges of clan strongholds and wallings of strategic points. Sieges were quicker: 3 months in 0654 versus 1 month in 0498. These imply more infantry, and thus the beginning of the new military system. Text evidence[67] implies an established bureaucracy in early 05c Lǔ, and thus an earlier beginning for the civil system. The first hint of the military revolution should thus be put, not at the beginning of Warring States as defined by the end of the CC chronicle, but earlier, at the beginning of Dìng-gūng's reign, c0510.

---

[65]The Shú clan was of recent origin; it derived from a brother of Sywǣn-gūng, a later Lǔ Prince. The Three Clans competed with the Lǔ ruler, but the Shú were loyal.

[66]For a European lull, when an old form of state had reached maximum efficiency and a new form of state had not yet emerged, see Strayer **Medieval** 89-111.

[67]For a brief review, see Brooks **Lore**.

Innovation. The Three Clans of Lǔ are deplored in orthodox commentaries. They had their bases at strategically located cities on the borders of Lǔ. By the time of Syāng-gūng (r 0572-0542), they were dominant at court: most military and diplomatic assignments went to them. This is usually considered to be bad. But clan domains may have been the periphery of innovation that was needed to show the path forward. Lǔ, as its chronicle entries, show, had been inching toward more rational procedures: a shift of interest away from the small doings of the ruling family, the appearance of functional terminology. But in making changes, Lǔ was hampered by existing structures, including the clan structures. The clans themselves, who governed directly, were less constrained, and the art of a more efficient management of resources may have been worked out first, or may have developed more rapidly, at the clan level.

Renewal. Another factor inhibiting systematic change in state management was the system of hereditary rule. Usurpation has a bad name, but there may be something to be said for it administratively. Lacking any formal procedure for rulership renewal, and no Spring and Autumn state had such a procedure, usurpation is one way to avoid the decline of hereditary houses, and to resist the inertia of the familiar. There were many incidents of the assassination of rulers in the Spring and Autumn. All of them eventuated in replacement from within the ruling lineage, but even that degree of renewal may be significant. It is thus noteworthy that the two greatest Spring and Autumn rulers, Hwán and Wv́n, came to power after murderous succession disputes. Later on, 05c clan strife did not destroy Jìn; it produced three strong successor states. The great age of Chí came in the 04c, when the Tyén clan, who long had ruled from behind the throne, finally usurped the throne and ruled in their own name. In Lǔ, where there was no usurpation, evidence points to Jāu-gūng's reign as the time when modernization begins to be visible. May it be that Jāu-gūng's exile (0517-0510) gave the clans an opportunity to rearrange some aspects of Lǔ state structure along new lines; lines which they had adopted in their own territories?

Classical China was a time when innovation was urgently relevant: when the states most successful in innovating were the ones most likely to survive. A need for change is opposed by every institutional tendency known to science. But equally, it produces some of the most interesting times known to history.[68] For better or worse, that kind of interest abounds in the Warring States period, and to that period we may now turn.

---

[68]Despite its name, the European Renaissance is most usefully viewed not as a rebirth (since it began, in science, by moving *beyond* Aristotle and Ptolemy) but as a textbook instance of competitive innovation among members of a multi-state system. Classical China is merely an earlier instance of such a situation. It is not the possibility of advantage, as such, but rather the danger *that another will exploit the advantage first,* that typically drives states to innovate.

2. The Economy

An equilibrium had been reached with the old landed warrior system. The states were defensively secure: no large state had conquered any other. If the large states wanted to continue as a multi-state system, nothing was lacking. They had enough army not to depend on alliances for their own protection. They had increased their land area, and they had also increased the efficiency with which that land fed their population.

But the larger states wanted more: they wanted to conquer their neighbors and rule a unified domain. For that, the old system was inadequate. The root of the problem was that each landed warrior took up *too much* land. Any new land gained by conquest or by clearing forest cover could be parceled out in new landholdings, but the military power *per land unit* was the same. The ruler, as a landholder, directly controlled little land, and so had little wealth. He had his court orchestra; he could supply his ancestral sacrifices; the tomb furnishings of the ruler of even a tiny state are impressive.[1] But personal wealth is not state power. State power, the ability to conquer and rule states of comparable size, could be enhanced only by increasing the military power per unit of land. This involved a military revolution, and the military revolution had to be supported, and thus preceded, by an economic and political revolution.

The obvious way to increase a state's land was to take more direct control of what land the state already had, much of which was taken up by elite warrior landholdings. Doing this therefore meant the end of the landed-warrior system. With the land came the people living on it, who would furnish the manpower for a larger army of a different kind. This meant a major change in the relation between ruler and populace. With the people came those engaged in trade, a profitable activity which the state had previously ignored, but which it would now incorporate into its own way of doing things. These changes took time, and each step in the process required its own support structure.

Officers had to learn how to lead the new mass army.[2] Before the army could be trained, there must be officials in charge of gathering resources for it.[3] To coordinate their work, a new and larger bureaucratic structure was required, with specific expertise and permanently assigned responsibilities.[4] All these resources, in both food and men, had to be accurately surveyed and allotted. This was done with a remarkable degree of economic understanding.

[1] For one example, see So **Music**; for the whole story, **Artistic**.

[2] For details, see Chapter 5, The Civilian Elite.

[3] For details, see Chapter 4, War and Peace.

[4] For details, see Chapter 3, The State.

The 05th Century

Lǔ Jāu-gūng had died in exile in 0510. His brother and successor Dìng-gūng (r 0509-0495) ruled from the capital, but had to accept the dominance of the Three Clans: for ten years, no member of the loyalist Dzāng or Shú clans is mentioned in the Lǔ chronicle. In 0499 Shú Sywæn was sent to make a peace treaty with Jvng. In 0498, the walls of the Jìsūn and Shúsūn clan fortresses were razed, reducing their power. Still, under Aī-gūng (r 0494-0468), members of the Three Clans led most military campaigns. The growing power of coastal Wú, to the southeast of Lǔ, also had to be taken into account. In 0488, Aī-gūng invaded the small state of Jū, and brought back its ruler, in this way asserting the local territorial ambition of Lǔ. It was twice resisted. In 0487, Wú invaded Lǔ. Almost simultaneously, Chí took a Lǔ city (in the next month, Aī-gūng sent back the ruler of Jū, and Chí returned that city). Here was a dilemma. It was solved by siding with Wú. Aī-gūng twice joined Wú in attacking Chí, but as a junior partner; no additions to Lǔ territory resulted. But Wú did at least stand by Lǔ: an 0484 Chí attack on Lǔ provoked a joint attack on Chí by Lǔ and Wú.

Land Tax. This did nothing for the land area of Lǔ; it may have increased the internal prestige of Aī-gūng. And his next initiative was internal: in 0483, the key *social* change was made: the assertion of direct control of land in Lǔ. This we know from an entry, three words long, in the Chūn/Chyōu chronicle:

2:1 (CC 12/12:1, 0483). 用田賦 Implemented land tax.

Salaried Officials. Grain from the elite landholdings now went to the state, and was used as salary for the new class of civil officials, including those who were not of the old warrior elite class, and thus had no permanent support of their own. Desire for wealth was the one foundation of the new civil service. In advising members of his client circle, Kǔng Chyōu 孔丘 of Lǔ (0549-0479), known to us as Confucius, added this important qualification:

> **Analects**; Lún Yǔ 論語 (LY). The house text of the Confucian school, compiled over the span 0479-0249. It continually adjusts the image of Confucius to agree with his increasing fame; it also invents sayings by him on issues arising long after his death. It is perilous as a source unless earlier and later layers are distinguished; see Brooks **Analects**.

2:2 (LY 4:5, excerpt, 0479). The Master said, Wealth and honor: these are what men desire, but if [the gentleman] cannot do so in accord with his principles, he will not abide in them . . .

The point here is not wealth, nor the social position which came with state employment (these are perfectly valid desires), but integrity. There are things the gentleman will not do; there are aspects of himself that are not for sale. The new civil servant has freed himself from the old personal loyalty to the ruler, and is now being coached in loyalty to a more general principle.

We can see Confucius' followers, not long after his death, struggling to define the proprieties of the new salary system and its expense accounts:

> **2:3** (LY 6:4, c0460). Dž-hwá went on a mission to Chí. Master Rǎn requested a grain allowance for his mother. The Master said, Give her a fù.[5] He said, I request more. He said, Give her a yǔ.[6] Master Rǎn gave her five *loads*.[7] The Master said, When Chì went to Chí, he drove sleek horses and wore light furs. I have heard that the gentleman relieves the needy, but does not enrich the wealthy.

The gentleman has an obligation of charity, but he does not abet profiteering. He fits into the old society, but is less at ease in the new salary-based society.

The Analects sayings are grouped in pairs. Often the second saying of a pair is a corrective to the first. As a corrective to LY 6:4, we have this passage about a salary which was *not* needed by the already well-off recipient:

> **2:4** (LY 6:5, c0460). Ywǽn Sž was the Steward [of the Jì clan]. They were going to give him nine hundred measures of grain, but he declined. The Master said, Was there no way you could have given it to the neighboring village 鄰里 or the county association 鄉黨?

We might expect that unneeded salary would be declined. This Ywǽn Sž does, *but he is wrong to do so*. He should have donated it to someone who needed it. The point is not whether one needs the salary, it is that the poor need support.[8] Consideration for others, and a focus on public rather than personal welfare, was to remain a central element in Confucian thinking.

Industry. Weaving had always been a specialty of rural women. It was now more efficient, and shifted focus from utilitarian hemp to more marketable silk. The wider availability of silk produced changes even in ceremonial usages:

> **2:5** (LY 9:3, c0405). The Master said, The hemp cap was customary, but now silk is cheaper. I follow the majority. To bow below [before ascending the ruler's platform] was customary, but now they bow above. It is presumptuous. Though I differ from the majority, I follow "below."

Silk production involved higher technology and greater initial investment than anything before it. Making silk thread implied ownership of a mulberry grove, to feed the silkworms, and the kind of weaving done at this time required a loom which was a very advanced piece of machinery.

---

[5]An allowance for one person for 16 days (the duration of the mission to Chí).

[6]An allowance sufficient to support *the whole household* for that period.

[7]Six times greater than the whole-household allowance; no longer a compensation for the expenses of the trip, but a profit level approaching that of a commercial venture.

[8]This is the "noblesse oblige" form of elite charity to the less fortunate, familiar in many feudal and postfeudal cultures. Note that part of this aid is given through an existing local association. For its later takeover by the government, see **#6:14.**

Trade. Between spinners and weavers, local traders played a necessary role. Here is a poem, perhaps of the 05c, about such a trader courting a local girl:

Shr 詩 "Poems." A repertoire eventually numbering 305 poems, mostly written during the 05c and 04c, and divided into Fv̄ng (popular), Yǎ (courtly), and Sùng (sacrificial); later became one of the Five Classics. Confucius did not compile or teach the Shr, though some of the poems were current in his day. Translations by Legge and Waley.

2:6 (Shr 58, excerpt, 05c).

58A   A peasant lad, and simple-seeming,
       Bringing cloth to trade for thread –
       It was not to trade for thread,
       But only to propose to me.

Later stanzas show that the marriage ended badly:

2:7 (Shr 58, excerpt, 05c).

58E   For three years I was wife to you.
       Nor did I my toil neglect.
       At dawn I rose; at night I slept.
       Never a morning to myself.
       My given word I have fulfilled,
       But ever harsher you became.
       My brothers disacknowledged me,
       Loudly did their laughter ring;
       And now that I think back on it,
       I only have myself to blame.

The whole poem is a sermon on the instability of merchant life and character.

Industry was stimulated by trade possibilities. The bronze works at Hóumǎ[9] were founded when Jìn moved its capital to that site in 0585, and were most active in the 05c. The workers lived nearby, in the partly subterranean houses of the period.[10] Some factories made coins or weapons; others, like Hóumǎ, made objects for sale, both to the Sinitic world and also to the northern steppe. Designs were influenced by steppe art motifs, some deriving from Persia, an empire which reached its height around 0450. There was also trade in silk and lacquer wares.[11] Steppe horses were traded at markets on the northern border.[12]

---

[9]At the time called Syīn-tyén; Hóumǎ is the modern site name. For an extensive illustrated account of the work of the foundry, see **Art**.

[10]von Falkenhausen **Waning** 462f.

[11]For the general situation, see So **Traders**. Several objects from this trade have been found at the Pazyryk site in the Altai; for its date, see Brooks **Textual**.

[12]Jade from the Altai was another major import; see Peng **Coinage** 255-260.

Divination. Trade involves uncertainties. For such matters, supernatural guidance is often sought. Shāng and Jōu rulers had used bone divination to read the will of the spirits. By the 05c, a form of divination was also available to private persons. There is reason to think that behind the Yì 易, the canonical divination text of 64 hexagrams, each composed of six lines, there lay an earlier and simpler system, one based on 32 five-line complexes or pentagrams:

> **Proto-Yì** (05c). Our reconstruction of a divination system based on 32 pentagrams, the core of the later hexagram-based Yì 易.

A pentagram, obtained by counting out stalks of the milfoil plant,[13] is a set of five whole (or odd) ▬▬ and broken (or even) ▬ ▬ lines. This one describes the various stages of a troubled and in the end (Line 5) unlucky trading venture. The text should be read from the bottom (Line 1) upward:

2:8 (Proto-Yì: Pentagram Lǔ 旅 "Travel," 05c).

> 5. ▬▬ Travelers first laugh; later weep and wail.
>   They lose their ox at the Yì River [the border]. Bad.
> 4. ▬▬ Travelers reach destination; get goods and weapons.
>
> 3. ▬▬ Travelers' inn is burned; they lose their escort. Critical.
>
> 2. ▬ ▬ Travelers halt; they hide goods and get an escort. Persist.
>
> 1. ▬ ▬ Travelers troubled. Whatever they choose is disastrous.

Reaching the market is lucky (Line 4), but they later lose their ox and cannot get their goods back home. Note the need for an escort – and weapons – in distant territory.[14] Travelers must rest (Lines 2-3); they need an understanding with those along the route. Early trade may thus have been partly in the hands of the pre-Sinitic peoples, who knew the paths, the inns, and the languages.[15]

By the late 05c, elite trade in luxury items, sometimes obtained from distant places,[16] was so familiar that it could serve as a metaphor for Confucius:

> **2:9** (LY 9:13, c0405). Dž-gùng said, I have a beautiful jade here. Shall I wrap it up in its box and keep it, or look for a good price and sell it? The Master said, Sell it! Sell it! I myself am just waiting for a buyer.

"Selling it" means finding an employer for the qualified civil servant.

---

[13]For one description of the method, see Wilhelm **I Ching** 1/392f.

[14]For a hexagram, with an emphasized line giving the specific prediction, see **#3:17**.

[15]For a modern retracing of an ancient route and its hazards, see Young **Journey**.

[16]Some jade came from Lake Baikal, far to the north. For the cutting of a rare jade, as delicate a matter as the cutting of a rare diamond in European culture, see **#5:62**.

Coinage. Cowry shell currency was used in Shāng, and in Warring States times, tiny metal coins imitating the form of cowry shells were issued by Chǔ. Useful items like forked metal spades and angled harvesting-knives were probably common in barter; small replicas of them (like the knife coin, above) were the oldest currency in the north. The spade money of Jōu circulated in the central states;[17] the knife money of Chí in the northeast.[18]

A tale about a minister protesting the Jōu issuance of heavy coins . . .

Gwó Yǔ 國語 (GY, c0300). A set of anecdotes arranged by state. The original GY had sections on Jōu, Lǔ, Jvng, Chí, Jìn, and Chǔ. GY was inspired by the DJ, and develops many motifs from the DJ.

2:10 (GY Jōu 3:5, excerpt, c0300). In the 21st year of Jǐng-wáng, they were going to cast large coins 大錢. Shàn Mù-gūng remonstrated, saying, It should not be done. In antiquity, disasters from Heaven came down, and they then . . . adjusted the ratio between light and heavy, to aid the people. When the people's worries were light, they made heavy coins.

. . . is surely a fable, but the year in which it is set (0524) is not implausible.[19] From other evidence we may infer that a practical currency existed by the 05c.

The 04th Century

Food had been the main economic concern of the Spring and Autumn state. The food supply had been steadily increased during that period by clearing forest for farmland, by introducing new crops, and by double cropping.

---

[17]The specimen illustrated above is probably from the northern state of Jàu.

[18]For the archaeological distribution, see Li **Eastern** 387-391.

[19]All round coins throughout Eurasia derive from those of Lydia (c0630). Early heavy coins were better suited for capital transfer than for ordinary buying and selling.

The next advance was metal tools (or metal tips for wooden tools).[20] Some Shr poems are ecstatic about the new results, while denying that they *are* new:

2:11 (Shr 290, excerpts, early 04c?).

> 290A   They clear the grass, they clear the brush,
> Their ploughs open up the ground.
> A thousand teams to plough and turn,
> Over the wetlands and the dry . . .
>
> 290B   . . . Then with their ploughshares all so sharp,
> They turn to the southern acreage.
>
> 290C   . . . Luxuriant stand the rows of shoots,
> Numerous are those who weed . . .
>
> 290E   . . . Not only do they this possess,
> Not only in the present time,
> But from of old it has been so.

So the managers are happy, but the work was hard for whose who did it. Complaints about popular hardship first appear from below the elite level.

> **Mwòdž** 墨子 "Master Mwò" (MZ), 04c-03c. The writings of the Micians, the sub-elite followers of Mwò Dí 墨翟. A key Mician concept was profit (social benefit; lì 利). The Micians later investigated logic and the art of defensive warfare. Translations by Mei and Johnston.

Here the Micians criticize the suffering caused by the new tax policies:

2:12 (MZ 20:3, excerpt, c0382). Modern governments have many ways to diminish the people. Their use of the people is wearisome, their levying of taxes is burdensome, and when the people's resources are not enough, those who die of hunger and cold are innumerable . . . Are not the ways of diminishing the people more numerous with the governments of modern rulers? When the sages were in charge of the government, there was none of this.

The ultimate argument here is shrewdly based. It does not just depict suffering; that would be merely an appeal to elite compassion. Instead, it makes the historical point that the present system is not the system of the ancient Sages; *it has no ancient precedent.*

Universal Sovereignty. In this society, even more than in other law-based societies (where legal precedent tends to govern), antiquity was prized. To label the new system *as* new was thus to score a telling point against it. One response was to *reconstruct* antiquity, to include in it such new ideas as the principle of central ownership. And so lines were added to one of the Shr poems, Shr 205.

---

[20]First of bronze, later of iron; see Wagner **Iron** sv ploughshares.

Methodological Moment. How do we know? Shī 205 is a soldier's song. It begins with three 6-line stanzas. All use one rhyme-sound, *except the second, which uses two*. The content of that stanza also marks an ideological change:

2:13 (Shī 205, excerpt, with rhyme pattern marked, early 04c?).

205A	I climb upon that northern hill,	–
	I pluck the medlars growing there.	A
	Assiduous, those officers,	A
	Morn and eve about their work.	A
	The King's affairs are never done,	–
	And for my parents I must grieve.	A
205B	Here beneath the Heaven so wide,	A
	None but are the King's own lands.	A
	Here within the ocean shores,	B
	None but are the King's own men.	B
	The noblemen are most unfair –	B
	And in the service, I alone am worthy.	B
205C	My four steeds go unceasingly,	A
	The King's affairs last endlessly.	A
	They compliment me on my youth,	–
	They praise me for my sturdiness –	A
	And while my body still is firm,	A
	I fortify on every side.	A

– it claims universal Jōu sovereignty. The irregularity of a passage in context, and the fact that the context is made smoother by its removal, are the standard signs of an interpolation. We can also see why it was added: *with that stanza*, the accepted Shī text supports a new idea: everything is owned by the King.

———••••———

The elite at this time had a certain presence at local ceremonies:

2:14 (LY 10:7b, c0380). When the country folk 鄉人 are drinking wine and the elders have left, he also takes his leave.

2:15 (LY 10:8, c0380). When the country folk are doing an expulsion (nwó 儺),[21] he takes his stand in his court dress on the formal stairs.

Like the Micians (**#2:12**), the Confucians deplored the new economy. They preferred the old decentralized system, with its lighter tax burden on the people:

2:16 (LY 11:14, c0360). The men of Lǔ were going to rebuild the Long Treasury. Mǐn Dž-chyēn said, How would it be to keep to the old lines? What need is there to build it on a new plan? The Master said, That man does not talk much, but when he *does* talk, he is sure to hit the mark.

This is not about architecture; it is against the new centralized agriculture.

---

[21]A **Missing Methodological Moment** should go here. What would it contain?

Trust. The Confucians ultimately relied on trust (syìn 信) between ruler and people, and not on food or other resources, as the real strength of the state:

> **2:17** (LY 12:7, c0326). Dž-gùng asked about government. The Master said, Enough food, enough weapons, the people having trust 信 in him. Dž-gùng said, If he had to let something go, of the three, which would be first? He said, Let weapons go. Dž-gùng said, If he had to let something else go, of the two, which would be first? He said, Let the food go. Since ancient times there has always been death, but if the people lack trust, he cannot stand.

Tax. How much of the farmer's crop does the state take? The custom was a tenth. In hard times, the state is tempted to tax more, but the farmer does not have it. The Confucians held that ruler and people must share the hardship:

> **2:18** (LY 12:9, c0326). Aī-gūng asked Yŏu Rwò, It is a year of scarcity, and there is not enough for my needs; what is to be done? Yŏu Rwò replied, Why not tithe?[22] He said, With *two* tithes, I do not have enough, how then should I tithe? He replied, if the Hundred Families have enough, what ruler will not also have enough? But if the Hundred Families[23] do not have enough, what ruler can expect to have enough?

But rulers *did* expect to have enough, in good years and bad. They got it by bringing new land under cultivation and cultivating old land more intensively. This required expert managers, and that need created a new class of official.[24] Here is the job description for the official in charge of the land survey:

> **Gwăndž** 管子 "Master Gwăn" (GZ), referring to Gwăn Jùng, the supposed minister of the 07c ruler Chí Hwán-gūng. These are in fact the writings of a Chí school of statecraft thought, dating from the accession of a new Chí ruler in 0357 to early Hàn. The group's distinctive focus was economics, including market economics. Translated by Rickett.

> **2:19** (GZ 4:7, c0312). To observe high and low ground, to assess fertile and barren soil, to observe what are the suitable uses of the land, to set the terms of labor service wisely, so the farmers, both before and afterward, can do their tasks at the proper season; to assure that the five grains, the mulberry and hemp, are thriving where they are planted – these are the duties of the Inspector of Fields.

The new system lacked the sanction of antiquity, and the Micians (#2:12) and the Confucians (#2:16) used that lack to argue against the bureaucratic state. To this challenge, one response was to invent an already bureaucratic antiquity.

---

[22]That is, collect the traditionally standard 10% of the crop.

[23]Băi-syìng 百姓 "the hundred families" at first meant the aristocracy; in some late 04c and in most 03c texts (as here), it came to mean instead "the common people."

[24]For the new manager class in early modern Europe, see Reynolds **Europe** 410.

And thus it was that, somewhere around the year 0320, an anecdote was inserted into the Dzwǒ Jwàn commentary under the year 0548:

> **2:20** (DJ 9/25:11, c0320). Wěɪ Yěn of Chǔ was Marshal. [Prime Minister] Dž-mù assigned him to adjust the tax rates and inventory the arms and armor. On the day jyǎ/wǔ, Wěɪ Yěn recorded lands and fields, calculated the extent of mountains and forests, defined the wetlands, distinguished high land and low, marked off salt and fresh, delimited the flood plain, raised small banks on level land between dikes, assigned soggy land for pasture, divided fertile fields into well-units, fixed taxes according to incomes, and assigned quotas of carriages and horses and foot-soldiers, along with quantities of armor and shields. When he had finished his task, he delivered the result to Dž-mù. This was proper.

This gave 04c resource managers the approval of the minister of a great state, two centuries earlier. The DJ narrator emphasizes that all this was in accord with proper procedure (lǐ 禮), this being the standard DJ term of approval.[25] What more could a tax collector want? For one thing, not to have to listen to remarks like this one, which cast doubt on the worth of the whole setup:

> **2:21** (LY 13:20, c0322). Dž-gùng asked, What must one be like before we can call him an officer? The Master said, In carrying out his own purposes he has a sense of shame; if sent on a mission to the Four Quarters, he does not dishonor his ruler's command – *he* may be called an officer. Dž-gùng said, I venture to ask which is next. He said, If his lineage and clan regard him as filial; if his county council regard him as fraternal. Dž-gùng said, I venture to ask which is next. He said, In word he is always faithful, in deed he is always effective: he may be a stubborn little man, but we may still rank him next. Dž-gùng said, Those who are now in government; what about them? The Master said, Ugh! Those dipper-and-scoop people; how are *they* worth calculating about?

"Dippers and scoops" are the officials' grain-measuring tools. There is a pun: those who do all this measuring have, themselves, no measurable value.

Markets. The Analects Confucians were not entirely at home in the new bureaucracy. They preferred the arrangements of the old palace state, where a small, culturally homogeneous circle managed affairs by personal experience and discretion. As in many elite cultures, judgement was a highly prized skill. This insistence on the personal element tended to align the Confucians against their modernizing opponents, the architects of the new state. The new managers did not want decisions made intuitively by individuals; they wanted objective standards and uniform and predictable outcomes. Among other mechanisms, they thought that the market mediated ideally between producers and buyers.

---

[25]LY and DJ are both Confucian texts; both quote "Confucius" in judging men and events. But they take different stands on some issues. The word "Confucian" thus does not denote a fixed ideology, any more than does the name of a modern political party.

Here is a piece on weapons procurement, which shows how selection was made from the goods offered by the various makers:

> **2:22** (GZ 6:4, excerpt, c0313) . . . Therefore, he assembles the world's finest products; he examines the sharp weapons of the various artisans. In spring and autumn, there are competitions to make a selection. The best and sharpest are given a superior rating. Until they have been inspected, the finished weapons are not used. Until they have been tested, they are not stored away. . .

The best is the best – and the best will be identified by the market process. One possible flaw in the system was the wealth available outside controlled markets:

> **2:23** (MZ 47:17, excerpt, c0305). The traders go to the Four Quarters, and their profits are multiplied. Despite the difficulties of barriers and bridges, and the hazards of robbers and brigands, they persist in doing it . . .

Which led to the problem of wealth-based corruption:

> **2:24** (GZ 3:21, excerpt, c0330). If merchants and traders are accepted at court, goods and wealth will start flowing upward . . .

If kept from the court, and thus from influence over policy, the merchants might still upset the social order by displaying their own wealth:[26]

> **2:25** (GZ 4:8, excerpt, c0312). The common people should not dare to wear mixed colors; the several artisans and the merchants and traders should not be allowed to wear long furs . . .

But at bottom, the proper functioning of the new society depended on markets, and these were part of the plan for organizing the countryside:

> **2:26** (GZ 5:6, excerpt, c0312). An area of six leagues (lǐ 里) is called a hamlet (bàu 暴). Five hamlets are called a section (bù 部). Five sections are called an assembly (jyẁ 聚). In each assembly, there must be a market (shr̀ 市); if there is no market, the people will be in want . . .

The price-fixing market concept is here applied to problems of procurement:

> **2:27** (GZ 5:5, excerpt, c0310). The market determines the value of goods. Thus, if goods are kept cheap, there will be no excess profits.[27] If there are no excess profits, the trades will be well organized. If the trades are well organized, the expenses [of weapons procurement] will be moderate . . .

The Chí theorists are distinctive in their concern for the economic basis of state power and for their interest in market forces. In their differences with the Analects Confucians, we can perhaps see the underlying social opposition, one familiar in many cultures, between old military merit and new money power.

---

[26]Sumptuary laws to control ostentation in the newly rich are common in postfeudal transitions; for Edo Japan, see Sansom **Short** 471-474.

[27]Setting prices low by government decree was also tried at Rome; it did not reckon with all the economic factors, and it did not work. See Finley **Diocletian** 147.

Attracting Population was a major policy goal. This was easier if people were unhappy where they were, and that situation had its artistic expression.

In this poem, the cry of the bird echoes the artisan's plaint, in a situation seemingly favorable but in fact full of "thornwood." A skilled craft like jade carving could be practiced anywhere, working with the stones of "other hills."

2:28 (Shr̄ 184, mid 04c).

> 184A   In ninefold marsh the crane-bird trills,
> its voice is heard upon the moor;
> Fishes hide in watery lair,
> or they linger by the shore.
>> Pleasant is that garden there,
>> with timber-trees all planted fair,
>> but all beneath, the deadwood spills,
>> and the stones of other hills
>> would suffice for making drills

> 184B   In ninefold marsh the crane-bird trills,
> its voice is heard upon the air;
> Fishes linger by the shore,
> or they hide in watery lair.
>> Pleasant is that garden there,
>> with timber-trees all planted fair,
>> but all beneath, the thornwood fills,
>> and the stones of other hills
>> would suffice to show our skills.

Some states sought to increase their attractiveness to farmers by appointing agricultural specialists. To the Analects people, this was beside the point:

> **2:29** (LY 13:4, c0322). Fán Chŕ asked to study agriculture. The Master said, I am not as good for that as some old farmer. He asked to study gardening. He said, I am not as good for that as some old gardener. Fán Chŕ went out. The Master said, A little man indeed is Fán Syw̄! If the superiors love ritual, then among the people none will dare not to be assiduous. If the superiors love right, then among the people none will dare not to be submissive. If the superiors love fidelity, then among the people none will dare not to respect the facts. If these conditions obtain, the people of the Four Quarters will come carrying their children on their backs. What use has he for *agriculture*?

Notice the sarcasm. Here is another Analects statement of the principle:

> **2:30** (LY 13:16, c0322). The Prince of Shv̀ asked about government. The Master said, When the near are happy, and the distant come.

In short, the real test of a government is whether people want to live under it.[28]

---

[28]This is the central idea of what we call populism; see further p157f.

In attracting population, the Chí theorists did not rely on the ruler's qualities (which the Confucians emphasized), but on the people's desire for wealth:

2:31 (GZ 1:1, excerpt, c0322).

If the state has much wealth,	A
the distant will come;	A
If open land is plentiful,	B
the people will remain.	B

From this angle, the desire for profit was not disruptive, but constitutive.

Beside the free farmers there were slaves, the product of the legal system. Near the Yēn state factory, dating from c0313, archaeologists have discovered several slaves, buried in their chains.[29]

Luxury. For the rich also, wealth had its attractions:

2:32 (Shr 115, early 04c).

115A   Mountain thornwood fair,
Marshland elmtrees spare;
Robes you have, and raiment fine,
But them you neither don nor wear;
Horses too, and carriages,
But in the chase you do not share.
Soon enough you will be dead,
And other men will have their care.

115B   Mountain medlars high,
Marshland yew-trees nigh;
Courts you have, and chambers wide,
But them you sprinkle not, nor dry;
Bells beside, and drums so grand,
But them you neither strike nor ply.
Soon enough you will be dead,
And other men will keep them by.

115C   Mountain lac-trees gay,
Marshland chestnuts gray;
Wine you have, and food so choice –
Why do you not every day your cithern play,
The better to enjoy yourself,
The better to prolong the day?
Soon enough you will be dead,
And others in your house will stay.

Here we see the spread of court luxuries – horses and carriages, fine clothing and rare foods, the musical resources of the court[30] – to private residences.

[29]See Wagner **Iron** 170-176 for industrial, corvée, and estate slave burials.

[30]Bells and drums are not amateur instruments; they imply a resident orchestra. Poems of enjoyment like Shr 115 were probably composed in the first instance for wealthy individuals like the ones implied here; their inclusion in the canon is secondary.

Women. When the basic issues of staying alive are solved, and in the preceding poem they have been handsomely solved, a climate favorable to sophistication is created. One sophisticated idea that turns up in the 04c is gender equity. This appears as a protest implicit in the last two stanzas of a Shr poem. Those stanzas put before us two children:

2:33 (Shr 189, last two stanzas, 04c).

189H   A son there will be born to him,
         And on a couch will he be laid.
         In robe of state he'll be arrayed,
         With tiny scepter he will play:
         Loudly will his crying sound –
             With crimson greaves he'll take his place,
             The Sovereign King of house and home.

189I   A daughter shall be born to him,
         And on the ground will she be set.
         With swaddling cloth will she be wrapped,
         Her plaything, but a bit of tile:
         No ornaments, no courtesies –
             Her place, to care for wine and food,
             And not to cause her parents grief.

Methodological Moment. These stanzas are late. How do we know? Shr 189 is congratulatory. It tells of the building of a house in stanzas B through E. Stanzas F and G add to this favorable prospect with a dream of future progeny. It is this prediction which is now followed by stanzas H and I, quoted above. Might the happy omen in stanzas FG have been the original end of the poem? Consider Shr 190, the next poem in the collection. It too is congratulatory, and ends with an omen of future prosperity, this time a dream of flocks and herds:

2:34 (Shr 190, end, 04c).

190D   Then the herdsman has a dream,
         Of fishes in their multitudes,
         Of banners waving on the wind.
         The Omener interprets it:
         "Fishes in their multitudes
         Betoken many fruitful years;
         Banners waving on the wind,
         Prosperity in house and home."

This corresponds to the dream and interpretation in Shr 189FG. From this we learn that such a prediction, a blessing for the person for whom the poem was made, is a valid way to end a Shr poem. Then Shr 189FG may have been the end of Shr 189, in which case Shr 189H and I are formally extraneous. The note of social complaint they convey is also inconsistent with what precedes. Form and content thus agree in suggesting that 189HI are a later addition.

The needs of the period led to systematic surveys, including this one:

> **Shān/Hǎı Jīng** 山海經 (SHJ), c0318; "The Classic of Mountains and Seas." Only its first 5 chapters are early; they cover territory from Burma to the Amur River, and from Japan to the virtually mythical west, listing resources and describing sacrifices to local deities.

Its mixture of resource information (useful for traders) and what look like mere travelers' exotica implies more than one audience. Here are some samples:

2:35 (SHJ 2A15-16, excerpt, c0318). 200 leagues west is Cháng-lyóu Mountain. Its spirit, the God of White, Shàu-hàu, dwells here. Its animals have striped tails, its birds have striped heads. There are many patterned jadestones . . .

280 leagues west is Jāng-v́ Mountain. It has no vegetation. It has much jasper and chrysoprase. Everything here is strange. There is an animal here that looks like a red leopard; it has five tails and one horn. It makes a sound like striking a stone; it is called the Jv̄ng 猙 . . .

2:36 (SHJ 2A21, c0318). 350 leagues west is the Heavenly Mountain. It has much gold and jade, and has green ocher. The Yīng River arises here, and flows southeast until it enters Tāng-gǔ. There is a spirit here; it looks like a yellow pouch, and is as red as a cinnabar fire. It has six legs and four wings; it is featureless, and has no face or eyes, but it knows how to sing and dance. [In fact, this is the Lord of the River 河伯].[31]

The bracketed comment is an effort to harmonize this strange landscape with more familiar gods. The route here followed led along the southern edge of the Tarim Basin, and was followed by the Silk Road traffic of later ages.

One meditation-based group warned of the danger of luxuries:

> **Dàu/Dv́ Jīng** 道德 (DDJ), c0360-0249. The text of a meditation group in Lǔ; Lǎu Dān 老聃 or Lǎudž was one of its leaders. The first text to reflect Dàuist philosophy. A selection was made in c0286 for the Heir Apparent of Chǔ (the Gwōdyèn text). Translations by Waley and Chan.

2:37 (DDJ 9, c0335).
> Than have it and add to it, better to stop.
> You may grind and polish, but you cannot keep long.
> Gold and jade may fill the hall, but none can ward them.
> The rich, high, and mighty but send themselves bane.
> When the work is done, he then withdraws –
> The Way of Heaven.

---

[31] For this northern god in his home habitat, see #6:68.

The Micians also deplored extravagance. One of their favorite targets was elaborate music performances, which they saw as outrageously superfluous:

> **2:38** (MZ 32:1-2, excerpt, c0320). Mwòdž said, A benevolent policy will pursue what gains benefits for the world and eliminates its disasters. If anything, when made a law, is beneficial to the people, it should be done; if not, it should not be done. Moreover, the benevolent in their care for the world do not think of doing those things which delight the eyes, please the ears, gratify the taste, or comfort the body. When these deprive the people of the means of clothing and food, the benevolent will not do them. So the reason Mwòdž opposes music is not that the sounds of bell and drum, cithern and psaltery, pipe and syrinx, are not pleasant . . . they are found not to be in accord with the deeds of the Sage Kings of antiquity, and not to add to the benefits of the people of the present day. And so Mwòdž proclaims, To have music is wrong.

Later in the essay, the Micians insist that music has no value for the people:

> **2:39** (MZ 32:4, excerpt, c0320). There are three things the people worry about: that the hungry cannot be fed, that the cold cannot be clothed, and that the weary cannot get rest. These three are the great worries of the people. Now suppose we strike the great bell, beat the sounding drum, play the cithern and psaltery, and blow the pipe and syrinx, can the wherewithal for food and clothing be procured for the people?

. . . and that if everyone took up music, farmers would not plough, women would not weave, and the economy in general would come to a standstill:

> **2:40** (MZ 32:12, c0320). Therefore Mwòdž said, If the gentlemen really wish to procure benefits for the world, and destroy its calamities, they cannot but prohibit such a thing as music.

Welfare. Most statecraft people did not forbid wealth, but they *did* want to avoid too great a wealth differential: the farmers had to be alive for the system to work. From the Confucians there now came a new idea about welfare:

> **Mencius** 孟子 (MC), 0320-0249. The interviews of Mencius with the rulers of his day, plus the texts of two successor schools, a southern or statecraft school (MC 2-3) and a northern, more philosophical school (MC 4-7; see Brooks **Nature**). Translated by Legge and Lau.

Mencius opposed the famine relief policies that had been adopted by some states. The King of Ngwèi had found that those policies did not work:

> **2:41** (MC 1A3, excerpt, 0320) . . . If things are bad inside the River, I move people east of the River, and move grain inside the River; if things are bad east of the River, I do the same. If I observe the governments of the neighbor states, none is as solicitous as the Solitary One. But the neighbor states' population does not decrease, and the Solitary One's population does not increase? Why is this?

Mencius instead advocated a *preventive* policy: in effect, rural self-sufficiency:

> **2:42** (MC 1A3a, excerpt, 0320) . . . If fine nets do not enter the pools and ponds, the fish and turtles will be more than can be eaten. If axes and hatchets enter the mountain forests only at the proper season, the timber will be more than can be used. When grain and fish and turtles are more than can be eaten, and timber is more than can be used, this will let the people nourish their living and mourn their dead without reproach . . .

Large planks were used for coffins, hence "mourn their dead without reproach." Notice also the emphasis on including some animal protein in the diet. This was later supplemented with a more precise, top-down, economic plan:

> **2:43** (MC 1A3b, excerpt, 0301). By every five-acre homestead let mulberry trees be planted, and those of fifty can wear silk. Let not the seasons for chickens, pigs, dogs, and swine be missed, and those of seventy can eat meat. From every hundred-acre farm let not the seasonal work be taken away, and a family of several can avoid starvation . . .

In other words, the best famine relief is leaving the people enough to live on. This amounts to a return to the paternalistic local arrangements of earlier times.

Social Classes. The state needs farmers. Government needed officers. Artisans usefully provide tools and weapons. This was widely granted, but merchants were a problem in social theory. To many, they were parasites, profiting from changes in grain prices to the disadvantage of the farmer, and importing luxuries which encouraged extravagance in the elite. Trade was first recognized by governments in Warring States times, and then only gradually seen as part of the state economy. This description of the four classes is from the turn of the century. Gwǎn Jùng, the legendary minister of 07c Chí, and himself supposedly a merchant in origin, is addressing the famous Chí Hwán-gūng:

> **2:44** (GZ 20, excerpt, c0300). Officers (shr̀ 士),[32] farmers (núng 農), artisans (gūng 工) and traders (shāng 商)[33] are the foundation of the state. They cannot be allowed to dwell together. If they dwell together, their words will be jumbled and their work disordered. It was for this reason that the Sage Kings always located the officers in places of ease, the farmers in the fields, the artisans in their workplaces, and the traders at markets and wells. Now when officers dwelt together in their separate place of ease, father spoke with father of right, and son spoke with son of filiality. Those who served the ruler spoke of respect, the old spoke of love, the young spoke of brotherliness. Day and night they acted thus, teaching sons and younger brothers. Their hearts were at peace therein; they did not look upon strange ways, that they might change to them . . .

[32]The term for the old military elite, who from the 05c had served in a civil capacity; the class of people from whom such officers come, though not the hereditary nobles.

[33]The local merchants are sometimes distinguished as gǔ 賈.

Thus did the sons of officers grow up instructed in the ways of the officer class, and became officers in their turn. Similar things are said of farmers, who talked of ploughs and scythes. But there is a departure at the end of that section:

> **2:45** (GZ 20, excerpt, c0300) . . . Thus the sons of farmers always became farmers. They were simple and acquired no devious habits. If there were exceptionally talented individuals among them who had the ability to become officers, they could be depended upon.

This is the only instance of class mobility in the system here described.

Artisans are next taken up, and last come the traders. Here is that section:

> **2:46** (GZ 20, excerpt, c0300). Now when traders dwelt together in their own place, they watched for times of disaster and famine, and attended to changes in the country. They studied the four seasons and examined local products to learn their market price. They bore burdens and assumed duties; they yoked oxen and harnessed horses, to range over the four directions. They estimated quantities and calculated values; they exchanged what they had for what they lacked; they bought cheap and sold dear. Thus it was that feather banners arrived unsought, and bamboo arrows abounded in the land.[34] The strange and the wondrous came in due season; the rare and the marvelous accumulated. Day and night they acted thus, teaching sons and younger brothers. They spoke of profit, they exemplified timeliness, they compared things to teach their value. From their youth up they practiced this. Their hearts were at peace therein; they did not look upon strange ways, that they might change to them. And so the teaching of fathers and elder brothers was effective without severity; the learning of sons and younger brothers was successful without strain. For this reason, the sons of traders always became traders.

The insight here is: all classes are productive, but each has its own subculture.

The 03rd Century

State control of rural life increased, fields were opened, trade was regulated. The Chí statecraft theorists liked to call these efforts "virtuous" (dv́ 德):[35]

> **2:47** (GZ 10, excerpt, c0295). What are the Six Aspects [of virtue]? They are: (1) opening up fields, (2) aiding housing, (3) promoting horticulture, (4) exhorting the people, (5) encouraging farming, and (6) repairing wells and buildings. This is called "enriching livelihood."

The aim of this "virtue" is rural infrastructure enhancement and higher yield, all of which, in addition to any other benefits, also benefit the state.

---

[34]These are military necessities, and symbolize the value of trade to the state.

[35]One sense of dv́ 德 "virtue" in the 05c already had a public dimension; see #5:17, which contrasts that sense with the more selfish desires of the commoner. We might think of it here as "common interest;" it is bad for the individual, but also for the state, if houses fall or crops fail. A certain amount of state supervision becomes inevitable.

The Mencians were also concerned about popular livelihood, but attacked it from a different angle. This piece of late invective rewrites a moderate speech of Mencius (#2:41) to read as a direct accusation of the Chí ruler:

2:48 (MC *1A4, excerpt, c0285) . . . There is fat meat in your kitchen and sleek horses in your stables, yet the people have a hungry look and outside your cities men die of starvation. This is showing animals how to devour men. . . . If one who pretends to be the father and mother of the people cannot, in ruling over them, avoid showing animals how to devour men, in what way is he a "father and mother" to the people?

The Chín theorists warned of the evils that come through trade,

---

Shāng-jyw̄n Shū 商君書 "The Book of Lord Shāng" (SJS). Chín statecraft writings from the late 04c to Hàn; none of them is safely attributable to Lord Shāng (d 0338). Translated by Duyvendak.

---

and wanted to hold all state functions to the bare minimum:

2:49 (SJS 20:6, excerpt, c0276). Farming, trade, and administration are the three permanent functions in a state. Farmers work the land, merchants import products, and officials oversee the people. The parasites of the three functions are six: age, dependency, beauty, love, ambition, and deportment; if these six become general, the state will perish. If farmers have more than subsistence, they will lavishly indulge the aged. If merchants have excess profits, there will be beauty and love, to the detriment of the wares. If officials are appointed but not used, then personal ambition and display of virtuous conduct will be the end. When the six parasites become customary, the army will be greatly defeated.

The eastern theorists, at approximately the same time, blamed rural hardship on bad choices made by the farmers. Here is part of a treatise on the agrarian, and thus (as also in the preceding passage), ultimately the military, situation:

2:50 (GZ 13:2, c0279). Go over the fields, look at the ploughing and weeding, calculate the amount of agricultural work, and whether the state will starve or thrive can be known. If ploughing is not deep and weeding is not assiduous; if proper use of the land is not considered and the fallow fields are weedgrown; if land ploughed is not always fertile, and land left uncultivated is not always barren; if in reckoning land against population, the uncultivated fields are many and the opened fields few, then even though there may be no floods or droughts, these are the fields of a starving state.

If so, and people are few, they will be unable to protect the territory; if so and people are many, the state will be poor and the people will starve. If in this condition they should meet with floods or droughts, then the many will disperse and not gather the harvest, and the remaining people will not be enough to mount guard, and the fortifications will be insecure.

Starving people cannot be used in war. If many have dispersed and do not gather the harvest, the state will become a wasteland. Thus it is said: A ruler who has territory but does not attend to ploughing and weeding is a ruler dependent on others for life. Thus it is said, "Go over the fields, look at the ploughing and weeding, calculate the amount of agricultural work, and whether the state will starve or thrive can be known."

Such is the importance of the mundane matter of checking to see if the tasks of the farmer are well performed, and the land has been well chosen. The same people farm and fight. The state's concern is not simply in their farming well, but in their being able to sustain the extra tasks of offensive and defensive war.

Technology. Whether it produced hardship or prosperity among the people, infrastructure support was economically rational *for the state*, and the technical level of resource exploitation (see #2:47) was therefore continually raised. The hand irrigation of fields from wells, a notably laborious and inefficient process, had been improved by the 03c by the introduction of water pumping machinery. This innovation drew an anti-technological reaction:

> **Jwāngdž** 莊 子 (JZ) "Master Jwāng," a collection of Dáuist and Primitivist texts deriving from many small groups. Most of it dates from the mid 03c. The Jwāngdž is famously humorous, but readers who see only the humor and not the suffering beneath the humor are missing the real point of much of the text. Translated by Watson.

2:51 (JZ 12:9a, c0270). Dž-gùng had gone south to Chǔ and was returning by way of Jìn. Passing by Hàn-yīn, he saw an old man who was about to water his garden. He had cut a channel leading up to the well, and was holding a bucket of water in his arms and emptying it out. Thus did he labor strenuously, for small result.

Dž-gùng said, There is a device which in one day can water a hundred acres. The effort is little, the result is great. Would you not like one? The gardener looked up at him and asked, What is it like? Dž-gùng said, It has a straight piece of wood for a beam, heavy in back and light in front. It lifts water as fast as if it were pouring out continuously, enough to make a flood. It is called the well-sweep.

The gardener flushed angrily, then he laughed and said, I heard this from my teacher: "Those with machines will have machine problems, and those who have machine problems will have machine minds. Once you have a machine inside you, the plain and simple is no longer there. When the plain and simple is not there, one's spirit vitality will not be stable. And those whose spirit vitality is not stable, the Way will not sustain." It is not that I did not know about it, but I would be ashamed to use it.

Dž-gùng was overcome with embarrassment; he cast his eyes down and did not reply.

After a bit, the gardener asked, Who are you? Dž-gùng said, A follower of Kǔng Chyōu. The gardener said, Aren't you one of those who study widely to copy the sages, the better to confuse the multitude? Who sing their sad song of one string so they can market themselves to the world? You should forget your spirit and breath, break up your body and limbs,[36] and then you will be getting somewhere! Your own person you cannot take care of, so what time can you spare to take care of the world? Go away and don't interfere with my work!

Dž-gùng cringed and paled; he was utterly at a loss. He traveled on for thirty leagues[37] before he recovered himself.

The Confucian Dž-gùng, who here represents the modernization of agriculture, is amusingly put to shame.

Work. One key idea of 03c Legalism is that there shall be no idleness and no unproductive effort. Here is a recommendation from Chín, that all activity (including intellectual activity) should be shifted to food production:

2:52 (SJS 3:1 excerpt, c0268). The means by which the ruler of men motivates his people are office and rank. The means by which a state thrives are agriculture and war. At present, the people all seek office and rank, not by means of agriculture and war, but by clever words and empty doctrines. This is what we call "wearying the people." The state of one who thus wearies the people will assuredly have no strength, and the state which has no strength will assuredly be destroyed.

Those who are good at running the state, in teaching their people, all make clear that there is only one way to acquire office and rank . . .

Note the theme of concentration: the simpler economy is the stronger economy.

Diet. despite effort below and technical support above, the overexploitation of food resources led to reduced rural diet. Here, fifty years after the Mencian program of #**2:42-43**, is a much more modest Mencian goal in this area:

2:53 (MC 7A22, excerpt, c0262). . . In a homestead of five acres,[38] if they plant the space by the walls with mulberry trees and the wife raises silkworms on them, the aged can wear silk; if there are five hens and two sows, and they do not miss their breeding season, the aged will not lack for meat. In a field of a hundred acres, if the husband cultivates them, then even a family of eight will not go hungry . . .

Even at best, only the elderly are sure of having any animal protein in their diet; the working members of the family live entirely on grain.

---

[36] A metaphor for losing the self in meditation.

[37] About ten miles; a good part of a standard day's journey.

[38] The mǒu 畝 is actually only one-sixth of an acre. We use the translation "acre" and others, such as "league" for the much shorter lǐ 里, as a cultural convenience.

The Less Portable Population. Attracting other people's population, as the 04th century had sought to do, was a reasonable goal; it was the basis of policy in several states. The converse was a wish to keep the state's own people from leaving. In the 03c, as times worsened, measures were taken to restrict the movement of population even *within* the state. A late passage in the Mencian writings suggests how far this had gone.

> **2:54** (MC 3A3b, excerpt, c0262). Neither in burying the dead nor in changing his abode shall a man go beyond the confines of his village.

Thus far the Confucians, proposing rules for the eastern states. Soon afterward, a similar policy also appears in the central states. King Lí of Ngwèi (r 0295-0243) put forth a law meant to keep certain questionable segments of the population in place. It was later incorporated verbatim into the Chín laws:

> **Shwèihŭdì** 睡虎地, in Yẃn-mv̀ng 雲夢, near Yǐng, at one time the capital of Chŭ. One grave at this site is that of a Chín law officer named Syǐ 喜, whose texts were buried with him. One of them, a brief diary of major events, fixes the date of burial at 0217. For translations of Syǐ's laws, see Hulsewé **Ch'in**, cited below as "Hulsewé."

This is how that concept reads as a law of Ngwèi:

> **2:55** (Hulsewé F1, excerpt, 0252). . . People sometimes leave the towns to go and live in the countryside, intruding among the widows and orphans of others, and demanding people's wives and daughters. This is against the old traditions of the state . . . Innkeepers, bondservants, and those who have married widows must not be allowed to form households, and must not be given land or houses . . .

This attempt to achieve social fixity is of a different kind, but has the same ultimate intent, as the Chí sumptuary legislation (#**2:25**).

The Magnates. Not all land was under the control of the several central governments. The collateral clans, which typically were descendants of one or another previous ruler of the state, kept their lands, and in some cases increased them. There were also newcomers, who were usually relatives of later rulers. Especially famous were four magnates of the 03c: Tyén Wv́n 田文 or Lord Mèng-cháng 孟嘗君 of Chí, Jàu Shv̀ng 趙勝 or Lord Píng-ywǽn 平原君 of Jàu, Wú-jì 無忌 or Lord Syìn-líng 信陵君 of Ngwèi, and Hwáng Syē 黃歇 or Lord Chūn-shv̄n 春申君 of Chŭ. Estate government, at least in legends dating from the Hàn period, was sometimes perceived as less harsh than state government, and several of the magnates are supposed to have taken in the indigent, treated them well, and thus acquired what amounted to private armies, numbering in the thousands. In later times, these men were regarded as having been superior to their rulers in generosity and in political understanding. How much of the tradition about the magnates is historical, and how much derives from Hàn sentimentality for bygone pre-Imperial ways, it is now difficult to say.

Agrarian Primitivism. One solution to the problem of rural poverty was rural simplicity. Separatist agrarian communities, whose patron deity was Shv́n Nv́ng 神農, the God of Agriculture, began to appear in the 03c. The Mencians here confront, and refute, an apologist for a socially simple system of this kind.

2:56 (MC 3A4, excerpt, c0261). There was a man who practiced the doctrines of Shv́n Nv́ng – Syw̌ Syíng, who came from Chǔ to Tv́ng. He went up to the gate and said to Wv́n-gūng, I, a man of distant regions, have heard that the Sovereign is practicing Benevolent Government, and I would like to be given a place to live and become one of your subjects. Wv́n-gūng gave him a place. His followers, numbering several tens, all wore rough clothing and hemp sandals, and wove mats for sale.

Chv́n Lyáng's followers, Chv́n Syāng and his brother Syīn, came from Sùng to Tv́ng with plough and ploughshare on their backs, saying, We hear that the Sovereign is practicing Sagely Government. We would like to be the people of a Sage. Chv́n Syāng met Syw̌ Syíng and was delighted. He dropped what he had previously studied, and began to learn from him.

Chv́n Syāng saw Mencius, and reported what Syw̌ Syíng had said: "The Sovereign of Tv́ng is truly a worthy ruler. Nevertheless, he has not yet heard the Way. A Worthy would get his food by ploughing in the fields beside the people; he would govern while preparing his own food. But Tv́ng has its storehouses and its arsenals. He is thus oppressing the people and thereby nourishing himself: how can he be called worthy?

Mencius said, Does Syw̌dž eat only grain he has planted?

He does.

Does Syw̌dž wear only cloth he has woven?

No; Syw̌dž wears hemp.

Does Syw̌dž wear a cap?

He wears a cap.

What kind of cap?

He wears a cap of plain cloth.

Did he weave it himself?

No; he exchanged grain for it.

Why does not Syw̌dž weave it himself?

It would be detrimental to his farming.

Does Syw̌dž cook in dishes and pans, and plough with an iron share?

He does.

Does he make them himself?

No; he exchanges grain for them.

To exchange grain for implements is not to oppress the potter or smith. Furthermore, when the potter and smith exchange utensils for grain, how can they be said to be oppressing the farmer?

Here is the key point: For the Mencians, trade is not intrinsically detrimental; it has its proper place in the ideal society. The Mencius passage continues . . .

And why does not Sywdž himself turn potter and smith, and from his own shop get things to use in his residence? Why all this flurrying about, exchanging things with the various craftsmen? Why does not Sywdž spare himself the trouble?

The business of the craftsmen cannot be done on top of farming.

And is it then only the ordering of the world that can be done on top of farming? There is the work of the great, and the work of the small. And with one individual, the wares of the craftsmen are all there; if he insists on making something himself before he will use it, this would lead the world off in all directions. Thus it is said, Some work with their minds, some work with their strength. Those who work with their minds govern others; those who work with their strength are governed by others. Those who are governed by others feed others; those who are fed by others govern others. This is the common principle everywhere in the world.

The radically egalitarian society of Sywdž is self-contradictory. Even in such a community, specialization and social hierarchy turn out to be necessary.[39]

Enterprise. Others sought their fortunes in the non-Sinitic coastal cultures. Ywè was surrounded by mountains, and little was known of it;[40] Wú, further north, was relatively accessible. This business story involves Wú:

2:57 (JZ 1:6, excerpt, c0240). In Sùng there was a man who knew how to make a preparation that would keep the hands from chapping. For generations his family had made a living by washing silk. A stranger heard of it, and offered to buy the formula for a hundred pieces of gold. The man called his family together and said, For generations, our family has been engaged in washing silk, and in all that time we have made no more than a few pieces of gold. Now, in one morning, we have a chance to make a hundred pieces of gold. I propose that we give it to him.

So the stranger got the formula and recommended it to the King of Wú. Wú was just then in conflict with Ywè. The King of Wú put this man in charge of the Wú forces. That winter, Wú fought a great naval battle, and inflicted a great defeat on Ywè. Wú divided up the new territory, and enfiefed the stranger with part of it.

The ability to prevent chapping of the hands was the same, but one used it to get himself a fief, whereas the other could never escape from the toil of washing silk. The level at which they made use of it was different.

---

[39]For a study of these agrarian primitivists, see Graham **Nung-chia**.

[40]Some coastal cultures of classical times have their contemporary counterparts. The name Ywè 越 (< Vyèt) survives in that of modern Vietnam 越南. In the Hàn text Shwō Ywæn 說苑 (11:13), a song in the Ywè language is first transcribed and then translated into Chinese; one transcription syllable (làn 濫, < làm) probably represents Vietnamese ðêm (< ðlem) "night." (Eric Henry, personal communication, 2010).

And this less successful story involves more remote Ywè:

> **2:58** (JZ 1:5, c0246). In Sùng there was a man who made ceremonial hats,[41] and took some to Ywè to sell. But the people of Ywè cut their hair short and tattoo their bodies,[42] so they had no use for the hats.

Some of the differences between the ways of Sinitic and non-Sinitic peoples could be commercially exploited, but others, as it turned out, could not.

Nature. A former merchant, who had risen to be a minister of Chín, commissioned a text in which the new science of cosmic coordination . . .

Lǔ-shr̀ Chūn/Chyōu 呂氏春秋 (LSCC) "Mr Lǔ's Almanac," 0241. The 12 core chapters, compiled under the patronage of the Chín minister Lǔ Bù-wéɪ 呂不韋, are based on a set of instructions for the work of the 12 months of the year. Translated by Knoblock and Riegel.

. . . was applied not just to farming, always a Chín focus, but to *all* the work of the state. Here is the eighth month, when the natural "balance" of the autumn equinox suggests the regulation of weights, and thus the promotion of trade:

> **2:59** (LSCC 8/1:4, c0241). In this month, one should build walls and outworks, establish cities and towns, excavate passages and pits, and repair bins and granaries. He then orders those responsible to hasten the people in gathering crops, seeing to silage and vegetables, and increasing stores and stocks. They urge them to plant [winter] wheat, so that on no account may the season be missed; those who do wrong should be in no doubt [that they will be punished].[43]

> **2:60** (LSCC 8/1:5, excerpt, c0241). In this month, day and night are equal. Thunder now begins to lessen . . . The Yáng force daily weakens, and waters begin to dry. When day and night are equal, unify weights and measures, adjust steelyard and balance weights . . .

> **2:61** (LSCC 8/1:6, excerpt, c0241). In this month, refurbish barriers and markets, attract merchants and travelers,[44] admit goods and commodities, and so facilitate the people's business. When all and sundry have come from the Four Quarters, when those of distant countries have all arrived, valuables will not be deficient, the superiors will not lack what they need, and the various kinds of business can go forward . . .

There is a distinct Mencian-economic air to this.

---

[41]Secured to the hair by a long pin, which will not hold in short hair. Unmentioned is the fact that the coastal culture of Ywè would have had different "ceremonies."

[42]Tattooing the face as well as the body is a trait of the coastal cultures. It may still be seen in Táɪwān (which lies opposite the old Ywè territory) and Okinawa.

[43]In contrast to this rigid outline, real farmers made many decisions to secure a decent chance of survival until the next year; for the Greek case, see Gallant **Risk** 114f.

[44]"Travelers" here is lǔ 旅; see the Proto-Yì pentagram of that name (#**2:8**).

Taxes on the land remained burdensome, speculators preyed, and the state itself sometimes bumbled. Here is a summary of conditions in the east:

> **2:62** (GZ 48, excerpt, c0235). In agriculture, monthly income is never enough; only at harvest is there a surplus. So if the ruler acts suddenly in collecting taxes and has no fixed time for them, the people will be forced to borrow at a rate of 2 for 1 in order to pay them. Work in the fields has a set schedule; if the rainfall is not sufficient, again the people will have to borrow at 2 for 1 to hire help. When merchants buy grain at 5 in the fall and sell it back at 10 in the spring, we have another borrowing at 2 for 1. Fees charged at customs barriers and in markets, taxes on stored grain, the 10% tax on yields, and expenses for firewood cutters and grooms over the four seasons, will add up to borrowing again at 2 for 1 . . .

Quite apart from the caprices of nature, farmers were caught between a greedy but inept government and greedy but all too competent money-lenders.

The solution in Chín was not to reduce the taxes imposed by the state, but to make room for them by eliminating the competition from the money-lenders, and concentrating all social energies in productive directions:

> **2:63** (SJS 25:3, excerpt, c0236). And so my teaching is, that if the people want profit, they cannot get it but by farming; if they want to avoid harm, they cannot do so but by fighting. If none of the people of the state but first engage in farming and fighting, then later they will get what they like. Thus, though the territory be small, the production will be large; though the populace be sparse, the army will be strong. If one can carry out these two principles in his own territory, then the Way of the Hegemon King lies open before him.

Thus did Chín nudge its human material toward the only activities it thought were of value to the state: farming and fighting.[45] It is a crude enough formula. Its implementation led to many casualties, both in war and on the home front.[46]

None of which matters in the least. What matters is this: By that formula, the rulers of Chín came in the fullness of time to be the masters of the world.

---

[45]The reluctance of Chín to acknowledge the importance of trade continued to be characteristic of the dynasties which followed Chín. This agrarian preference in Chinese economics, the idea that state income should be based on activities which the state itself can properly encourage, intrigued the Europeans when they first learned of it through the reports of Jesuit missionaries. The first group of European economic theorists, the Physiocrats, imitated the Chinese system of agriculture-based taxation. Only later did European economic theory shift in a mercantile direction.

[46]So also the concluding paragraph of Gallant **Risk** 196: "Poverty became more profound and widespread. Famines did not . . . The "razor-thin" line separating the bulk of the peasantry from destitution was shaved, not severed. The system of survival strategies continued to work, and they survived." We may say that the accountants of the Sinitic states had also calculated, perhaps not kindly, but well. Well enough.

3. The State

The Spring and Autumn ruler and his senior warrior elite, with a modest palace staff, together did what was needful: the war and diplomacy of the time. In the Warring States, the structure of government grew larger. Efforts were made to keep that structure responsive to the will of the ruler, as well as effective in its task; this was accomplished by laws, and by an insistence on the chain of command: the ruler's orders should be obeyed at all levels. Some of the serving elite, who identified themselves as followers of Confucius, had other ideas: they disapproved of law and preferred a form of social control based on lǐ 禮 or ceremonial propriety. They held that rulers should be chosen like officials: by merit and not by heredity. By still others, the ruler's role was seen in a more aggressive way, one agreeable to the conquest agenda of the age. An incipient science appeared: a new understanding of nature as a system. All this intellectual ferment, which centered around the state and its purposes, made the late 04th century the Golden Age of early Chinese thought.

In the end, rulers were strengthened by the loyalty the state was able to develop among the people, and by the special relationship of rulers to Heaven. Alternatives to hereditary rulership were conceived, but none developed.

The 05th Century

States began to be defined in loyalty terms. In some early 05c texts . . .

> **Hóumǎ** 侯馬 is a site near the old Jìn capital at which pits containing oath (or "covenant") texts of c0496 have been discovered; similar finds were made at nearby Wv̄n-syèn 溫縣. See Weld **Covenant**.

. . . we find that people in large numbers are being made to swear allegiance to one subfaction within the House of Jàu, itself a clan within Jìn:

3:1 (Hóumǎ 1.9, c0496). If Hú dares not to bare heart and vitals in serving his lord, or dares not to obey in all particulars Jyā's covenant and the commands issued at Dìng-gūng and Píng-sz̀, or . . . dares to work for the restoration of Jàu Ní and his descendants to the territories of the state of Jìn, or dares to adhere to a covenant with them, may the far-seeing former rulers [of Jìn] at once know of it, and may ruin befall my lineage.

These pressures within Jìn were to divide the state by the end of the century.

Law was now in operation among the general populace. Confucius, with his military heritage, preferred strict justice (punishment of the right people):

3:2 (LY 4:11, 0479). The Master said, The gentleman likes justice; the little man likes mercy.

Justice must be uniform to be just. Exceptions and exemptions would spoil it.

Confucius' followers *were* prepared to dissent from erroneous verdicts, which to them implied a failure of the state, and not a fault in the individual:

> **3:3** (LY 5:1, c0470). The Master said of Gūngyě Cháng 公冶長, He is marriageable. Though he has been in durance, it was not his fault. And he gave him his daughter to wife.

The adroitness to avoid being punished by a bad government, one which had not the Way, was desirable in one qualified to serve a good government:

> **3:4** (LY 5:2, c0470). The Master said of Nán Rúng 南容,[1] When the state has the Way 道, he will not be cast aside. When the state has not the Way, he will keep clear of penalties and punishments. And he gave him his elder brother's daughter to wife.

Lǐ 禮, or ceremonial propriety, was preferred by the Confucians to law as a means of social control. Like law, it prohibited certain actions, but unlike law, it was positive: it enjoined certain attitudes, including respect between persons grounded in something other than fear. The historical Confucius had said:

> **3:5** (LY 4:13, 0479). The Master said, Can one run the country with propriety and deference (禮讓)? Then what is the obstacle? But if one *cannot* run it with propriety and deference, what good is propriety?

Propriety is not ornament; it is the way government itself is supposed to work. Deference or unassertiveness (ràng 讓) is an aspect of lǐ behavior. The ideal warrior is energetic in action but indifferent to the *rewards* for action. Law, by contrast, is a conditioning of the many by external rewards and punishments.

The Nature of the Ruler was another current issue, and one that the Shī also addressed in depth. As with the folk Shī, these more courtly topics were subject to revision as time passed, and as the needs of the period changed.

The whole idea of a unified state was of Jōu origin, and Jōu rulers were the natural models for those who aimed at a Jōu-like supremacy. As between the *two* Jōu Kings, the precursor Wˊn-wáng was at first more highly esteemed; his merits were thought to overshadow Wǔ-wáng's merely military success against Shāng. The virtue of Wˊn-wáng was sometimes seen in lǐ or sacrificial terms:

> **3:6** (Shī 268, undivided and unrhymed, 05c?).
>
> > Pellucid and shining bright –
> > The ordinances of King Wˊn.
> >
> > He established the sacrifices,
> > And now they have their fulfilment:
> > The good omens of Jōu

This ritual persona would presently be replaced by a much more military one.

---

[1]LY 11:6 (c0360) makes him a member of the elite Nán'gūng clan, but the point of #**3:3-4** is that Confucius, whose court rank was low, could not make exalted matches.

The Tripartition of Jìn. The rival clans of Jìn were six: the eventual victors, Jàu, Ngwèi, and Hán, plus the Jr̀ 智, Fàn 范, and Jūng-háng 中行 clans. The last two were of little account; their lands were absorbed by the Jr̀ in 0454. At the battle of Jìn-yáng in 0453, the Jr̀ were destroyed by the other three, Jàu Syāngdž being the great figure among the victors. This caught the imagination of later ages: tales of revenge on behalf of the Lord of Jr̀ gained a permanent place in the literature of lost causes.[2] In 0424, new rulers succeeded in Ngwèi, Hán, and Jàu, and these were acknowledged as Lords (hóu), that is, as rulers of their respective domains, by the still ceremonially important Jōu King in 0403.

Of the three, it was Ngwèi Wv́n-hóu (r 0424-0387) of whose reign tales of administrative excellence were later told. Lǐ Kwēi 李悝 of Ngwèi (05c) was later claimed to have produced the Fǎ Jīng 法經, a master canon of the laws of all the states, but that claim is clearly untenable.[3] An earlier claim was based on the text Lǐdž 李子 "Master Lǐ," attributed to Lǐ Kwēi in the Hàn Dynasty; it credits him with inventing the ever-normal granary, but that policy is first mentioned in Hàn, and the Lǐdž was probably written to give it the sanction of ancient credentials.[4] Ngwèi may indeed have been ahead of the other Jìn states, Jàu and Hán, in the modernization process which seems to have begun in Chí,[5] but what its actual 05c legal and economic policies were, we do not now know.

Other traditions identify Ngwèi 魏 (under the name of Wèi 衛) with the process of textualization in the Confucian version of the Shr̄ repertoire:

3:7 (LY 9:15, c0405). The Master said, When I returned from Wèi to Lǔ the music was put right, and the Yǎ and Sùng found their proper places.

This passage was written by Dzv̄ng Ywǽn 曾元, Dzv̄ngdž's elder son, who had inherited Dzv̄ngdž's position as head of the Analects school. His younger brother Dzv̄ng Shv̄n 曾申 had succeeded Dž-syà in the proprietorship of the Shr̄, and the information in this passage is thus probably authentic. At least the earliest poems in the court (Yǎ) and ritual (Sùng) sections of the Shr̄ were probably added at this time, along with many more poems associated with Wèi, which (as Shr̄ 26-64) now make up a quarter of the entire Fv̄ng section.

And so we come to the end of the 05c. Law and economic policy were making progress, though in ways that can no longer be precisely specified, and Confucian cultural propaganda was beginning to be organized in textual form.

---

[2]A famous example is the Vengeance of Yẁ-ràng; #**4:58-59**. For the lore of the later Roving Avengers, see Watson **Records** 3/409f (SJ 124) and Liu **Knight**.

[3]For its refutation, see Pokora **Canon**.

[4]For its acceptance in Latter Hàn (1c), see Swann **Food** 67. For the 20c American version of the 01c Chinese price equalization policy, see Bodde **Wallace**.

[5]In this light, the Battle of Mǎ-líng in 0343 (see p69 below) takes on something of the character of a symbolic trial of strength between the old East and the new Center.

The 04th Century

Jìn had been divided in the 05c; the throne of Chí was usurped in the 04c.[6] But rulership was strengthened – by new concepts of rulership, new theories of the state, and a reshaping of legal practice. The revolutionary idea that there are laws of nature as well as laws of men, which might have been a challenge to the position of the hereditary rulers, became in the end a further source of strength.

Chí. The exile Chv́n 陳 clan, in Chí called Tyén 田, had become the power behind the Chí throne. In 0481 they killed the ruler, but let his heir succeed. In 0375 the ruler died *without* an heir. The head of the Tyén clan took the throne, and at his death was given the epithet Hwán-gūng. Here is the inscription on a bronze vessel with which the second Tyén ruler sacrificed to his father:

3:8 (Chí inscription, excerpt, 0357).[7] In the 6th month, on the cyclical day gwěɪ/wèɪ [#28], Yīn-dẕ, the Lord of Chv́n 陳, said, My August late father, the filial and martial Hwán-gūng: may his great desire be magnificently achieved! Let it be Yīn-dẕ who extols his August deceased father's glory; extends the line of the High Ancestor, the Yellow Emperor; fulfils and follows the work of Hwán of Chí and Wv́n of Jìn; summons the feudal lords to his court . . .

This is an open appeal for future domination of the entire Sinitic world.

---

[6]Not necessarily a bad thing for the state of Chí; see p38.
[7]For the full text and a discussion, see Doty **Bronze** 614f.

The work of "Hwán and Wv́n" (page 27f) was the unification of the states, and the Yellow Emperor was regarded as the ancestor of all the Sinitic peoples. To claim his as one's ancestor was to claim ascendency over all.

Mǎ-líng. In 0343, Chí defeated Ngwèi at Mǎ-líng, in Ngwèi territory. So encouraged was the Chí ruler that he proclaimed himself a King, taking the title of the Jōu rulers and implicitly annexing the former Jōu Mandate of Heaven. The Lǔ Confucians, defenders of Jōu tradition, expressed this outrage as the adoption by the Jì clan of ceremonies to which they were not entitled:

> **3:9** (LY 3:1, 0342). The Master said of the Jì, Eight rows of dancers performing in his courtyard: if this can be borne, what cannot be borne?

Only the King was supposed to have that many dancers. Another denunciation:

> **3:10** (LY 3:2, c0342). The Three Families used the Yūng song as a recessional. The Master said, "Assisting princes standing by / the Son of Heaven in majesty" – where in the halls of the Three Families was *this* drawn from?

The King Ideal. The Yūng song (Shr̄ 282) celebrated the peaceful reign of the Jōu King; so did Shr̄ 268 (#**3:6**). But in line with the 04c ideological shift,[8] later poems make Wv́n-wáng, not his son Wǔ-wáng, *himself* a conqueror:

> **3:11** (Shr̄ 241, excerpt, mid 04c).
>
> 241G   . . . God said to King Wv́n:
> > Take thought for your enemies,
> > join with your brothers;
> > with your scaling ladders,
> > with your towers and rams,
> > assault the walls of Chúng

This shows its lateness by its mention of 04c siege techniques. In another poem, Wv́n-wáng is portrayed not only as a victor, but as *a victor over Shāng:*

> **3:12** (Shr̄ 255, excerpt, mid 04c).
>
> 255G   King Wv́n said, "Oh, alas!
> > Oh, alas, you Yīn[9] and Shāng!
> > It is not that God on High gave no blessings,
> > but Yīn used not the ancient ways.
> > Even if you lacked men old and wise,
> > you had your laws and punishments.
> > But to these you gave no heed,
> > and the Great Command is now cast down.

The old ideal of cultural influence has here been replaced by an exclusively military image. Royal "virtue" consists only in the fact of military conquest.

---

[8]For the militarization of 04c culture, see further p99f, 113f.

[9]Yīn (the dynastic name used by Shāng in its later years) is here a poetic synonym.

The Hegemon Concept was also being rethought. The Dzwǒ Jwàn gives the hegemon three different titles, which suggest an increasingly violent ideal. The first, Mv́ng-jǔ 盟主, "Arbiter of Covenants," corrects abuses of power:

> **3:13** (DJ 9/26:14, excerpt, c0360). [The Jìn minister Jàu] Wv́n-dž said to the Lord of Jìn, Jìn is Arbiter of Covenants. If any Lord infringe on another, then [Jìn] should interfere, and compel the return of the territory. Now, the towns taken by Wū Yv́ [and given to Jìn] are in this category, and to covet them is not to be Arbiter of Covenants. I beg to return them. The Prince said, Very well, but who can we send? He replied, Syẁ Lyáng-dài can do it without military force. The Lord of Jìn sent him.

The Mv́ng-jǔ gains his authority by virtue (DJ 6/7:8, 9/9:5, 9/26:7); he does not throw away the lives of the people (6/6:3a) or weary them (10/1:1).

The next title is Hóu-bwó 侯伯, "Chief of the Lords" or simply Bwó. He both supports and punishes. Small Syíng is being aided by Chí, Sùng, and Tsáu:

> **3:14** (DJ 5/1:3b, c0334). In summer, Syíng moved to Yí-yí, and the Lords walled it. This was to relieve distress. In general, the Hóu-bwó relieves distress, shares catastrophe, and punishes the guilty. This is proper.

In a third set of passages, the hegemon is called Bà 霸, the term usually used for "hegemon" in Warring States theory. The Bà at one point is described thus:

> **3:15** (DJ 4/1:5, c0318). To be friendly with states that observe the rules of propriety, to help those that have the potential for stability and strength, to complete the separation of those that are divided and disaffected, and to overthrow those that are full of disorder and confusion – this is how a Prince with the role of Hegemon proceeds.

The Bà functions not to preserve the states, but to weed out the weaker ones. Hegemon theory, like King theory, edged toward a mere-conquest concept.

Methodological Moment. These three titles might reflect a real evolution during Spring and Autumn, or it might reflect evolution of DJ theory. Which? We reason: If Chí Hwán-gūng was always called a Mv́ng-jǔ, and Jìn Wv́n-gūng always a Hóu-bwó, and if later rulers were always Bà, we would have a plausible evolution in real time. But this is not what happens: Jìn Wv́n-gūng is identified by *all three terms* (Mv́ng-jǔ 9/31:6 and 10/29:5, Hóu-bwó in 5/23:8 and 10/9:3, Bà in 5/27:4 and 10/3:1). If all three terms are used of the same person, they cannot define different phases. It is then not the *hegemon*, but the DJ *theory* of the hegemon, that is evolving here.

Then the Hegemon concept was simply that: *a concept*, invented in the 04c to legitimize the idea of replacing the Jōu sovereign in his regulatory function, and to give theoretical support to increasingly aggressive contemporary rulers.[10]

--------••••--------

[10]For these DJ theory changes, see Brooks **Hegemon** and Brooks **Heaven**.

Other Kings. The Chí assertion of Kingship was imitated in other states: Ngwèı in 0334, Jàu in 0325, Chín in 0324, Yēn in 0320, and Sùng in 0318. Lǔ did not openly take that title, but it did make four ritual hymns which celebrated its ruler Syī-gūng (r 0659-0627) in ways that ranked him with the Jōu kings:

3:16 (Shī 300, excerpt, late 04c).

300F Tàı-shān towers high;
the Land of Lǔ looks up to it.
It also possesses Gwēı and Mv̀ng,
stretching to the Furthest East,
as far as the states along the Sea.
The Hwáı tribes in submission come;
none but is obedient.
– Such are the deeds of the Lord of Lǔ.

These hymns became part of the canon: they are the present Shī 297-300.

Sùng, which *had* a royal past, produced five sacrificial hymns, supposedly from Shāng times; these were eventually included as Shī 301-305. With their inclusion, "Shāng" took its place beside Jōu as defining Sinitic culture.

Predictions were also used to authenticate contemporary rulers. By this time, the earlier pentagram system had been expanded into the present Yì:

> **Yì** 易 "Changes," 04c. A divination system of 64 hexagrams, expanded from the proto-Yì. The added text refers to higher culture: sacrifice, war, and Shāng events. Claimed to be a Jōu text, but archaeology shows that Jōu continued to use Shāng bone divination. Translated by Wilhelm.

The Dzwǒ Jwàn people moved from Lǔ to Chí in c0320, and there invented omens for Chí. One (DJ 3/22:1b), meant to legitimize the Tyén usurpation, described an Yì divination for the founder of the Tyén clan. The result was Hexagram 20 (觀), "View," with the fourth line emphasized:

3:17 (Yì, Hexagram 20 Gwàn 觀 "View," 04c).

6. ▬▬ Viewing his life.
For a gentleman, no blame.
5. ▬▬ Viewing my life.
For a gentleman, no blame.
4. ▬ ▬ **Viewing the Splendor of the State.**
Favors being the guest of a King.
3. ▬ ▬ Viewing my life.
Decide between advance and retreat.
2. ▬ ▬ Viewing through a crack.
Favors persistence by a woman.
1. ▬ ▬ Youthful view.
For a humble man, no blame. For a gentleman, humiliation.

The prediction of future greatness for the Tyén family is obvious.

Philosophy of the State first appeared in Chí, under the Tyén rulers. The earliest political thinkers are anonymously preserved in the Gwǎndž; later ones like Shv̄n Bù-hàı and Shv̀n Dàu left their names attached to their ideas.

The first questions asked by the Gwǎndž thinkers were about control:

3:18 (GZ 3:1, excerpt, c0356). In a state of a myriad chariots, the soldiers must have leaders. Its area being extensive, the countryside must have administrators. Its population being large, the bureaus must have heads. In shaping the people's future, the court must have a policy . . .

3:19 (GZ 1:4, excerpt, c0355). Put the state on a firm basis. Accumulate in inexhaustible granaries; stock in undepletable storehouses . . . Use the people 民 in nonconflicting offices. Make clear the road to certain death [punishment]; open the gate to certain gain [reward]. . .

The system should be efficient, without overlapping responsibilities. Society was controlled by rewards and punishments. The punishments were severe:

3:20 (GZ 7:12, excerpt, c0350). [The ruler] is severe with the remiss and lazy, to shame them [and others]. He punishes those who break rules or make mistakes, to discipline them. He executes those who violate prohibitions, to terrify them.

3:21 (GZ 7:13, excerpt, c0350). If [the ruler] is firm and consistent, the deviant and depraved will be fearful. When the deviant are changed and the depraved are reformed, no sooner will an order go out than the people will already be moving.

The system must not have a mind of its own; it must reflect the ruler's will.

In 0376, Hán conquered Jv̀ng, and moved its capital there. There presently appeared a philosopher of state who had been born in Jv̀ng, but who in his adult years is said to have served as minister to Hán. His doctrines . . .

> **Shv̄n Bù-hàı** 申不害, c0400-0337, was a Legalist thinker and perhaps minister in Hán. A collection of sayings attributed to him (some of them genuine) still existed in Hàn. The Hàn work was later lost, and is now known only from quotations, which have been collected in Creel **Shen**.

. . . are concerned with how the ruler can avoid danger but still control the new bureaucracy. This art was later called shù 術 "skill, administrative adroitness."

3:22 (Shv̄n Bù-hàı #1:1, c0350). If one wife monopolizes a husband, other wives are thrown into disorder; if one minister monopolizes the ruler, the rest of the ministers are overshadowed. Thus a jealous wife has no difficulty breaking up a family; an unruly minister has no difficulty in breaking up a state. So the wise ruler has all his ministers come forward together like the spokes of a wheel, so that none can monopolize the ruler.

The human resources of the larger state need to be fully exploited – one cannot have only a few ministers – but also fully dominated. There must be no source of command, no center of power, other than the ruler.

Another comment on the danger of a single favored minister:

> **3:23** (Shv̄n Bù-hài #1:2, c0350). The reason a ruler of men makes his walls and ramparts high and secures his gates and doors is to prepare against robbers and bandits. But the one who assassinates the ruler and takes his state does not necessarily do it by climbing over the walls and ramparts or battering down the gates and doors. He blocks off what the ruler knows, limits what the ruler hears, and thus monopolizes what he commands; he possesses his people, and he takes his state.

The ruler is always in danger. His safety lies not in the personal-valor heroics of Spring and Autumn, but in the more expert state structure of the 04c:

> **3:24** (Shv̄n Bù-hài #1:3, c0350). Now, suppose that Wū Hwò or Pv́ng Dzǔ were to bear on their back a weight of a thousand jyv̄n and carry in their bosom the value of a precious jade; let Mv̀ng Bv̄n[11] or Chv́ng Jīng wear a sword as sharp as Gān Jyāng and go along to guard him; if he travels by a deserted road, robbers will still plunder him. Now, the strength of the ruler of men is not as great as that of Wū Hwò or Pv́ng Dzǔ, and his valor is not as great as that of Mv̀ng Bv̄n or Chv́ng Jīng, and the value of that which he is watching over is greater than that of a precious jade or a thousand of gold. Can he expect not to lose them?

The Dàuists of the Dàu/Dv́ Jīng group were also venturing into state theory. They advised working with fewer resources, and acting only inconspicuously. The extreme of inconspicuous action is undoubtedly wú-wéı 無爲, or *in*action:

> **3:25** (DDJ 10, c0337).
>
> > In supporting your soul and holding the One,
> > > can you be without divergence?
> > In concentrating your breath and achieving Weakness,
> > > can you be like the newborn?
> > In cleansing and cleaning your mystic vision,
> > > can you be without stain?
> > In loving your people and governing your state,
> > > can you be without knowledge?
> > When the gates of Heaven open and close,
> > > can you play the female part?
> > In seeing and understanding in all four directions,
> > > can you be without activity 無爲 ?
> >
> > Give birth to them, rear them:
> > give birth but do not possess,
> > act but do not depend.
> > Be chief, but do not manage –
> > > This is the Mystic Virtue.

---

[11]A swordsman of legendary ferocity, mentioned also in Mencius; Gān Jyāng was the most famous sword of antiquity, and so on with the others named in this passage.

4th Cent,
Golden Age of
Chinese thought

Philosophical Interactions. Shv̄n Bù-hài's idea that wealth is hard to guard (#**3:24**) turns up recognizably in the DDJ:

3:26 (DDJ 9, excerpt, c0335).

> Gold and jade may fill the hall, but none can ward them.

These theories were not thought up in some vacuum; the theorists responded to each other's work, copying the good ideas or opposing the erroneous ones. Such was the interactive nature of the 04c Golden Age of Chinese Thought.

By way of exchange, DDJ ideas turn up in the *second* layer of Shv̄n Bù-hài, and were probably added in the generation after Shv̄n Bù-hài himself:

3:27 (Shv̄n Bù-hài #1:5, c0318). One good at ruling will rely on stupidity, take his stand in inadequacy, adopt a stance of not daring, hide himself in lack of purpose (wú-shř 無事). He will hide his motives and conceal his tracks, and show the world a picture of inactivity (wú-wéi 無爲). Thus those near will be close to him, and those far away will cherish him.

> If he shows people that he has too much, they will take it away; if he shows people that he does not have enough, they will give to him. The hard are broken; the endangered are sheltered. Who moves is insecure, who stays still is at peace.

Here is the image of a humble and unassertive ruler, who prospers solely through the spontaneous generosity and sympathy of his people. The Gwǎndž people adopted this tactic of attraction and conciliation:

3:28 (GZ 2:25, c0317). To summon the distant, use "wú-wéi" 無爲 on them. To ingratiate the near, talk "wú-shř" 無事 to them. It is only the traveler who goes by night who really has it 獨有也.

The cynicism is obvious. The wise ruler "goes by night:" keeps his plans secret and operates in the dark; his purposes are unknown to those he persuades.

The DDJ people had earlier rejected expert knowledge, recommended by the statecraft experts of the time, as having a bad effect on the people:

3:29 (DDJ 19, c0340).

> Eliminate Wisdom 智, discard Eloquence 辯 –
> and the people will profit a hundredfold.
> Eliminate Craft 巧, discard Profit 利 –
> and robbers and thieves there will be none.
> Eliminate Transformation 化, discard Concern 慮 –
> and the people will again be filial and kind.

The part about robbers and thieves was later picked up by the Confucians . . .

3:30 (LY 12:18, c0326). Jì Kāngdž was worried about robbers, and asked Confucius. Confucius replied, If somehow you were to have no desires, then even if you offered them rewards, they would not steal.

. . . who also believed in the cultural influence of the elite. Thus did ideas pass back and forth among rival schools in the late 04th century.

The Problem of Conquest. It had been thought that no conqueror could replace a local ruler because only a descendant could secure blessings from the ancestral spirits. Here the Prince of Yẃ relies on that protection:

> **3:31** (DJ 5/5:8, excerpt, c0316) . . . The Prince said, My sacrificial offerings have been abundant and pure; the spirits will not forsake me, but will sustain me. His minister replied, I have heard that the spirits do not accept the *persons* of men, it is their *virtue* to which they cleave . . . If Jìn should take Yẃ, and cultivate virtue, and on that basis present fragrant offerings, will the spirits vomit them out?

And in the story, his state is destroyed. Ritual protections no longer protected.

Nor did Heaven itself necessarily care about what lay below. The Dàuists had put forth a picture of an uncaring universe and a similarly inactive ruler:

> **3:32** (DDJ 5, excerpt, c0320).
> Heaven and Earth are unkind:
>   they treat the Myriad Creatures like straw dogs.
> The Sage is unkind:
>   he treats the common people like straw dogs . . .

. . . that is, without favoritism. Heaven simply does what it does.

Jì-syà. The Chí invasion of Yēn, urged by Mencius in 0315, led to disaster in 0314, when other states drove Chí from Yēn.[12] In 0313, the King of Chí gathered six experts at Jì-syà 稷下 and charged them to analyze the rise and fall of states. Three were from Chí, and three from other states. One was:

> **Shv̀n Dàu** 慎到, c0350-c0280, of Jàu. Some parts of his work as known in Hàn have been recovered from later quotations by Thompson.

Shv̀n Dàu developed the Dàuist idea of an uncaring universe:

> **3:33** (Shv̀n Dàu #1-2, c0310). Heaven has its light; it does not care about men's darkness. Earth has its riches; it does not care about men's poverty. The Sage has his virtue; he does not care about men's perils.
>   Though Heaven does not care about men's darkness, they can open up doors and make windows, and will surely obtain their own light thereby, so Heaven need not concern itself.

The Sage, like Heaven and Earth, provides a model for an orderly society.

> **3:34** (Shv̀n Dàu #6, c0310). That the Sage possesses the world is because he has received it, not taken it. The relation of the common people to the Sage is that they nourish him; they do not expect the Sage to nourish them, so the Sage need not concern himself.

Things happen naturally, but also sufficiently, in the impersonal universe.

---

[12]For Mencius and the Yēn Incident, see further p135.

Position. The Sage's power does not depend on his personal qualities:

3:35 (Shv̀n Dàu #12-13, c0310). When [the exemplary good ruler] Yáu was a commoner, he could not bring order even to the people next door, but when [the archetypical bad ruler] Jyé was Son of Heaven, he could bring confusion to the entire world. From this we may see that excellence is not enough of itself to cause the many to submit, but that situation 勢 and position 位 are enough to make even the excellent submit.

Shr̀ 勢 means the power latent in a situation. The *ruler* is not powerful; it is the *ruler's position* that is powerful. From this, it is but a step to the idea that the state could run on its collective ability, whatever the character of the ruler:

3:36 (LY 14:19, c0310). The Master had spoken of Wèi Líng-gūng's lack of the Way. Kāngdž said, If so, why was he not destroyed? Confucius said, Jùngshú Yw̌ had charge of visitors and guests, Invocator Twó had charge of the ancestral shrine, Wángsūn Jyǎ had charge of military strategy. That being so, how should he be destroyed?

Here is the root idea of a proto-constitutional sovereignty. It went nowhere.

A Dàuist Response. Conventional statecraft theory sought to transform 化 the people, to make them orderly and dutiful. The DDJ Dàuists objected:

3:37 (DDJ 37, c0310).

> The Way ever does nothing,
>   but there is nothing that is not done.
> If lords and kings could keep to this,
>   the Myriad Things[13] would be transformed of themselves 自化 .

Shv̀n Dàu had a third idea: the concept of accommodation (yīn 因), or going along with an untransformed reality, administered by impersonal law.

3:38 (Shv̀n Dàu #28-29, c0310). It is the Way of Heaven that the results of accommodation are great, and the results of transformation are small. By 'accommodation,' I mean accommodation to the human reality.

No man but acts out of self-interest. If I alter men so as to make them act in *my* 我 interest, there will be no one whom I can employ.

The more a ruler shapes men to his personal wishes, the less the state interest can be carried out. Even in giving rewards, the ruler must not be personal:

3:39 (Shv̀n Dàu #61, c0310). If a ruler 君人 puts aside law and governs by himself, punishments and rewards, confiscations and bestowals, will issue in accord with the ruler's own wishes. Then those who receive rewards, however appropriate, will have hoped for more, and thus be unsatisfied; those who incur penalties, however appropriate, will have hoped for less, and thus be discontent.

Predictability is the basis of harmony; personal elements will wreck the system.

---

[13] All beings; here, all men.

The system must thus work like a machine. One way to make it do so is to organize not only the government, but the countryside:

3:40 (GZ 5:6, excerpt, resuming **#2:26**, c0312). . . five assemblies 聚 are a county 鄉, four counties are a region 方, and are organized officially. When organization is complete, establish a town 邑.[14] Five families 家 are a group 伍,[15] ten families are a unit 連 . . .

The passage goes on to detail the obligation of each of these entities to supply a certain quota of material for the army: armor, men, or chariots.

Law was punitive in nature, and prescribed behavior even within the family. The oldest Mician tract already implies a working legal system, complete with an enforcement mechanism of sorts, protecting life and property:

3:41 (MZ 17:1, excerpt, c0390). Suppose someone enters another's orchard and filches his peaches and plums. When others hear of it, they will think it wrong; and the high officials will punish him if they can catch him . . .

Researching law from supposedly ancient texts like the Shū . . .

> **Shū** 書 "Writings" or "Documents," 04c-03c. Purported speeches of ancient rulers. Half the Shū were lost in Hàn; the present texts for those titles are 3rd century forgeries. Translated by Legge and Karlgren.

. . . requires care; specifically, it requires a certain amount of analytical technique. The two Shū texts most often cited as evidence for Jōu law, the Kāng Gàu and the Lw̆ Syíng, actually focus on 04c and 03c legal issues.

The Kāng Gàu 康誥 purports to be a speech of Jōu-gūng to his brother, who is enfiefed in the former Shāng capital area. He is to judge the people, but by whose laws? The text says, by the laws of Shāng (also called Yīn):

3:42 (Shū 37:11, excerpt, c0355) . . . Do you, in announcing verdicts, follow the penal laws of Yīn.

3:43 (Shū 37:20, excerpt, c0355) . . . When I think of the people, I see they are to be led to happiness and tranquility. I think of the virtue of the former wise Kings of Yīn, whereby they tranquilized and regulated the people, and rouse myself to realize it.

But other parts of the same document say instead, by the laws of Jōu:

3:44 (Shū 37:16, excerpt, c0278) . . . You must deal speedily with [such] persons according to the penal laws of Wv́n-wáng . . .

What is going on here?

---

[14]In contrast to the towns of mediaeval Europe, which were often horizons of economic opportunity, these Chinese towns are government control points.

[15]The term group (伍) is borrowed from military usage; see **#4:61**.

Methodological Moment. There is an internal contradiction in Shū 37. Where are its boundaries? In terms of Legge's divisions, §1-14 and §20-24 assume continuity with Yīn (Shāng) traditions, whereas §15-19, which decree death for violations of filial piety (the respect a son should show to his father), invoke instead the laws of Jōu. The pattern looks like this:

A A A A A A A A A A A A A A A A **B B B B B** A A A A A

The aberrant segment is well-defined, making a good case for an interpolation. Also, (a) filial piety first became a high-profile issue in the late 04c,[16] and (b) as states continued to rule culturally diverse territories, it was probably difficult to retain local law, and necessary to impose the law of the central government, here symbolized by "Jōu." The B interpolation updates A in both these senses.

That B is late also appears from external evidence. The 04c Dzwǒ Jwàn quotes only from the A section of our present Kāng Gàu, whereas Sywńdž and other 03c texts quote from B as well as A. That is, no 04c text is aware of B. It follows that B itself is probably an 03c addition to A.

———————••••———————

State and Family were the two foci of personal obligation. They came into conflict in the late 04c, a conflict ultimately resolved in favor of the state. An early statement of the relation between state (gwó 國) and family (jyā 家) is:

> **3:45** (LY 12:20, excerpt, c0326). Dž-jāng asked, how may an officer[17] be successful? The Master said, What do you mean by "successful?" Dž-jāng replied, In the state, sure to be known; in the family, sure to be known. The Master said, This is being known, not being successful. As for success: His character is straight, he loves the right; he inquires into words and observes appearances; he is considerate of those below him – in the state, sure to be successful; in the family, sure to be successful.

Euthyphro. The conflict between family and state had been explored in Plato's early 04c dialogue Euthyphro, in which a son informs the state about a crime committed by his father; Socrates proves that Euthyphro (whose name means "upright") does not really understand filial piety. Alexander conquered Bactria, the transfer point for the silk trade, in 0327, and imposed Greek culture on it. For the first time, Greek ideas were located where Chinese traders could encounter them, be intrigued by them, and spread them on their return.

---

[16]The 05c Analects (see Brooks **Analects**), though it discusses virtue at great length, never mentions filial piety; that value appears once in LY 11:5 (c0360) and then often in LY 2 (c0317). This does not mean that filial piety was a recent virtue, but only that filial piety *first enters the Confucian statecraft discourse* in the late 04c.

[17]"Officer" is shr̀ 士, a term of military origin, later (as here) applied to literate civil servants. The translation "scholar-knight" is an attempt to capture this dual character, but the shr̀ is not very similar to either the European scholar or the European knight.

Greek Philosophies impact on Chinese thought in 4th century BC.

Thus we have the story of "Upright Gūng," which is about filial piety:[18]

> **3:46** (LY 13:18, c0322). The Prince of Shv̀ said to Confucius, In our country there is a certain Upright Gūng. His father stole a sheep, and the son gave evidence against him. Confucius said, The upright ones in my country are different from this: a son will screen a father, and a father will screen a son. There is a sort of uprightness in this too.

The Upright Gūng motif often recurs in later writings. Filial piety was unopposable; it is the one conventional cultural value that is never satirized, even in the irreverent Jwāngdž. But in its own way, law too was unopposable.

Collective Responsibility, which is implicit in the Upright Gūng dilemma, was an important concept in Legalist thinking. It first appears in the Gwǎndž:

> **3:47** (GZ 4:5, excerpt, c0315). Collective guilt: If [an infraction] is by family members, it extends to the head of the family; if by the head of a family, it extends to the head of the group of ten or five; if by the head of a group or ten or five, it extends to the clan head . . .

The presumption is that (1) everyone is responsible for what occurs at the next lower level, and (2) to conceal a crime is itself a crime. Yet filial piety in this system was a virtue recognized by the state, one to be reported and rewarded:

> **3:48** (GZ 4:5, excerpt, c0315). Filiality and respect for elders, loyalty and fidelity, ability and goodness, refinement and talent: if displayed by a family head's senior and junior family members, male and female slaves, servants and menials, or visitors and guests, [the family head reports it to the group of ten or five], the group of ten or five reports it to the clan head, the clan head reports it to the district marshal . . .

These are virtues of subordination; the basic virtue *is precisely* subordination.

There is further evidence for collective responsibility in the Kāng Gàu. Two Dzwǒ Jwàn quotations from it are not found in either the A or the B segment; they are *not in our text of the Kāng Gàu*. They were probably replaced when the more severe Kāng Gàu B material was added. They read, in full:

> **3:49** (Shū 37, lost passage, quoted at DJ 5/33:6, c0322). In the Kāng Gàu it says, If the father is unkind, or the son disrespectful, if the elder brother is unfriendly or the younger brother unsubmissive, [guilt] does not extend from one to the other (不相及也).

> **3:50** (Shū 37, lost passage, quoted at DJ 10/20:4, c0322). In the Kāng Gàu it says, With father and son, elder and younger brother, guilt does not extend from one to the other (罪不相及).

Methodological Moment. These arguments for an *exception* to the rule *imply* a rule, and are thus evidence for a co-responsibility rule in the late 04c.

———————•••••———————

---

[18]For Greek echoes in Chinese texts after 0327, see Brooks **Alexandrian**.

The Lw̌ Sýing 呂刑 (Shū 55) is supposed to be a speech by the 010c Jōu King Mù-wáng. Like the Kāng Gàu, it is one of the most quoted Shū texts. It represents a humanizing trend in legal theory, though it does so by the ungallant device of blaming the cruelty of the law on somebody else. The text has two parts, of which the second or B (Legge §14-22) is defined by promising, at its beginning and its end, to "make punishments a blessing" (祥刑). Part A (§1-13) attributes cruel punishments not to Sinitic tradition, but to the Myáu 苗:

> **3:51** (Shū 55:3, excerpt, c0330). The Myáu people did not use persuasion, but kept order by punishments; they made a penal code of Five Cruelties and called it Law . . .

The Myáu are "destroyed" to protect the culture. Somehow the same cruel five punishments are still used, but at least there shall be no undue influence . . .

> **3:52** (Shū 55:11, excerpt, c0330) . . . In adjudicating cases, they shall not be influenced by intimidation, nor by wealth . . .

. . . and intentionality (終) shall be considered in deciding guilt:

> **3:53** (Shū 55:13, excerpt, c0330) . . . Heaven, in keeping order among the people, allows us one day [for judgement]. Whether [a crime] is unintentional 無終 or intentional 惟終 depends upon the person . . .[19]

The later B section extends the A rule against improper influence. It also proposes dismissing doubtful cases which would involve punishments . . .

> **3:54** (Shū 55:17, excerpt, c0288). If there is doubt about the five punishments, the punishment should be forborne; if there is doubt about the five penalties, the penalty should be forborne . . .

. . . and has an elaborate system for the commutation of punishments into fines:

> **3:55** (Shū 55:18, excerpt, c0288). When the punishment of branding is doubtful, and forborne, the penalty is a hundred rings,[20] but first make sure that the offense was committed. When the punishment of cutting off the nose is doubtful, and is forborne, the penalty is twice as much . . .

The penalty in lieu of death is a thousand rings. The text gives the number of ancient crimes as 3,000. This is pure fantasy: no *later* law code was that large.[21] But commutation was real; we will encounter it in 03c Chí and Chín.[22]

The 04c Micians, householders rather than farmers, found law protective. These Lw̌ Sýing B statements are meant to further civilianize law; to make it a blessing and not a curse for those who live under it.

micians & civilianizing law ↗

---

[19]The phrase here is cryptic; the principle is more fully spelled out in Kāng Gàu A, where even a severe crime, if unintentional (有大罪非終), is to be forgiven.

[20]A ring of metal (in the majority opinion, copper) contained six ounces.

[21]Nor was any ancient code. For the Hittite laws (200 clauses), see Roth **Law** 213f.

[22]Commutation was commonplace in the Ancient Near East; see Roth **Law** passim.

The Gwǎndž Legalists had tended to exclude the human dimension . . .

3:56 (GZ 3:18, c0332). Maintaining territory depends on fortifications; maintaining fortifications depends on armies; maintaining armies depends on men; maintaining men depends on grain.

. . . and to rely only on things they could be sure of controlling. The Analects group had insisted on the importance of people's *feelings* toward the state:

3:57 (LY 12:7, c0326). Dž-gùng asked about government. The Master said, Enough food, enough weapons, the people having trust 信 in him. Dž-gùng said, If he had to let something go, of the three, which would be first? He said, Let weapons go. Dž-gùng said, If he had to let something else go, of the two, which would be first? He said, Let food go. Since ancient times there has always been death, but if the people lack trust, he cannot stand.

They also found inadequate the whole idea of government by compulsion:

3:58 (LY 2:3, c0317). The Master said, Lead them by government and regulate them by punishments, and the people will evade them with no sense of shame. Lead them with virtue and regulate them by ritual, and they will acquire a sense of shame – and moreover, they will be orderly.

Lǐ will achieve *as a byproduct* what law struggles, and fails, to achieve directly.

Custom. The Analects Confucians, who were now shifting their position (see #3:2), did not want a system of laws; they wanted a social order achieved by more spontaneous means. Justice before the law no longer attracted them; they wanted, not justice, but prevention:

3:59 (LY 12:13, c0326). The Master said, in hearing lawsuits, I am no better than anybody else. What is required is to bring about a situation where there *are* no lawsuits.

And they sought social transformation through moral influence from above:

3:60 (LY 12:19, c0326). Jì Kāngdž asked Confucius about government, saying, If I kill those who have not the Way to support those who do have the Way, how would that be? Confucius replied, You are there to govern, what use have you for killing? If you desire the good, the people will be good. The virtue of the gentleman is the wind, the virtue of the little people is the grass. The wind blowing on the grass will surely bend it.

Bending the grass means changing the people. But how long would it take to change them to create a civic order, so that law itself would be superfluous?

3:61 (LY 13:11, c0322). The Master said, If good men ran the state for a hundred years, one could finally rise above cruelty and abolish killing – true indeed is this saying!

Four human generations. At least this does not underestimate the difficulty.[23]

---

[23]For the process of changing customs in modern France, see Weber **Peasants**.

Needless to say, no 04c state could afford to wait that long to get its civilian house in order before going to war. The social insight of the Confucians is sound, and their candor about the requisites for a spontaneously law-abiding state is admirable, but the timetable did not recommend the method. The mass army drillmaster stood ready to produce a docile populace in just a few weeks.

Legal Practice is first directly known, from the inside, in late 04c Chǔ:

> **The Bāushān** 包山 **Texts** (0322-0316) are from the tomb of the highest Chǔ law official, the Intendant Shàu Twō 邵佗. They include a large set of legal documents. See Weld **Chu**.

The Bāushān legal documents tell us a good deal about law and legal practice in a Sinicized state at the end of the 04c.[24] They reveal social and political conservatism in Chǔ, along with advanced legal procedures. The Chǔ King had his "traveling palaces" (syíng-gūng 行宮) at which he held court in various parts of his domain, as he doubtless imagined the Jōu Kings had done, though litigants are often ordered to appear in Yǐng, the Chǔ capital. Next below the King was Intendant Shàu Twō, himself the descendant of a Chǔ ruling family. He too traveled, to investigate things or render decisions on the spot.

Dated documents name years by the major event of the year preceding. The roster of recognized "major events" is suggestive:

- 0322. Chǔ general defeats the army of "Jìn" (Ngwèi)
- 0321. Embassy from Chí
- 0320. The Chǔ Prince of Lǔ-yáng repairs the wall of Jv̀ng.
- 0319. Embassy from a state whose name is now lost to history
- 0318. Embassy from Sùng
- 0317. Embassy from "Eastern Jōu," presenting sacrificial meat
- 0316. Chǔ general rescues a threatened city.

These are all events which increase, or recognize, the power of Chǔ.

Individuals might complain of wrongs both personal and administrative:

3:62 (Bāushān #97, excerpt, 0317) . . . has taken his wife. . .

3:63 (Bāushān #102, excerpt, 0317) . . . have judged illegally.

Petitioners who did not appear for their hearing prompted an investigation, and a finding of probable fact might lead to the case being taken up by the state:

3:64 (Bāushān #29, c0317). 8th month, day #11. Jōu Rv́n, a man of the Magistrate of Lyáu, was assigned a date. On day #20, he did not appear at court. Investigation determined that there had been injury . . .

There is no clear separation between what we call civil and criminal law.

[24]For a full account of the more personal documents, see Cook **Death**.

Absorbed Territories. At least some Chǔ districts (syèn 縣) were headed by a Prince (gūng 公), not a civil appointee. These previously independent districts had their own law officials and police. Interaction between them and the state could be cumbersome: one case in the district of Tāng, whose police are called the police of Yīn, and involving counter-accusations of the murder of a brother, was several times referred back and forth between the state and the district; at one stage, no less than 211 witness gave their testimony under oath. The impatience of the higher authorities led to this official note:

> **3:65** (Bāushān #135, excerpt, 0317) . . . This case has long gone without final judgement. The King orders that all be brought to judgement.

Accused persons who flee were a problem in this case. Another deals with the omission of a few "gentlemen" (jyẃndž 君子) from the tax roll, presumably as a personal favor. In another, officials conspire to falsify a population register; all of them flee before they can be arrested.

The legal system was also in charge of agricultural loans in gold:

> **3:66** (Bāushān #108, excerpt, c0317) . . . granted them seven yì of gold for the planting . . . The deadline passed without the gold being repaid.

In fairness be it added that according to the records, some of these loans *were* repaid, in full or in part, by the due date.

On the whole, the Chǔ system is functioning well, if not always promptly, in its tasks of controlling the population and supporting the infrastructure. The law is publicly known, and it is generally effective.

Science. The cogency of nature as a model for the state was increased at this time by concepts which seemed to give a deeper understanding of nature, amounting, in the opinion of the time, to a *science* of nature. It suggested the possibility of resonant interaction between the human and the natural realms. The key concepts included Yīn/Yáng dualism, the Five Element theory, the implications of the new Yì divination system, the model of the seasonal cycle, and several ideas usually associated with the Chí philosopher Dzōu Yěn.

Yīn/Yáng 陰楊 is probably a version of early Persian dualism;[25] it first appears in Chinese texts in the 04c. The words themselves are old: Yīn 陰 was the dark side of a mountain; Yáng 陽 the sunlit side. As cosmic forces they were complementary. Their first theoretical application may have been medical: a way of rationalizing the effects of heat and cold. The association with the light and dark parts of the year was also early. Yīn/Yáng dualism had all the suggestive power of any binary opposition, and it quickly became influential.

---

[25]Bactria, where eastern and western trade routes met, had been part of the Persian Empire until its conquest by Alexander. Persian dualism was widely diffused: the Jews encountered it during their Babylonian exile (06c), and one Greek theory regarded the world as formed from the interaction of two opposing forms, Light and Darkness.

Concepts of Change proliferated in the highly analytical late 04c.

The Five Elements were a late idea.[26] They were early associated with the older five directions (the cardinal four plus the center), five colors, five notes of the scale, and five planets. From the five planets they probably took their name Wǔ Syíng 五行, "the Five Walkers." Besides simply defining a five-part group, they were also thought of as an endlessly recurring cycle,[27] in which each stage "destroyed" the preceding one:

water > fire > metal > wood > earth[28]

The Yì with its system of 64 hexagrams envisioned a wilder kind of change. If emphasized lines in a hexagram are changed to their opposite, the resulting hexagram gives the outcome. Any one hexagram might therefore conceivably become *any of the others*. This was attractive to small states, which could never catch up with their rivals except by some sudden and discontinuous leap.

Here is how the DJ writers applied changing-hexagram analysis to the question of whether Jìn should have supported Jv̀ng against Sùng in 0486:

> **3:67** (DJ 12/9:6, c0318). Jàu Yáng of Jìn divined [by the bone method] about going to the aid of Jv̀ng . . . [three interpreters commented on the result; all advised against doing so]. Yáng Hǔ divined by the stalk method with the Jōu Yì. He obtained hexagram Tài 泰 going to Syw̄ 需. He said, Sùng just now is in a fortunate position; it may not be engaged . . .

Tài "The Great" is auspicious, but here it gets bogged down in Syw̄ "Delay."

The Seasonal Cycle was another paradigm of change for the ruler:

> **3:68** (GZ 7:14-15, c0323). He should model himself on Heaven by extending benevolence to all, and imitate Earth by being impartial. He should make a third with the sun and moon; a fifth with the four seasons.

One way for a ruler to imitate Heaven was to take charge of the traditional seasonal activities of planting and harvesting:

> **3:69** (DJ 10/25:3b, excerpt, c0320). There are duties of government and the administrative services . . . in accordance with the four seasons.

Later, detailed work schedules appeared. Seasonality was essential:

> **3:70** (GZ 8, excerpt, c0310). In spring, if the winter schedule is followed, there will be chill; if the autumn schedule is followed, there will be thunder; if the summer schedule is followed, there will be stunting.

---

[26]The original number, probably of Indian origin, seems to have been six; they appear in DJ 6/7:8 (c0358) as water, fire, metal, wood, earth, and grain. Similarly, the four elements of Empedocles (05c) are identical with a related Indian set of four.

[27]Also translated as "Five Phases," to emphasize their cyclical-succession aspect.

[28]This is the "destructive" sequence as given in DJ 6/7:8; other authorities differ. The "generative" sequence is usually given as wood > fire > earth > metal > water.

In the twelve days when the aura (chì 氣) of earth is emerging, give warning about spring tasks. In [the next twelve days], begin ploughing. In [the next], make distributions. In [the next], repair gates and doorways. In [the next], bring males and females together. In the twelve days including the Chīng-míng festival, issue prohibitions . . .

The number eight is honored in this season. The ruler wears green[29] clothing, tastes sour flavors, listens to music in the jywé 角 mode . . .

All this met with healthy disbelief on the part of some practical men:

Sūndž Bīngfǎ 孫子兵法 "The Art of War of Master Sūn" or Sūn Bìn, the victor of Mǎ-líng (0343). Compiled c0360-c0305, with an addendum (Sūndž 13) in c0262; later attributed to a mythical 06c general. The first of the early Chinese military texts. Translations by Giles and Sawyer.

3:71 (Sūndž 6, excerpt, c0320). So the Five Elements have no constant conquest order, the Four Seasons have no constant duration, Night and Day may be short or long, and the Moon waxes and wanes.

That is, the Five Elements have *no* constant order, and thus no predictive value.

Dzōu Yěn 騶衍 of Chí (c0347-c0276) was the leading figure of the Jì-syà theoreticians. His career, which shifted from Chí to Ngwèi to Jàu to Yēn,[30] suggests knowledge of a secret, albeit fallible, method. It may have been a theory of astral/terrestrial correspondences, which maps the constellations onto the states, so that an event in a constellation portends an event in that state.[31]

The possessor of such a system might be invited by any ambitious state, but then dismissed if a major event turned out badly. Dzōu Yěn's career moves can be mapped onto events in just that way. In 0295, Ngwèi was attacked by Chín, in 0294 it fought a drawn battle, in 0293 it suffered a great defeat. This might have led to an invitation to Dzōu Yěn in 0293. He may have lost prestige in Ngwèi after another defeat, with loss of territory, in 0290. A move to Jàu (which had lost a battle to Chín in 0289) may have occurred in that year. Jàu then enjoyed several years of calm; a joint action with Yēn against Chí in 0284 was successful. The King of Yēn came to Jàu in 0283, and may have hired Dzōu Yěn away in that year. That King died in 0279, and Dzōu Yěn ended his days in Yēn, in the house the King had built for him. One book he wrote in Yēn was The Master of the Cycles; it may have dealt with the Five Phases theory. It is with that theory that he has chiefly been associated in later times.

---

[29]Chīng 青 covers colors from light green to dark blue; we translate by context.

[30]For these details we follow SJ 47, which seems to derive from a genuine tradition.

[31]The system includes Wú (conquered in 0468), but not Jv̀ng (conquered in 0376). The roster is: Hán, Sùng, Yēn, Wú, Ywè, Chí, Wèi, Lǔ, Jàu, Ngwèi, Chín, Jōu, Chǔ.

The 03rd Century

This is the century of the military showdown. In the east, Chí Mǐn-wáng, who ruled from 0300, was eager for conquest. After long delay for preparation, a delay which the Gwǎndž theorists urgently advised, he attacked Sùng in 0285. And conquered it, but allied states drove him from Sùng and from Chí itself. He died far from his capital in 0284, and Chí never again ranked as a major power. Its eclipse favored its western rival: Chín.

Lord Shāng or Wèi Yāng, a general of Chín, had defeated Ngwèi in 0342; he was given the fief of Shāng and a ministership in 0341. His reputation in other states was military, but Chín tradition (found in the Shāng-jywn Shū) claimed him as a statesman, and it is possible that he applied military discipline (harsh punishments, no exemptions for nobles) to the civilian population also. As in Chí, reward and punishment are the root axioms of 03c Chín legal theory:

3:72 (SJS 9:2a, excerpt, c0295). Now, the nature of men is to like titles and salaries and to hate punishments and penalties. A ruler institutes these two things to control men's wills . . .

But in contrast to eastern thought, the SJS firmly rejects antiquity arguments:

3:73 (SJS 7:2c, excerpt, c0288). The Sage neither imitates the ancient nor cultivates the modern . . . the Three Dynasties had different situations, but they all managed to rule. Thus, to *rise* to the Kingship, there is one way, but to *hold* it, there are different principles.

Governing conquered territory requires attention to the specific situation.

Chín conquered the Chǔ capital Yǐng in 0278, but presently Chǔ made a counterattack. The tone of the SJS becomes more absolutist from this point on. It is clear that all power in the state *belongs* to the state, and none to the people:

3:74 (SJS 20:1, excerpt, c0276). If the people are weak, the state will be strong; if the state is strong, the people will be weak. Therefore, the state which possesses the Way will be concerned to weaken the people.

Mician Theory favored law. The Micians were the ideal citizens of the new state, who accepted law as protecting them from criminal behavior. They expected law to protect the good and punish the bad, and in government, they expected meritocracy: the employment of the virtuous. These expectations were so blatantly violated by 03c governments as to provoke this angry denunciation:

3:75 (MZ 10:5, excerpt, c0275) . . . But when the art of judging is not understood, though virtuous men may compare with Yǔ and Tāng, with Wvn and Wǔ, there will be no commendation. And though some relative of the ruler may be lame and dumb, deaf and blind, as evil as Jyé or Jòu, there will be no condemnation. Thus does reward not come to the virtuous, nor punishment to the evil . . .

From the Mician viewpoint, the evil are favored and the virtuous are neglected. The new system has failed to produce a moral government.

The Mician answer to these ills was still the reward and punishment system. but now reorganized as a meritocratic reporting system at each social level:

3:76 (MZ 13:7, excerpt, c0273) . . . Let the Son of Heaven announce and proclaim to the masses of the world: "If you see someone who loves and benefits the world, you must report it; if you see someone who hates and harms the world, you must report it." Whoever, on seeing someone who loves and benefits the world, reports it, is like one who himself loves and benefits the world. If his superior can get him, he will reward him; if the masses hear of him, they will praise him. But whoever, on seeing someone who hates and harms the world, fails to report it, is himself one who hates and harms the world. If his superior can get him, he will punish him; if the masses hear of him, they will oppose him . . .

Not to put too fine a point on it, the people have here become the police force, or if one prefers, the merit recruitment and reproval agency, of the state.

In some parts of the world, law limits the ruler. Chinese law did not arise in that way. It functioned to *empower* the ruler. Law made the state easier for the ruler to control, whoever the ruler might be. This merely set things up for a usurper, like the Tyén usurpers in Chí. As the Jwāngdž people pointed out:

3:77 (JZ 10:1a, excerpt, c0257) . . . Of old, the neighboring towns of Chí could be seen from each other; the cries of dogs and chickens could be heard from each other; where its nets and seines were spread, what its ploughs and spades turned, was an area of more than two thousand leagues. It filled all the space within its four borders. In its establishing of temples and shrines or altars of soil or grain, in its governing of its cities and towns, its districts and regions, its counties and hamlets, what was there that did not model itself on the Sages?

But Tyén Chʻngdž in a single morning killed the ruler of Chí and stole his state. And was it only the state he stole? With it he stole the laws which Sagely wisdom had devised. And so Tyén Chʻngdž gained the name of a thief and a bandit, but he himself rested as easy as Yáu or Shùn. Small states dared not denounce him, large states dared not attack him, and for twelve generations his family has held the state of Chí . . .

That twelfth Tyén ruler, King Jyèn (r 0264-0221), favored Confucianism. He responded to the Chǔ threat by reactivating, and attempting to Confucianize, the Jì-syà theory group. Chí thought was still cosmological in character . . .

3:78 (GZ 40, excerpt, c0250). Yīn and Yáng are the grand rationale of Heaven and Earth; the Four Seasons are the great cycle of Yīn and Yáng. If punishment and amnesty correspond to the seasons, they will beget good fortune; if they are adverse, they will beget disaster . . . In summer, if one carries out the spring schedule, there will be windstorms; if one carries out the autumn schedule, there will be floods; if one carries out the winter schedule, there will be shedding [of leaves]. . .

. . . but that routine had not protected the state against recent disasters such as the near-destruction of Chí following its 0285 conquest of Sùng.

So to the new Jì-syà, King Jyèn in 0258 invited the Confucian Sywndž.

Sywndž 荀子 (SZ). The preserved writings of the 03c Confucian Sywn Kwàng (c0310-c0235) of Jàu. Of its 32 chapters, most are authentic; some additions are as late as early Hàn. Translated by Knoblock.

Sywndž had begun as a student of ritual and music at the court of Lǔ. At first he followed traditional Confucian philosophy, but later diverged from it. He was the most abrasive controversialist of his day, though this did not prevent him from appropriating what he thought was good in others' ideas. As of 0258, Sywndž was a well-known figure, but had not yet gained a court position.

Sywndž considered his 0258 appointment in Chí as a mandate to bring Confucian light to the erring Chí philosophers. To counter the Chí theory of a determining Heaven, he wrote what he surely intended as a thoughtful and considerate account of the subject. It is still considered to be his masterpiece:

3:79 (SZ 17:1, beginning, c0257). The course of Heaven is constant. It does not survive because of Yáu, nor perish because of Jyé. If you respond to it with order, there will be good fortune; if you respond to it with disorder, there will be misfortune. If you strengthen basics and keep expenses low, Heaven cannot afflict you. If you follow the Way faithfully, Heaven cannot bring disaster on you. So flood and drought cannot cause famine, cold and heat cannot cause sickness, strange and weird events cannot cause misfortune. If basics are neglected and expenses wasteful, Heaven cannot make you rich; if food is scarce and initiative lacking, Heaven cannot make you whole; if you forsake the Way and act irrationally, Heaven cannot make you fortunate . . .

3:80 (SZ 17:4, excerpt, c0257). Are order and chaos due to Heaven? I say, Sun and moon, stars and constellations, the calendrical markers, were the same for Yǔ and Jyé. With Yǔ they led to order; with Jyé they led to disorder: Order and chaos are then not due to Heaven. Are they due to the seasons? I say, crops sprout and grow in spring and summer; they are gathered and stored in autumn and winter. These too were the same for Yǔ and Jyé. With Yǔ they led to order; with Jyé they led to disorder. Order and chaos are then not due to the seasons . . .

3:81 (SZ 17:7, excerpt, c0257). When stars fall or trees creak, the country is terrified. They ask, Why is this? I reply, No reason; these are things that happen when Heaven and Earth change, or Yīn and Yáng mutate. We may marvel at them, but it is wrong to fear them. As for eclipses of sun and moon, unseasonableness of wind and rain, or the uncanny appearance of a strange star, there is no age but has had them . . .

All this tact and eloquence did not convert the cosmologically committed philosophers of Chí to a more human-centered view. Relations at Jì-syà became so uncomfortable that in 0254, Sywndž departed for a less philosophical post, as the Chǔ governor of newly conquered Lǔ.

Seasonal Theories continued to flourish in Chí. From there they spread to Chín, where they were used as the framework of Lǔ Bù-wéi's Chín statecraft compendium, completed in 0241. We have previously (#**2:59-61**) seen its rules for mid-autumn. Here is how LSCC begins the year:

> **3:82** (LSCC 1/1:1, excerpt, c0241). The correlates of this month are the cyclical days jyǎ 甲 (#1) and yī 乙 (#2), the Sovereign Tài-hàu, his assisting spirit Gōu-máng, creatures with scales, the note jywé, the pitch Tài-tsòu, the number eight, sour tastes, rank smells, and the offering at the door. At sacrifices, the spleen is given the prominent position.
>
> The east wind melts the ice, dormant creatures begin to stir, fish push up against the ice, otters sacrifice fish, and migrating geese head north.

> **3:83** (LSCC 1/1:4, excerpt, c0241). In this month . . . the King distributes the tasks of agriculture and orders that field inspectors lodge at the eastern suburban altar. They must see that people keep boundaries and borders in good repair, and that care is taken as to the straightness of the pathways between fields. They are to carefully survey the mounds, slopes, ravines, plains, and marshes to see which have soils and landforms suitable to the growth of the five grains. In all this they must personally instruct the people, and personally take part in the work . . .

Another LSCC chapter deals with the concept of impartiality (gūng 公): fairness, evenhandedness, not favoring one thing over others:

> **3:84** (LSCC 1/4:1-2, excerpts, 0241). In the past, when the Sage Kings governed the world, they always put first impartiality: if they acted impartially, the world would be at peace. This peace was obtained by impartiality. When we examine the records of antiquity, there are many examples of the world being won and lost. Those who gained it, did so by impartiality; those who lost it, did so through partiality. Whenever sovereignty is established, it is from impartiality . . .
>
> The world is not one man's world; it is the world's world. The harmony of the Yīn and Yáng does not favor one species; the sweet dews and seasonable rains are not confined to one creature. The ruler of the myriad people does not attend to only one person . . .
>
> A man of Chǔ lost his bow, but declined to look for it. He said, A man of Chǔ lost it, a man of Chǔ will find it; why should I look for it? . . .
>
> Heaven and Earth are so great that they give birth to things but do not regard them as their children; they bring to completion but do not regard them as their own. The myriad creatures all are nourished by them, and receive benefits from them, but no one knows where they come from. Such was the virtue of the Three August Ones and the Five Sovereigns.

The King of Chǔ sees no difference between himself and any other man of Chǔ. The state, similarly, must be as capacious as Heaven, inclusive as Earth, indifferent as sun, impartial as rain. Only in this way can the state be over all. Thus ran one conception of how Chín should prepare itself to rule the world: with no sense of locality or special privilege, like nature itself.

Science? In the end, the Two Forces, the Four Seasons, and the Five Planets did not develop into the concept of a law of nature; a world order independent of the political order, and superior to it: something that could be appealed to against the ruler. The new cosmic symbolism instead strengthened the old association of the ruler with Heaven. Interest in the planets led to more accurate calculation of eclipses, but not to a countervailing system of political thought.[32]

Theory. At first, Chí had been the source of statecraft theory for the west. In the mid 03c, we see a movement back in the other direction. Here is a late Gwǎndž view of how the state works. It is contemporary with the core LSCC, but it shows more influence from Chín harshness than the LSCC itself:

> **3:85** (GZ 45, excerpt, c0240). Subordinate serving superior should be like echo answering sound; minister serving ruler should be like shadow following shape . . . If the people respect the orders of the ruler and carry them out, should there be injury or loss and they are penalized, they would hesitate, would begin to consider outcomes, and so depart from the law. Once ministers and commoners begin considering outcomes, they will bring forward their own judgement, the law will be in ruins, and orders will not be carried out.

Judgement is forbidden: obedience is more important than results..

By contrast, the LSCC, however ostensibly Legalist, preserves a certain place for Confucian values. Here, it returns to the Upright Gūng theme (#3:46). In Chín, this reaffirmation of the old Analects position was rather daring:

> **3:86** (LSCC 11/4:3, c0241). In Chǔ there was one Upright Gūng. When his father stole a sheep, he reported him to the authorities. The authorities arrested the thief and were about to execute him, when his honest son requested that he be allowed to take his place and be executed. He said to the officer, When my father stole a sheep I reported him – is this not the very meaning of honesty 信? Now that my father is about to be executed, I take his place – is this not the very meaning of filiality 孝? If you execute one who is both honest and filial, who will the state pardon? When the King of Chǔ heard of this, he did not execute the man.
>
> When Confucius heard of it, he said, Different indeed is Upright Gūng's kind of honesty. It was merely at the expense of his father that he was able to get his reputation. It would be better to be dishonest than to practice the "honesty" of Upright Gūng.

This writer[33] contemptuously rejects the idea that there can be a compromise between the paramount duty to one's father and the requirements of the state.

---

[32]Compare the momentous implications of Kepler's astronomical discoveries for European political theory, and indeed for the future of European states.

[33]Whoever he was. In all, probably about eight contributors, of somewhat different philosophical background and policy proclivities, took part in writing the LSCC.

Hán Fēı 韓非 came from Hán to Chín, and was there executed, probably (as the earliest tradition says) for a failed intrigue against a court rival. Under his name there now circulate a large body of statecraft writings which are widely regarded as typical of Warring States Legalism . . .

> **Hán Fēıdž** 韓非子 (HFZ). Statecraft writings, attributed to Hán Fēı (executed in Chín in 0233) but actually written during the 02c by a succession of Hàn statecraft theorists. Translated by Liao.

. . . but that attribution can be refuted in a **Methodological Parenthesis** (they ignore the core Warring States problem of conquest, and focus on court intrigue and other concerns of a unified empire; successive chapters are inconsistent in doctrine, but mirror the changing fads of the 02c Hàn court). Hán Fēı himself was real enough, but the theories later associated with his name belong to the intellectual history of the Hàn Dynasty, and will not concern us here.

Chín Laws. The requirements of the Chín state are known in some detail, thanks to the Shwèıhǔdì documents,[34] which contain the case files of the Chín law official Syǐ. These files give us a look at the actual administration of law under Chín, and of the logic of the Chín judges. Here are some samples.[35]

Chín offered promotion to those who had cut off heads or otherwise distinguished themselves in battle. But there were refinements:

> **3:87** (Hulsewé A91, c0220). If any wish to surrender two degrees of rank to liberate one person – their own father or mother – who is a slave, or if bond-servants who have been [given the lowest rank] for having cut off a head ask to surrender that rank to liberate a wife who is of servile status, this is to be permitted. They are to be liberated and made commoners.

Rank amounts to a kind of currency with the state, and as such, it can be exchanged with the state for other social goods.

> **3:88** (Hulsewé C13, c0220). When the produce of the lacquer plantations is inferior, the Overseer is fined one suit of armor; the Director, Assistant Director, and Assistants are fined one shield each; the men are fined twenty sets of armor lacings each. When the produce of the lacquer plantations is inferior for three years, the Overseer is fined two suits of armor and is dismissed; the Director and Assistant Director are each fined one suit of armor.

This develops the idea of commutation of mutilating punishments (#**3:55**), but with a new twist: the penalties benefit the state by contributing to its armory. Even justice serves the ends of conquest.

---

[34]See p60.

[35]For a complete translation of the Shwèıhǔdì laws, see Hulsewé **Ch'in**.

There is considerable precision in the defining of legal offenses:

3:89 (Hulsewé D14, c0220). A husband steals 300 cash. He informs his wife, and he and his wife consume it in eating and drinking. How is the wife to be sentenced? If there had been no previous plotting, this is to be considered a case of "receiving" 收. If they had previously plotted, [she gets] the same punishment. A husband steals 200 cash and hides 110 in his wife's apartment. How is the wife to be sentenced? If she knew that her husband had stolen them, it is to be considered a case of theft. If she did not know, it is a case of "keeping" 守 ill-gotten gains.

Chín, like Chí before it, grouped households into fives 伍. Movements of individuals were restricted. This emerges in several rules on false accusation:

3:90 (Hulsewé D80, excerpt, c0220). When one of a group of five denounces another, hoping to escape punishment, and it is inaccurate, he is to be punished with the punishment he had hoped to escape.

3:91 (Hulsewé D93b, excerpt, c0220) . . . To denounce someone, saying he has left the state, when he did not cross the border or did not leave without permission, is carelessness in denouncing. How should he be sentenced? This is a case of carelessness in denouncing. It is punishable by tattooing and being made a forced laborer.

Sometimes further information was requested about a still incomplete case:

3:92 (Hulsewé E16, c0220). Tattooing a Female Slave. A public officer 公士[36] of such-and-such village brought in adult woman B, and deposed: I am a household official of Grandee 大夫 A of such-and-such village. B is A's slave. A has asked me to say, "B is insubordinate. I ask that B be tattooed and have her nose cut off." On being interrogated, B said, "I am A's slave woman." She has not been accused of any other crime.

The Assistant herewith informs the Head of the District of [the above information]. Inquire whether things are as he says. Determine her name, status, village, crimes of which she has been accused or sentenced, and whether she has been again interrogated. Report in writing.

Let it be noted that this is not a particularly cruel system. It is a *severe* system, but not an exercise in terror: it aims at a recognizable kind of justice. Enough pressure will be applied to get the system to work as intended

The intent of the system is manifest. Some mutilating punishments are kept from earlier times. But the fines it sets are weapons, and go to the armory, and the penal servitude it mandates is so much hard labor, and is sent to the walls.

Here then is the Spring and Autumn state, re-equipped with laws and land, stripped down again to its ancient essentials, and fine-tuned for war.

---

[36]The lowest Chín rank; here, a private and not a government official.

4. War and Peace

The Spring and Autumn host (shr̄ 師), the elite chariot force, had been led by the ruler or his delegate, usually a relative. To achieve more, a mass infantry army (jywn 軍) was needed, led by an expert, the general (jyàng 將). The transition to that kind of army had begun at the end of the 06c (page 37). One question for the state was, how to get ordinary people to fight for the state? That was solved by compulsion, and by the cultivation of a national identity.

The next question was, Given victory, how to incorporate the new territory? The answer was to use centrally appointed officials, not hereditary local rulers. The precedent was small conquests like Láng (page 24), which had been taken by Lǔ in early Spring and Autumn, or Dzv̄ngdž's city of Wǔ-chv́ng (page 127), a late Spring and Autumn border strongpoint with a Lǔ-appointed governor.

The third question was, Why do this at all? Why not live at peace, as a system of mutually friendly states, trading back and forth and killing no one? So asked the Micians, the least predictable of the classical schools of thought.

The 05th Century

The New Soldiers were commoners. They did not have the elite warriors' lifelong training and ingrained dedication. They had to be forced to serve, and they did not like it much. This poem may be based on an early marching song. In what became the orthodox interpretation, it goes like this:

4:1 (Shr̄ 36, Bèi #11, 05c?).

36A   Worn down, alack; worn down, alack,
        Why do we not go back?
        Were it not our ruler's will,
        What would we be doing in the chill?

36B   Worn down, alack; worn down, alack,
        Why do we not go back?
        Were it not to serve our sire,
        What would we be doing in the mire?

The original may have been sharper, but even read in a loyal way, it was felt to be too negative. Later, a more enthusiastic soldier piece was added to the Shr̄:

4:2 (Shr̄ 133, Chín #8, excerpt, 04c?).

133A   That you've no clothes, how can you say?
        With you I'll share my robes so long;
        The King is raising troops today,
        And I've made ready a spearshaft strong –
        Together we will march along . . .

The problem of how to get the common people to fight for the new style state has here been solved (or so we are told) by eager volunteers.

Weapons for the infantry were in part retained from earlier periods. Basic for the foot soldier was the dagger-axe (gv̄ 戈), a knife-blade lashed to a pole:

The gv̄ went back to Shāng. New at this time was the jĭ 戟 or halberd, which had a thrusting point; sometimes the slashing blade of the gv̄ was added to the jĭ. The compound bow was the basic elite weapon. Elite warriors now also carried a full-length bronze sword, no longer a mere dagger as in Spring and Autumn. Armor of lacquered leather was available to the chariot warriors; the crossbow, which could drive a bolt through such armor, would soon appear.

The 04th Century

A Plan for Peace. Antiwar sentiment appears in an already developed form at the beginning of the 04c, in what was probably a speech by the founder of the Mician movement, Mwò Dí. The appeal of the speech is to law, but also to an intuitive sense of what is right (yì 義) and what is unkind (bù-rv́n 不仁).[1] The Micians supported law; they merely asked that the state's law against murder should be consistently applied to the activities of the state itself:

> **4:3** (MZ 17:1-3, c0390). [1] Suppose someone enters another's orchard and filches his peaches and plums. When others hear of it, they will think it wrong, and the high officials will punish him if they can catch him. Why? Because he has injured another to benefit himself. Suppose someone steals another's dogs and pigs, his chickens and shoats; the wrong 不義 is worse than entering another's orchard and filching his peaches and plums. Why? Because the injury to the other is more, so the bù-rv́n 不仁 is greater, and the guilt is heavier.[2]

---

[1]Modern persons tend to think of "right" as something conferred by a law, but yì is rather a prelegal "right;" simple social expectation.

[2]The injury is an attribute of the *victim*. If it was caused by chance, no guilt exists; guilt is an attribute of a *doer*. It is the "unkindness" of the deed, the doer's knowledge that it is harmful, that proves guilt. For intentionality 終 in 04c theory, see p80 n19.

If he enters another's barn and takes his horses and oxen, the bù-rv́n is greater than stealing another's dogs and pigs, his chickens and shoats. Why? Because the injury to the other is more. If the injury to the other is more, then the bù-rv́n is greater, and the guilt is heavier. If he kills an innocent man, strips him of gown and robe, and takes his axe and sword, the wrong is greater than entering another's barn and taking his horses and oxen. Why? Because the injury to the other is more, so the bù-rv́n is greater, and the guilt is heavier. With these things, the gentlemen of the world know to condemn them and call them wrong. But if we come to making a great attack on some state, they do *not* know to condemn it. Instead they go so far as to praise it, and call it right. Is this not what we should call failure to understand the difference between right and wrong?

[2] Killing one man they call wrong, and will surely judge it to be a capital crime. Extrapolating from this, killing ten men is ten times more wrong, and should incur ten capital punishments, and killing a hundred men is a hundred times more wrong, and should incur a hundred capital punishments. With these things, the gentlemen of the world know to condemn them and call them wrong. But if we come to the case of making a great and wrongful attack on some state, they do *not* know to condemn it. Instead they go so far as to write down their exploits to hand on to later ages. So they really do *not* know it is wrong, and so they write them down to hand on to later ages. If they knew it was a great wrong, why would they write it down to hand on to later ages?

The first two paragraphs establish a hierarchy of wrongs, with war at the top. The next paragraph proves that the ruling elite actually do regard war as right. The final section connects the two, showing that the ruling elite are utterly confused about right and wrong, and thus unfit to rule. It goes like this:

[3] Now, suppose there were a man who, when he saw a little black, called it black, but when he saw a lot of black, called it white: we would consider that this man did not know the difference between black and white. Or if when he tasted a little bitter he called it bitter, but when he tasted a lot of bitter he called it sweet: we would surely consider that this man did not know the difference between sweet and bitter. Now, when some small wrong is done, they know enough to call it wrong, but when a great wrong is done – attacking a state – they do not know enough to call it wrong; they even go so far as to praise it, calling it righteous 義. Can this be called knowing the difference between right and wrong? From this we may know that the gentlemen of the world are confused in their judgements of right 義 and wrong 不義.

longest Mician work

This speech is remarkable for its length (longer than any other known piece of 05c or early 04c prose), and its seeming acquaintance with step-by-step legal argumentation, but especially for its criticism of the governments of the day.

With this attack on the war policies of the great states, there began an open discussion of public issues; a phenomenon later called the "Hundred Schools."

It takes little wit to oppose war, but how would *peace* work? Three later essays give the Mician answer. (1) Love: People should extend love beyond their own families, avoiding the hatreds from which wars grow. (2) State frugality removes the economic motive for war. In particular, (3) the lavish funerals[3] in which the elite increasingly indulged should be more modest.

Love. The "universal love" doctrine (jyēn ài 兼愛) conflicts with the deeply rooted filial piety value: the limitation of concern to one's own family. The Micians argued that universal love includes, and thus guarantees, filial love:

> 4:4 (MZ 14:3, excerpt, c0386). If the world loved others equally – if they loved others as much as they loved themselves – would any be unfilial? If they regarded their fathers and elder brothers as themselves, who would be unfilial? Would any be unkind? If people regarded sons and younger brothers as they did themselves, who would be unkind? So the unfilial and the unkind would not exist.
>
> Would there still be robbers and thieves? If people regarded others' households as their own, who would steal? If they regarded others as themselves, who would thieve? So robbers and thieves would not exist.
>
> Would there still be great officers throwing other clans into confusion, and feudal lords attacking other states? If they regarded others' clans as their own, who would cause disorder? If they regarded others' states as their own, who would attack? So great officers disordering other clans, and feudal lords attacking other states, would not exist.
>
> If all the world would love others equally, state and state would not attack each other; clan and clan would not disorder each other; there would be no robbers or thieves; ruler and subject, father and son, would be filial and kind. And so the world would come to be well ordered.

Frugality. This piece (abbreviated in #2:12) stresses the burdens of war, and prescribes state frugality to cure state greed for other people's wealth:

> 4:5 (MZ 20:3, excerpt, c0382). Modern governments have many ways to diminish the people. Their use of the people is wearisome, their levying of taxes is burdensome, and when the people's resources are not enough, those who die of hunger and cold are innumerable. Moreover, the rulers make war and attack a neighboring state. The war may last a whole year, or at minimum, several months. Thus men and women cannot see each other for a long time. Is this not a way to diminish the people?[4] Living in danger, eating and drinking irregularly, many become sick and die. Hiding in ambush, setting fires, besieging cities and battling in the open fields, innumerable men die . . .

---

[3]The oldest essay against extravagant funerals is lost, and thus is not quoted below.

[4]The early European demographers were also concerned that people should be able to marry, and thus procreate, at the ideal age. In modern times too, population is power.

The Micians did not merely denounce *palace* extravagance, they deplored inessential ornament of every kind. This position ran counter to a general wish not to lower the current standard of living. How then does one urge frugality? The Micians approach the subject with the idea of *doubling* social benefit:

> **4:6** (MZ 20:1, excerpt, c0382). When a Sage governs a state, the benefits to that state can be doubled. On a larger scale, when he governs the world, the benefits to the world can be doubled. This doubling is not from the taking of foreign territory, it is from eliminating, in both state and family, everything that is useless: this is enough to double the benefit. When a Sage King governs, when he issues an order or undertakes an enterprise, employs the people or uses resources, he does nothing but what has utility. Thus his use of resources is not wasteful, the people's strength 德 is not wearied, and the profits of his enterprises are many.
>
> Why do we make clothing? To protect against cold in winter and heat in summer. The art of making clothing is to make one warm in winter and cool in summer. Decorations and ornaments we will not add; we will get rid of them.
>
> Why do we make dwellings? To protect against wind and cold in winter, and heat and rain in summer. We add whatever gives strength. Decorations and ornaments we will not add; we will get rid of them . . .

[margin note: on Sage rule and maximum utility]

All is to be minimal, in order to maximize the final social benefit. This position was later taken up by various Legalist and primitivist thinkers, and in that form found its way into mainstream perceptions. But as a program in its own right, the Mician vision of the peaceful society attracted no practical attention.

The Micians nevertheless continued to assert their basic antiwar doctrine. At mid-century, they sarcastically characterized the warring rulers in this way:

> **4:7** (MZ 18:5, excerpt, c0362). Those who admire war say, They could not gather and use their masses, so they perished. I *can* gather and use my masses. If I then go to war with the world, who will dare not to submit?

Using the masses involved an extensive system of governmental organization, as the Chí theorists tell us:

> **4:8** (GZ 3:1, excerpt, c0356). In a state of a myriad chariots, the soldiers must have leaders. Its area being extensive, the countryside must have administrators. Its population being large, the bureaus must have heads. In managing the people's future, the court must have a policy . . .

But the same essay then goes on to point out, very much in the Mician vein, that government extravagance dooms the organizational effort:

> **4:9** (GZ 3:5, excerpt, c0356). If land has been brought under cultivation, but the state is still poor, it is because boats and carts are sumptuously ornamented, and terraces and palaces are spread over vast areas . . .

[margin note: nexus of Micion and legalist philosophy on excess extravagance.]

Legalists and Micians were at one in decrying the extension of the old palace luxuries into the more affluent modern age.

(Sun Tzu)

The Art of War was being developed in Chí at this time; its stages are recorded in the Sūndž (page 85). The mass army could do things that the old chariot force could not, such as operate on hilly or marshy ground. From the oldest layer in the Sūndž, we have this very elementary paragraph:

> **4:10** (Sūndž 9, excerpt, c0360). To cross mountains: follow the passes, search out tenable ground, occupy the heights. If the enemy hold the heights, do not ascend to engage them in battle. This is the way to deploy an army in the mountains.

Don't fight uphill. This, the most basic principle of land warfare, did not need to be stated for the old chariot force, which only operated on level ground. For low and wet ground, where all movement is difficult, we have this:

> **4:11** (Sūndž 9, excerpt, c0360). To cross salt marshes and wetlands, focus on quickly getting free of them; do not remain. If you do battle in marshes or wetlands, stay in areas with marsh grass, and keep groves of trees at your back. This is the way to deploy the army in marshes or wetlands.

That is, keep moving, and protect your back. A later terrain list focused not on ground as such but on the tactical implications of a particular type of terrain:

> **4:12** (Sūndž 11A, excerpt, c0340). When there are mountains and forests, ravines and defiles, wetlands and marshes, or where the road is hard to negotiate, it is entrapping terrain. Where entry is constricted and return indirect, or where with few they can strike our force, it is encircled terrain . . . On entrapping terrain, keep moving. On encircled terrain, use strategy.

Combat is to be avoided where possible. This agrees with the mindset of Spring and Autumn warfare (page 24): get it done, but with the least possible loss.

At first, the new-style leader had to consider the feelings of the recruits:

> **4:13** (Sūndž 9, excerpt, c0360). If you impose punishment on the troops before they have become attached to you, they will not be submissive, and if they are not submissive, they will be difficult to employ. If you do not impose punishments after the troops have become attached, they cannot be used. Thus, if you command them with the civil and unify them with the martial, this is what we call being able to take [command of] them.

Later on, the element of persuasion vanishes, and orders are followed:

> **4:14** (Sūndž 11A, excerpt, c0340). Throw the troops into a situation in which there is nowhere to go, and they will stand fast to the death. Faced with death, what can they not achieve? Officers and men will put forth all their strength. When troops and officers are in peril, they are not afraid; when there is nowhere to go, they are resolute; when deep [in enemy territory] they pull together. When there is no alternative, they will fight.
>
> Thus, the troops: without specific orders they will be ranged aright, without assigned objective they will succeed, without prior conditioning they will be cohesive, without previous instruction they can be relied on.

Preconditions of troop cohesiveness and success.

Mǎ-líng. In 0343, Chí troops led by Tyén Pàn, but with Sūn Bìn as their commander, defeated a Ngwèi army at Mǎ-líng – *in the Ngwèi home territory*. This raised the possibility that one state might conquer a distant rival, and thus unify the world. So encouraged was the Chí ruler that in the following year he abandoned the title Prince (gūng 公) and assumed the title King (wáng 王), which until then had been solely held[5] by the Jōu ruler.

Chí was now openly committed to a policy of unification by military force. The second phase of the Warring States period had begun.

PUBLIC CULTURE

Not everything in the period was produced by individuals, or even states. There were also texts generally known and commanding wide acceptance. The Shī, performed at more than one regional court, and thus the common property of the diplomatic elite, are the prime example. Within its circle,[6] there was also the Dzwǒ Jwàn, with its more detailed pictures of a more recent antiquity. In both texts, over the 04c, we can observe the effect of war on the public culture. It was this: war insinuated itself ever more intimately into the public culture. Here are two contrasts, one from each of these more or less public texts.

Shī 268. In this older poem, Wv́n-wáng, celebrated as the first Jōu King, has the character we would expect from his posthumous title (wv́n 文, "civil" as contrasted with wǔ 武 "military"): preparing, not achieving, the conquest. His role here is to establish the ceremonies on which the identity of Jōu rested:

> 4:15 (Shr 268, 05c?) Pellucid, and shining bright[7] –
> The ordinances of King Wv́n.
> He established the sacrifices.
> And now they have had their fulfilment:
> The good omens of Jōu.

Shī 285. Here, in a hymn whose words were partly taken from an old dance song, are the two in their usual relationship: Wv́n preparing, Wǔ achieving:

> 4:16 (Shī 285, 05c?) August were you, King Wǔ,
> Incomparable in your glory.
> Well had labored King Wv́n,
> Opening a path for those to follow;
> Then did Wǔ receive it,
> Conquering Yīn, ending its cruelties;
> And firmly establishing your merit.

This is the picture that we all knew.

---

[5]In the Sinitic world. The non-Sinitic state of Chǔ had always called its rulers Kings.

[6]Which seems to have included both the Micians and Mencius; see Brooks **Heaven**.

[7]Brightness is the standard attribute of the sacred, in this and other cultures.

Stunningly different is the Wv́n-wáng we meet in one long and late poem: a conqueror rather than a preparatory builder.

Shr̄ 241 recounts the exploits of some previous rulers, and then orders Wv́n-wáng to make war in his turn:

4:17 (Shr̄ 241E, 04c) God said to King Wv́n:
> "Be not content to remain idle,
> Or to follow your own liking."
> And so he first ascended the heights:
> The people of Mì were disrespectful,
> Daring to oppose our great domain.
> He invaded Rwǎn and beset Gūng.
> The King was majestic in his wrath,
> As he set in order his forces
> To block the opposing forces,
> To secure the prosperity of Jōu,
> To respond to All Under Heaven . . .

The crime of Mì, it would appear, is a wish not to be conquered by Jōu. This is resented, not of course by the Jōu, who are dutiful throughout, but by God on High (Shàng Dì 上帝), who evidently has charge of everything that is. Next, God orders the King to proceed against Chúng (**#3:11**), and the poem ends:

241H
> Towers and rams[8] wrought steadily,
> The walls of Chúng towered high.
> The captives were brought forward in rows,
> Heads were cut off in great number;[9]
> These he sacrificed; these he offered,
> These he annexed; these he subdued –
> In the four directions, none resisted.
> Towers and rams wrought constantly,
> The walls of Chúng held stoutly firm.
> These he attacked; these he beset,
> These he cut off; these he destroyed –
> In the four directions, none opposed.

This recasting of King Wv́n as a conqueror of cities undoubtedly reinforced the militarization of 04c Warring States society – victory is now to be achieved, not by virtuous waiting, but by vigorous fighting.

The appearance of the term All Under Heaven (tyēn-syà 天下) is ominous. The object of conquest is no longer the other Sinitic states, or them plus the long-intermingled non-Sinitic states, but the entire world, which is to be brought into the Sinitic sphere at the command of a universal Sinitic God.

[8]Siege devices of the 04c and later; not known in the days of early Jōu.

[9]Not ears (as a token representing heads), as in later usage. The heads and the still live captives were all offered as trophies of the victory.

Methodological Moment. How ancient, how widely distributed in the Shr̄, is this sensitive term tyēn-syà? Checking in the concordance (it is not necessary to know Chinese), and eliminating occurrences in the included commentary, we find one other case: Shr̄ 205B1 溥天之下. And from an earlier Methodological Moment (page 46), we know the status of Shr̄ 205B: It is an interpolation.

Right.

------•••••------

Dzwǒ Jwàn. The Shr̄, Dzwǒ Jwàn, and early Chinese literature in general, do not abound in battle descriptions. Those who approach this literature with the Iliad ringing in their ears are courting disappointment. Battles in DJ serve chiefly as background for moral conversations between individuals. But those conversations do reflect attitudes to war in the period when DJ was composed, that is, most of the 04c. Here are two stages in that evolution.

(1) The Battle of Bì. J̀vng was the pivot state in the attempts of Chǔ to penetrate the north, and those of Jìn and other states to prevent it. J̀vng has just been defeated by Chǔ, and has made peace with Chǔ. Jìn had sent out a force to aid J̀vng, but on finding that J̀vng and Chǔ have made peace, most of the Jìn leaders counsel withdrawal, citing Chǔ's magnanimity and good civic order. We join the story just as the Jìn force has reached a decision point. Our speaker urges that respect for good order in Chǔ requires that Jìn withdraw its army:

> **4:18** (DJ 7/12:2, excerpt, c0315). When they reached the [Yellow] River, they learned that J̀vng had made peace with Chǔ. Hwándž wished to return, saying, We did not get to J̀vng in time, and we will now merely weary our people: what is the use of that? If Chǔ returns and then moves [again], it will not be too late [to react]. Swéı Wùdž said, Good. I have heard that in using an army, one waits for an opportunity and then moves. But when the virtue [of a state], its use of punishments, its administration, its conduct of affairs, its regulations, and its rituals have not changed, it cannot be opposed.[10] We should not carry out this mission.
>
> When the Chǔ army attacked J̀vng, it was moved by anger at its duplicity, and [then] by compassion for its humility.[11] When it rebelled, [Chǔ] attacked it; when it submitted, [Chǔ] forgave it – its kindness and its severity were both perfect. To attack the rebellious is severity; to be mild with the submitted is virtue . . .

[10]Have not changed from the ideal state in which they anciently were. That a virtuous state cannot be successfully attacked is a common thought in 04c and 03c texts, both Chinese and Indian. This DJ story develops the theme at enormous length.

[11]Its duplicity in siding with Jìn, and the abject stance of its ruler toward Chǔ once it had been conquered by Chǔ. These are emotionally and morally intelligible responses, and thus do not justify Jìn's proceeding against the Chǔ force.

In the year just past, [Chǔ] entered Chv́n. Now iit has entered Jv̀ng. But its people are not worn out, its ruler is not the object of resentments or complaints: its administration is along correct lines. When its troops are arrayed in formation, its traders, farmers, artisans, and merchants are not hindered in their occupations, and footsoldiers and elite warriors are on good terms; its undertakings do not conflict . . .

When virtue is established, when punishments are implemented, when the administration is perfected, when affairs are timely, when regulations are followed, when the rules of propriety are respected – how should we make them an enemy? When one sees a possibility, one advances; when one is aware of difficulties, one withdraws: this is the correct ordering of an army. To annex the weak and attack the deluded: this is the correct principle of war. Will you for the present so order the army, and so form your plans? There are still the weak and deluded; why must it be Chǔ?

The speech concludes with a flurry of Shr̄ and Shū quotations. It is met by a rejoinder representing the warrior's code of personal honor:

[Syēn Gǔ, second in command of the army of the center] said, It will not do. The way Jìn became Hegemon was the might of its armies and the strength of its officers. Now, we have lost the loyalty of the Lords:[12] this cannot be called strength. We have an enemy whom we do not pursue; this cannot be called might. If through my actions we lose the Hegemony, it would be better if I should die. And still more, having formed our army and gone forth, if we retreat on hearing that the enemy is strong, it would be unmanly. If commanded to be a leader of the army, but in the end to be unmanly – the lot of you may be capable of this, but I will not do it.

And as Assistant Commander of the army of the center, he crossed the River.

The outcome, reached after pages of further debate among both the Jìn and Chǔ leaders, is an attack, and a defeat, for Jìn. The contrast is between a deliberative and morally sensitive advisor, who knows the civil strength conferred by sound institutions, and an impetuous old-style military man, who is aware of nothing but his own personal valor and shame.[13]

---

[12]That is, Jìn has lost Jv̀ng, which is now allied with Chǔ.

[13]Just this contrast, and this approval of the deliberative option, is expressed by "Confucius" in LY *7:11, an 04c interpolation in an 05c Analects chapter. We add it as #4:19 – The Master said to Yén Ywǣn, "When they use him, he acts; when they cast him aside, he waits – it is only you and I that have this, is it not so?" Dž-lù [eager to ask a question with himself as the answer] said, "If the Master were in charge of the Three Armies, who would he have as associate?" The Master said, "One who would rush a tiger or breast a river, who would die without a regret – I would *not* associate with. What I need is one who manages with caution, and prefers to succeed by consultation." The DJ story may be taken as a long dramatization of this principle.

So far our first example, which shows that awareness of moral categories leads to military success. It is more or less what we would expect from the DJ. The next example is famous precisely because it violates that expectation.

(2) The Battle of the Húng River. Sùng had invaded Jv̀ng:

4:20 (DJ 5/22:8, excerpt, c0315). An officer of Chǔ attacked Sùng to relieve Jv̀ng, and the Prince of Sùng was about to give battle. The Grand Marshal strongly remonstrated, saying, It is long since Heaven abandoned Shāng.[14] You wish to raise it again, but that will not be permitted." He did not listen. In winter, in the 11th month, on the 6th cyclical day, at the new moon, the Prince of Sùng and the officer of Chǔ battled at Húng River. The men of Sùng had formed their ranks, but the men of Chǔ had not yet finished crossing. The Marshal said, They are many and we are few. While they have not yet finished crossing, I ask permission to strike them. The Prince said, It cannot be done. When they had finished crossing but had not yet formed their ranks, [the Marshal] again made his request. The Prince said, It cannot yet be done; when they are in formation, then strike them. The Sùng host was severely defeated, the Prince was wounded in the thigh, and his personal guard were slain. The people of the state all blamed the Prince. The Prince said, A gentleman will not inflict a second wound, he will not take captive the gray-haired. When the ancients made war, they did not attack those in awkward situations. This Lonely One, though a remnant of a defeated state, will not sound the drum[15] against those not drawn up.

[Marshal] Dž-yw̌ said, Our ruler does not understand battle. A stronger enemy in an awkward situation or not drawn up is Heaven helping us. If we could drum against them in that situation, is that not permissible? We would still be anxious about [the outcome]. As for today's strong ones, they are all our enemies. Even if there are aged among them, if we take them we should keep them captive; what has it to do with "gray hair?" In teaching war, we stress the principle of shame,[16] seeking that [our soldiers] should kill the enemy. If we wound, but the enemy is not yet dead, why should we not inflict a second wound? If we forbear a second wound, we might as well not wound at all. If we forbear with the gray-haired, we might as well submit to them. The Three Armies are to be used for advantage. Its bronze [trumpets] and drums are to rouse fighting spirit. If we are to use it to advantage, then attacking them in an awkward situation is permissible. When spirits are high and morale is strong, to drum against the foe is permissible.

[handwritten margin note: on the ethics of war. Chǔ v. Sùng]

Here is the modern, the expedient, note in warfare.[17] What works is good.

[14]It was the Shāng heritage that was preserved in Warring States Sùng.
[15]The signal to attack was given by the drum.
[16]Shame at failing in duty to the state.
[17]We add a marginal **#4:21** (Sūndž 1:26, c0303). "Attack where he is unprepared."

These are the contrasting Dzwǒ Jwàn examples. As the notes show, they have resonances in other 04c texts, particularly the military theory of the Sūndž. These and the Shr̄ examples record the militarizing of contemporary culture, and even the contemporary culture's idea of its own past. That process would continue into the 03c as well.

Chín, which had lagged behind Chí, now began to produce military theory. At first, Chín celebrated not the skill of the general but the organizational prowess of the government. This essay, probably presented to King Hwèi of Chín, portrays a belligerent populace which did not need to be induced to fight, but only to have its fighting spirit directed against other states:

> **4:22** (SJS 10 core, c0324).[18] The whole art of war is founded on victories of administration, so that the people do not contend, or if they do contend, it is not from personal motivation: they take their motivation from their superiors. Thus, the effect of the government of a King is to make the people shy of squabbling in the square, but bold in battling with the bandits.[19] As the people grow accustomed to attacking difficult situations with all their strength, they will accordingly come to make light of death.
>
> The soldiers of a King are not arrogant in victory or resentful in defeat. They are not arrogant in victory because the strategy (shù 術) leading to victory is clear to them. They are not resentful in defeat because they know where they have fallen short in executing it. If over time the administration holds the winning strategy, it will be strong enough to reach the Kingship. If the people are submissive and listen to their superiors, the state will be rich and its armies victorious. One who can walk this path will be able to maintain Kingship indefinitely.
>
> Thus the general in using the people is like the driver of a fine horse: he must keep it up to the mark.

The aggressiveness of the Chín populace doubtless worked in Chín's favor. Another saying, part of which is attributed by some to the 04c theorist Shv̀n Dàu,[20] picks up the theme of the superiority of the untrained soldier:

> **4:23** (LSCC 8/3:1, excerpt, c0241). A current maxim says, If you collect people from the marketplace and go to war with them, you can be victorious over another's well-paid and trained troops. The old, weak, and worn-out can be victorious over another's picked men and drilled soldiers. Disorganized convicts can be victorious over another's mobile formations and fixed ranks. Hoes, harrows, and plain clubs can be victorious over another's long spears and sharp weapons 利兵.

This sounds counterintuitive. How is it supposed to work?

---

[18]The core is recovered by removing some phrases later added from the Sūndž.

[19]A standard term for enemy soldiers, who are always seen as wrongful intruders.

[20]Thompson **Shen** p290 (#105).

Citizenship. One possibility might be the determination of the convinced citizen and grateful subject. So Mencius claimed in 0320:

> **4:24** (MC 1A5, excerpt, 0320). If the King gives the people a benevolent government, being sparing of punishments and fines and frugal in imposing taxes and levies, they will plough deep and weed carefully, and their able-bodied in days of leisure will cultivate filiality, fraternity, loyalty, and good faith. At home, they will thus be able to serve their fathers and older brothers; outside the home, they will be able to serve their elders and superiors. With nothing but sharpened sticks, one can use them to oppose the strong armor and sharp weapons of Chín and Chǔ.

Instead of the already bellicose populace of SJS 10 (#**4:22**), we have a grateful and thus motivated populace. *This is something government can do.*

Position. Back east, the Sūndž moved from specifics to principles. Its most famous concept is shr̀ 勢, "position," a situation seen as the ground of possible action. The dual attack of Chí on Lǔ in 0556 (#**1:49**) now finds its realization: the front and flank of the single army give it a flexible two-army potential:

> **4:25** (Sūndž 5, excerpts, c0318). Sūndž said, Controlling many is like controlling few; the principle is to distinguish units by size. Fighting against many is like fighting against few; the principle is to assign responsibilities and penalties.[21] That the mass of the Three Armies can be made to receive the attack of the enemy and never be defeated, is the principle of flank (chí 奇) and front (jv̀ng 正). The army's advantage, like throwing a stone against an egg, consists in the principle of empty and full.[22] In combat, we use the frontal attack to hold, the flank attack to win.

The two forces are not separated, but coordinated against the same object.

> Therefore the general who is good at flank attacks is as inexhaustible as Heaven and Earth . . . Military situations consist of no more than flank and front, but the variations of flank and front are innumerable. Flank and front grow out of each other, just as a jade ring has no ends: who could exhaust them?[23] . . . Thus those who are good at moving the enemy assume a certain disposition (syíng 形), and the enemy must conform to it. I offer something, and the enemy must accept it. I tempt him with advantage, and await him with my troops.[24] Therefore, one good at war seeks victory from the position (shr̀), and does not assign responsibility to men. Thus he is able to select his men, and master the situation (shr̀).

The novel idea here is strength against weakness. But superior strength must be concealed (as in the flank attack), not flaunted (as in the frontal attack).

---

[21] Syíng-míng 形名, a principle which is also used to control the civil bureaucracy, means assigning tasks and holding individuals responsible for their accomplishment.

[22] The "empty" are the undefended or lightly defended points in the enemy situation.

[23] An opposed flank attack may become a holding action; one shifts into the other.

[24] The general who can compel the enemy's movements holds the tactical initiative.

Secrecy. Somewhat later, in arguing with its philosophical contemporaries, the DDJ insisted that its treasures were too subtle for ordinary minds:

4:26 (DDJ 41, excerpt, c0306).

> The clear Way seems worthless,
> The bright Way seems commonplace,
> The advancing Way seems like withdrawal.

The last line may have caught the fancy of the Sūndž compilers, who in putting the last touches on their work added this, on war as a Way of Dissimulation:

4:27 (Sūndž 1, excerpt, c0305). War is a Way of deception. Thus when you are capable, show him incapacity; when you are putting something in motion, show him that you are not. When you are near, show him that you are far; when you are far, show him that you are near. With the seemingly attractive entice him, with seeming disorder take him.

[handwritten marginalia: Position and Perception]

Better Weapons. The crossbow was developed in Chǔ from a folk weapon of the southern peoples.[25] The improved version, with a high-precision bronze trigger mechanism, could drive a bolt through leather armor; it was known in Chí by the late 04c[26] and is mentioned in Sūndž 5 (c0318) and 2 (c0311). Long bronze swords appeared. By the 03c, Chǔ was making sword blades of steel.

All this took money. But there was a way to shift some of the cost to the enemy: this was to *plunder* the enemy. Here are two reflections on that policy:

4:28 (Sūndž 2, excerpts, c0311). Sūndž said, Operations of war require a thousand fast four-horse chariots, a thousand leather-covered [supply] carts, and ten myriad men with armor. Provisions for a thousand-league march campaign, what with internal and external wastage, the needs of the consultants, such materials as glue and lacquer, and the provision of carriages and armor, will come to a thousand of gold per day. After that has been secured, a host of ten myriad may be raised . . .

If you obtain your equipment from within the state, but rely on seizing provisions from the enemy, then the army's food supply will be enough.

4:29 (MZ 19:3, excerpt, c0326). They cut down grainfields and fell trees; they tear down the inner and outer walls and fill in ditches and ponds; they seize and kill sacrificial animals and burn down ancestral temples; they kill the people and exterminate the aged and weak . . .

It may be doubted that this will win the affections of the conquered.

---

[25]The older form, an untended setbow with a release device and a poisoned arrow, was still known or remembered among the Myáu 苗 of southwestern China in the early 20c, as witness this tale: ". . . strung his crossbow and set it on the old tiger's path. They . . . slept until next morning, then went to see whether the tigers had come . . . At midnight the tigers *had* come, and had run into their bow and crossbow, and the poisoned arrow had pierced the old tiger's liver." (Graham **Songs** 124).

[26]For details, see Wagner **Iron** sv Crossbow.

The Micians, now themselves in office, had come to accept just (義) war. They made a distinction in terms:

> **4:30** (MZ 19:5, excerpt, c0326). The warring lords would gloss over their conduct with counter-arguments, saying, Do you condemn aggression and attack as wrong and not beneficial? But in ancient times, Yw̌ made war on the Myáu, Tāng attacked 桀 Jyé,[27] and King Wŭ attacked 紂 Jòu.[28] Yet these are held to be Sage Kings. How do you explain this? Mwòdž said, You have not examined the terms of my teaching, and you do not understand its purport. That is not what one calls "aggression" 攻, but rather "punishment" 誅.

Defensive Warfare. The Micians still opposed bad wars, and even took the field against them. Having acquired a capability in defensive warfare, they hired themselves out to threatened cities. This made sieges more difficult:

> **4:31** (Sūndž 8, excerpt, c0334). Some cities are not to be assaulted . . .

> **4:32** (Sūndž 3, excerpt, c0312). The highest realization of warfare is to attack the enemy's plans, the next is to attack their alliances, next to attack their army, and last to attack their cities . . . This tactic of attacking cities is adopted only when it is unavoidable . . .

So in less than a generation, the difficulty of sieges has increased.

Separately, Mician antiwar propaganda was having its effect, and the Chī statecraft people deplored that result:

> **4:33** (GZ 4:9 "Nine Ways To Lose It," excerpt, c0310).
> 1. If disarmament theories prevail, the passes will not be defended.
> 2. If "universal love" theories prevail, the soldiers will not fight.

The Northern Steppe. The states bordering on the northern grasslands, Chín in the west, Jàu in the center, and Yēn in the east, had been expanding into that area, but toward the end of the 04c, there was a counterpressure: something like a unified military leadership had recently emerged in the steppe, and mounted archers were troubling the border. This provoked a reference to the supposed ancient minister Gwǎn Jùng, who by his organization of the state of Chí had saved all the Sinitic states from conquest by the non-Sinitic hordes, or so it was thought, at this time:

> **4:34** (LY 14:17, excerpt, c0310) . . . The Master said, Hwán-gūng was the leader of the Lords, and united All Under Heaven; the people down to the present receive the benefit of it. Without Gwǎn Jùng, we would be wearing our hair long and lapping our robes to the left . . .

Meaning, we would have been conquered by the northern peoples, and would now be culturally absorbed into their way of living.

---

[27]The evil last ruler of the Syà dynasty, killed by the founder of Shāng.

[28]The evil last ruler of the Shāng Dynasty, killed by the founder of Jōu.

But just that change was happening. Horses had been *driven* for centuries, but trousers were now adopted, to permit the *riding* of horses. The stirrup and the long cavalry sword appeared somewhat later. By the middle of the 03c, cavalry had become part of Sinitic warfare.

Methodological Moment. Most evidence suggests that the pressure which led to adoption of non-Sinitic clothing (胡服) for at least the Sinitic cavalry, occurred in the late 04c (the Shr̄ Jì 15 date is 0307). Why not earlier? Because the earlier Analects passage which implies the existence of a steppe political organization and thus combined steppe military pressure . . .

> **4:35** (LY 3:4). Lín Fàng asked about ritual. The Master said, Great indeed is this question! In ceremonies, than lavish, be rather sparing; in funerals, than detached, be rather moved.

> **4:36** (LY 3:5). The Master said, The Yí and Dí [peoples] *with* rulers are not the equal of the several Syà states *without* them.

> **4:37** (LY 3:6). The Jì were going to sacrifice to Mount Tài. The Master said to Rǎn Yǒu, Can you not save the situation? He replied, I cannot. The Master said, Alas! Who will say that Mount Tài is not as good as Lín Fàng?

. . . is an obvious interruption, and thus a later insertion.[29] It was added to a mostly ritual chapter (LY 3, c0342) because clothing had ritual meaning.

————·•••·————

Two Geostrategies. The problem for Chí was that it needed more army, and more army required more land, and the only land into which it could now expand was the neighboring Sinitic states. This it did, but with evil results. In 0315, the King of Yēn abdicated in favor of his minister. His heir's supporters resisted. Chí, advised by Mencius, entered Yēn and restored order. Chí then *annexed* Yēn, thus doubling its area. This (page 135) provoked a reaction from other states, which in 0314 combined to expel Chí from Yēn and establish an heir as King of Yēn. This restored what we now call the balance of powers.

[handwritten margin note: Chí's invasion of Yēn]

The shock of this disaster was also felt in Lǔ. The DDJ school had always advocated caution. On the brink of the Chí venture, they issued this warning:

> **4:38** (DDJ 29, excerpt, c0315).
> Some wish to conquer the world and control it;
> I see they will not be able to succeed.
> The world is a sacred vessel; it cannot be controlled.
> Those who would control it will spoil it;
> Those who would grasp it will lose it.

---

[29]This is one of the few Analects interpolations noticed by the commentators as interrupting a thematic pair (mention of Lín Fàng). See further Brooks **Analects** 127.

Once the results were in, DDJ yet more strongly warned of overreaching:

4:39 (DDJ 30, c0314).

> He who by Dàu would aid the leader of men
>> will not wish to be stronger in arms than all the world.
>
> The good man will get his result and nothing more;
>> he will not dare use it to take a position of strength.[30]
>>
>> He will get his result and not flaunt it,
>> get his result and not be vain of it,
>> get his result and not brag of it.
>
> This is called
>> Get your result but be not strong –
>> Such things are like to last for long.

Flaunting your strength will only lead to reprisals from other states.

Chín, in the west, had an advantage: it could expand into areas whose conquest did not provoke a military response from the Sinitic states. In 0316, it had entered the large but remote and non-Sinitic realm of Shǔ, conquered it, and begun to develop it as a food-producing area.[31] The absorption of this region, which doubled the area of Chín, passed without any notice in the east. What *was* noticed was that Chín (engaged in digesting its tremendous addition) was less active against its neighbors, Ngwèi on the east and Chǔ on the south. This lull was taken as an omen by a late passage in the Dzwǒ Jwàn, which is certain that the cruelties of Chín Mù-gūng[32] prove that savage Chín must fail:

4:40 (DJ 6/6:3b, excerpt, c0319) . . . Not only had he no example to leave to his successors, he further led his best men to their deaths; it will be difficult for Chín to occupy a place of authority among the states. Thus does the Gentleman know that Chín will never again march to the east.

Seldom have more foolish words been spoken. Chín soon resumed its pressure on the east. After victories over Ngwèi from 0313 to 0303, Chín joined Ngwèi, Hán, and Chí to attack non-Sinitic Chǔ in 0301, winning a major battle in 0300.

Mencius in c0310 was asked about a case in Dzōu where troops had abandoned their officers. He responded by urging benevolent government:

4:41 (MC 1B12, c0313). Dzōu and Lǔ had a skirmish. Dzōu Mù-gūng asked, Thirty-three of my officers died, and none of my subjects died in their defense. If I should execute them, there would be too many; if I should *not* execute them, I would be letting go those who looked on as their superiors died and would not save them. What should I do?

---

[30]He will not advertise his strength to other states, lest he attract their hostility.

[31]For the process, see Sage **Ancient**. For the strange statuary (the Sinitic states at this time had no statuary at all) and distinctive metal work of Shǔ, see Bagley **Ancient**.

[32]For the text of the poem used as evidence for this negative view, see **#8:1**.

Mencius answered, In a bad year or a time of famine, the old and weak among milord's subjects who are rolled into ditches and canals, the strong who scatter to the four quarters, are several thousands. Milord's treasuries are full, his storehouses overflow, yet among his officers, there are none to report the situation to him. This is a case of the superiors despising and scorning their inferiors. Dzvngdž said, "Take care, take care; what goes forth from you will return again to you." So if the people, now or later, have a chance to get back at them, milord should not treat it as a fault. If milord would put in practice a benevolent government, the people would come to feel at one with their superiors, and would die for their leaders.

Morale, or so Mencius wishes the world to understand, is the decisive military factor, and only his kind of governmental benevolence can create morale.

Confucian Pacifism. Just as the Micians were accepting the idea of just war, the ritualistic Analects Confucians turned *against* war. By the end of the century (#**5:77**), they refused even to *discuss* war. But the war went on.

The 03rd Century

A new Art of War appeared about this time in the central states:

> **Wú Chǐ** 吳起 or Wúdž, "Master Wú," c0295. Attributed to Wú Chǐ in the time of Ngwèi Wǔ-hóu (early 04c). A second layer (c0270) associates him with Ngwèi Wv́n-hóu (late 05c). Translated by Sawyer.

It advances the art of conquest, an art which had eluded Spring and Autumn, by telling how to take over the political infrastructure of a conquered state:

4:42 (Wú Chǐ 4:1, excerpt, c0295). Now, the commanding general of the Three Armies should combine both military and civilian abilities.

4:43 (Wú Chǐ 5:10, c0295). The way to attack and besiege enemy cities is this: When the walls have been breached, enter the buildings and take over all the wealth and offices; the tools and animals. Where the army encamps, do not cut down trees, destroy dwellings, take away crops, slaughter domestic animals, or burn granaries. Thus you demonstrate to the people that you have no desire to oppress them. Those who wish to surrender should be allowed to do so, and permitted to live in peace.

Again Geostrategy. Sùng, the heir of ancient Shāng, had urged its claims as an important state, and sought to have its sacrificial hymns added to the Shr̄. One of the hymns claimed Heavenly sanction for the Shāng (or "Yīn") empire:

4:44 (Shr̄ 303, excerpt, c0320).

> Heaven bade the Dark Bird
> to come down and bear the Shāng
> who dwelt in the lands of Yīn so wide.

> Of old, God bade warlike Tāng
> to partition the frontier lands.
> Of those lands he was assigned to be Lord;
> Into his keeping came all realms . . .

This cultural initiative was successful (the Shāng hymns are still there, as Shr̄ 301-305). But militarily, Sùng was weak. Chí attacked in 0286, and Sùng ceased to exist. But as with Yēn in 0314 (page 135), other states joined to expel Chí from Sùng in 0285 and went on to occupy Chí itself, driving its ruler into exile and death. Chín, by contrast, once again expanded into less culturally sensitive areas; in this case, non-Sinitic Chǔ. In 0278, Chín took the Chǔ capital Yǐng, and Chǔ moved its capital down the Yángdž River. Some territory was regained in the following year, but from this time onward, Chǔ was essentially an eastern state. This in turn drastically altered the strategic position of Ngwèi, which was now exposed on two sides to pressure from Chín.

After Sùng. The end of Sùng made a great impression. So did the fate of Chí. Responses varied. Some offered advice on a better *way* of fighting:

4:45 (DDJ 68, c0285).

> A good officer is not bellicose,
> A good warrior does not get angry;
> One good at subduing the foe does not engage,
> One skilled at using others puts himself below.
> This is called the Virtue of Not Contending . . .

Others later tried a philosophical approach, based on larger considerations:

4:46 (JZ 25:5b, excerpt, c0264). Dài Jìn-rv́n said, There is something called a snail. Is the Ruler familiar with it? The Ruler replied, Yes.

There is a state on the snail's left horn, called Clash. There is a state on the snail's right horn, called Mangle. Sometimes, in contending over territory, the two go to war. The piled-up corpses number in the myriads, and they pursue the defeated for a week and a half before returning. The Ruler said, Ha! This is merely a piece of rhetoric, is it not?

Your subject begs to show the Ruler the truth of it. According to the Ruler's view, as one moves outward in the Four Directions, and up and down, is there an end? The Ruler said, There is no end.

Does he know that if he lets his mind wander in the Endless, and then with that perspective returns to the lands we know, it will be uncertain that, in comparison, those lands even exist? The Ruler said, Yes.

Among those states is Ngwèi. Within Ngwèi there is Lyáng. In Lyáng there is the King. Between the King of Lyáng and the King of Mangle, is there a difference? The Ruler said, There is no difference.

The visitor then went out, but the Ruler kept on sitting there, uncertainly, as though he had forgotten something.

He had forgotten *himself.* Or more exactly, his former idea of himself.

Spying. As the military manuals came to be widely read, and generals on all sides came to know the same things, the former tactical edge vanished. One way to regain the initiative was to know in advance what the enemy would do. The proprietors of the Sūndž thus added a chapter to their work, which gave sophisticated advice on getting, and also on planting, military information:

> 4:47 (Sūndž 13, excerpts, c0262) . . . One who confronts his enemy for years in order to strive for victory in a decisive battle, yet who because he grudges rank, honor, and a few hundred pieces of gold, remains ignorant of his enemy's situation, is devoid of humanity . . . The reason the wise prince and able general conquer wherever they go . . . is foreknowledge. Foreknowledge cannot be elicited from spirits or gods, or by analogy with past events, or from calculations. It must be obtained from men who know the enemy situation. There are five types of secret agents to be employed: the local, the inside, the double, the expendable, and the living . . .

Note the emphasis on humanity: an intelligence war produces fewer casualties.

The Chín theorists defended war by analogy from legal punishments:

> 4:48 (SJS 18:1, excerpt, c0256). If by war one would abolish war, then even though it *is* war, it is permissible. If by killing one would abolish killing, then even though it *is* killing, it is permissible. If by punishment one would abolish punishments, then even if they are severe punishments, they are permissible . . .

[margin handwriting: Chín theorists on "just" war.]

The text admits the people's dislike of fighting, but only to advise how it may be overcome. Family pressure is one way; local control is another:

> 4:49 (SJS 18:2b, excerpt, c0256). War is what the people hate, but he who can make the people delight in war will become King. With the people of a strong state, a father seeing off his son, or an elder brother his younger brother, or a wife her husband, will all say, If you are not successful, do not return. They will also say, If you die through breaking the law or disobeying orders, we too will die. If the villages are orderly, deserters will have no place to hide, and stragglers no place to go . . .

All earlier efforts against the war machine having proved unavailing, the late Mencians turned to pure invective. They pilloried Lyáng Hwèi-wáng, whose own son had fallen in battle, as a monstrous butcher:

> 4:50 (MC 7B1, c0255). Mencius said, Unbenevolent was King Hwèi of Lyáng! The benevolent extend from those they love to those they don't. The unbenevolent extend from those they don't love to those they do.
>
> Gūngsūn Chǒu asked, What do you mean?
>
> King Hwèi of Lyáng for the sake of territory made pulp of his people, sending them to war. Suffering a major defeat, and being about to resume but fearing he might not win, he drove the youth he loved to his death. That is what is meant by "from those they don't love to those they do."

This inversion of the Mician idea of extrapolating from love of kin to love of all men (#4:4) abandons persuasion for abuse. At least it is effective abuse.

Militarization of the intellectual sphere continued in the 03c. It is perhaps saddest to observe in the Micians, who had been the most organized, and the most articulate, of the antiwar thinkers. But the need to talk the language of those around them affected the Micians, as it must affect any advocacy group. Of their last ethical essays, this one shows the process especially clearly:

> **4:51** (MZ 5, excerpt, c0263). Our Master Mwòdž said, A state has seven disasters. What are the seven disasters? When the walls and moat cannot be guarded but palaces and chambers are in order: this is the first disaster. When an adjacent state comes to the border but no neighbor state comes to our aid: this is the second disaster. When first they exhaust the people's strength on useless projects and reward incapable people; when the people's strength is exhausted in trivialities and rewards are wasted on visitors: this is the third disaster. When officials protect their salaries and travelers are received with affection; when the ruler creates laws to punish the officials and the officials are in fear and dare not resist: this is the fourth disaster. When a ruler thinks himself wise and does not inquire into affairs, when he thinks himself safe and does not make preparations; when the neighbor states plot against him and he does not know enough to take measures: this is the fifth disaster. When those who are trusted are disloyal and when the loyal are not trusted: this is the sixth disaster. When stored and planted grain is not enough for consumption; when the high officials are not sufficient to manage; when rewards do not give happiness and punishments to not inspire awe: this is the seventh disaster.
>
> If these seven disasters exist in a state, there will be no altars of soil and grain; if with these seven disasters one tries to guard the wall, the foe will arrive and the state will fall. When the seven disasters obtain, the state will surely meet with disaster.

Military, economic, and organizational shortcomings are magnified in severity if they exist in a context of general war. Of the primary Mician tenets, universal love is gone, opposition to war is gone: war is here whether we like it or not. Only frugality is left, and frugality is important only as a way to avoid defeat.

Sywndž had become the governor of much of the old Lǔ and Sùng territory in 0254. In 0250 he took part in a Chǔ military mission to Jàu. In those discussions, he thus characterized the quality of Chín's armies:

> **4:52** (SZ 15:1d, excerpt, c0250) . . . The use of the people in obligatory services is stern and harsh. They are coerced with authority, restricted to a narrow life by deprivation, urged on with incentives and rewards, and intimidated with punishments and penalties. Those in subordinate and humble positions are made to understand that only by success in combat can they hope for benefits from their superiors. Men must endure deprivation before they are employed, and some accomplishment must be achieved before any benefits are obtained, but as the accomplishments increase, so do the rewards. Accordingly, a man who takes the heads of five enemy soldiers has five households assigned to him.

Because of this policy, soldiers have become exceedingly numerous, the fighting strength of the army is very formidable, its ability to remain in the field has been much prolonged, and Chín's taxable territories have been greatly extended. That there have been four consecutive generations of victories is due, not to mere chance or luck, but to calculation . . .

Sywndž also notes the fears of Chín:

4:53 (SZ 15:3, excerpt, c0250) . . . Chín for four generations has had only victories, but it has always been apprehensive lest the world should unite to oppose it . . .

Efforts *were* being made at this time to form an anti-Chín alliance; the First Emperor of Chín would later refer to them.[33] Exactly what the efforts were is buried under a Hàn literature of wishful thinking.[34] They failed due to the eastern states' fear of each other, as is shown by the alliances that crushed Chí in 0314 and in 0285: they would only unite to prevent one of their number from dominating the rest. A permanent union of these states could have reached military equilibrium with Chín, but the popular loyalties on which the strength of these states rested, and their own separate agendas, precluded that outcome.[35] Victory would go to the strongest single state.

The End of Lǔ. For a while, it seemed that the strongest one might be Chǔ. Chǔ had cautiously annexed the southern part of Lǔ and Sùng in 0255/54, without provoking reprisals from any other states, and installed Sywndž as its governor. In 0249, it completed the task by annexing the northern part, bringing to an end the sovereignty of Lǔ, as well as the local Confucian and Mician schools. The Micians in Lǔ seem to have seen this coming. In the last of their writings, they let Mwòdž write the epitaph of the Mician movement as the defenders of cities. They had failed, and even their memory was fading:

4:54 (MZ 50, c0250). Gūngshū Pán had completed some cloud-ladders for Chǔ, and was preparing to attack Sùng with them. Master Mwòdž heard about it, and starting from Chí, he traveled for ten days and ten nights until he reached Yǐng. There he had an audience with Gūngshū Pán. Gūngshū Pán said, What instruction has the Master for me? Master Mwòdž said, In the north there is someone who has insulted your subject. I should like to arrange for you to kill him. Gūngshū Pán was not pleased. Master Mwòdž said, I ask permission to present ten pieces of gold. Gūngshū Pán said, My principles are firmly against killing. Master Mwòdž rose, bowed twice, and said, I beg leave to explain.

---

[33]For the Chín Emperor's inscriptions see #**8:9**, and even more forcefully #**8:28**.

[34]Massively preserved in the diplomatic stories of the Jàn-gwó Tsv̀ (below, p116).

[35]For the equally forlorn notion of a political union of Britain and France against a stronger enemy in 1940, see Churchill **Finest** 204f.

In the north, I heard you were making ladders and preparing to attack Sùng. What offense has Sùng committed? The Land of Jīng[36] has an excess of land, but not enough people. To kill what you have not enough of in order to contend for what you have an excess of cannot be said to be wise. To attack Sùng when it has committed no offense cannot be said to be benevolent. To know this, but not to contest [the Chŭ plan] cannot be said to be loyal. To contest it but not to succeed cannot be said to be forceful. To refuse to kill few out of principle, but yet to be ready to kill many, cannot be said to show a sense of proportion.

Gūngshū Pán said, Agreed. Master Mwòdž said, Then why not desist? Gūngshū Pán said, It cannot be done; I have already spoken of it with the King. Master Mwòdž said, Why not present me to the King? Gūngshū Pán said, Very well.

Master Mwódž saw the King, and said, Suppose someone were to discard his own decorated carriage, but his neighbor has a shabby cart, and he wants to steal it? Suppose he were to discard his own embroidered robe, but his neighbor has a short jacket and he wants to steal it? Suppose he were to discard his own fine meat, but his neighbor has some chaff, and he wants to steal it? What kind of man would that be? The King said, he would have to be a kleptomaniac.

Master Mwòdž said, The territory of Jīng is 5000 square leagues in extent; the territory of Sùng is 500 square leagues in extent. This is like the decorated carriage and the shabby cart. Jīng has its Ywn-mvng Park, which is full of rhinoceros and deer, and the fish and turtles, the gars and gators, in the Jyāng and Hàn rivers are the most plentiful in the world; Sùng is said to possess not even pheasants or rabbits; foxes or badgers. This is like the meat and the chaff. Jīng possesses tall pines, figured catalpas, pin oaks and cedars, camphor trees; Sùng has no tall timber. This is like the embroidered robe and the short jacket. Your subject, on comparing these three things to the plans of the King's servants to attack Sùng, finds that there may be a similarity.

The King said, Excellent. But all the same, Gūngshū Pán has made the cloud ladders for me, and I am determined to take Sùng. Thereupon he received Gūngshū Pán. Master Mwòdž took off his sash to represent the city wall, and used small sticks to represent the various weapons. Gūngshū Pán deployed his weapons in nine attacks on Sùng, and Master Mwòdž nine times countered them. Gūngshū Pán's devices of attack were exhausted, while Master Mwòdž still had defensive stratagems to spare.

Gūngshū Pán was embarrassed, but said, I know how I can refute you, but I won't tell. Master Mwòdž said, I know how you can refute me, but I won't tell. The King of Chŭ asked what it was.

[36]This archaic variant is evidently more courtly than the common name "Chŭ."

Master Mwòdž said, Master Gūngshū's idea is to kill me, and when he has killed me, he thinks there will be no one to defend Sùng, so it can be attacked. But your servant's disciple Chín Gǔ-lí and three hundred others are manning the defenses for me, and atop the walls of Sùng they await the bandits from Chǔ. Though you kill your servant, you cannot avoid them. The King of Chǔ said, Excellent. I beg permission not to attack Sùng.

Master Mwòdž passed through Sùng on his return. It was raining, and he wanted to take shelter in the gateway, but the gate warden would not admit him. Thus it is said, Those who create order in secret, the multitude do not know of their achievements. Those who make war in the open, the multitude know all about.

And in that year, 0249, the Sùng lands which had been invaded in 0286 by Chí were after all added to the territory of Chǔ. Chǔ would not keep them long.

Chí thought it might still have a chance. A new Chí military treatise . . .

> **Sžmǎ Fǎ** 司馬法 (SMF), "The Marshal's Art of War," c0248. Written in Chí. Despite a Confucian coloring, it is in places more draconic than its predecessors, the Sūndž and the Wú Chǐ. Translated by Sawyer.

. . . argued, with SJS (**#4:48**), that war is waged for the purpose of *ending* war:

4:55 (Sžmǎ Fǎ 1, excerpt, c0248). Authority comes from war and not from men. For this reason, if one must kill men to give peace to the people, then killing is permissible . . . If one can only stop war with war, then even if it is war, it is permissible.

The Lǔ-shř Chūn/Chyōu also accepted war, in terms taken from the Sžmǎ Fǎ:

4:56 (LSCC 7/2:4, excerpt, 0241). Weapons are truly justified when they are used to punish cruel rulers and free their suffering people . . .

4:57 (LSCC 8/2:4, excerpt, c0241). One uses a tool of ill omen when one cannot help it . . . One kills some to allow others to live . . .

Heaven permits, and indeed requires, ruthlessness toward one's own people.

The chariot warriors' ethos of prowess and personal loyalty was obsolete in the new age of mass warfare, but it lived on in a tradition of elite vengeance. The archetype of vengeance stories is that of the desperado Yẁ Ràng 豫讓, set in the epic days of the tripartition of Jìn (page 65). Excerpts survive in the core LSCC (0241); the whole story is preserved in a Hàn-dynasty collection:

> **Jàn-gwó Tsv̀** 戰國策 (JGT). A collection of 497 tales from the personal exploit and (especially) the diplomatic intrigue literature of early Hàn. Edited by Lyóu Syàng in c022. Translated by Crump.

The Yẁ Ràng tale is not so much about Yẁ Ràng as about the ideal of honor.

The tale begins:

4:58 (JGT #232, excerpt, c0245). Yẁ Ràng, the grandson of Bì Yáng of Jìn, first served the Fàn and Jūng-háng clans, but was unhappy. He left them and went to the Lord of Jr̄, and the Lord of Jr̄ showed him favor. When the Three Jìn states divided the territory of the Lord of Jr̄, Jàu Syāngdž hated the Lord of Jr̄ more than the others, and made his skull into a drinking vessel. Yẁ Ràng fled to the mountains, and said, Alas! A knight will die for one who knows his worth; a maid will beautify herself for one who loves her. I will repay the insult to the Jr̄ clan.

He changed his surname and name, became a [mutilated] convict, and entered the palace on the pretext of plastering the privy, intending to assassinate Syāngdž. Syāngdž went to the privy, but he grew suspicious. He held and questioned the plasterer. It was Yẁ Ràng, who had sharpened the edge of his trowel into a blade; he said, I wished to repay the insult shown to the Lord of Jr̄. The attendants wished to kill him, but Syāngdž said, He is a man of honor 義; I will merely take care to avoid him. The Lord of Jr̄ is dead, and has left no posterity behind him, but this, his subject, goes to such lengths to avenge the insult to him. This is one of the worthiest men in the world. In the end, he released him.

Yẁ Ràng lacquered his body until it was ulcerated, shaved his hair and removed his eyebrows, and scarred himself to change his appearance. Disguising himself as a beggar he went forth to beg. His wife did not recognize him, and said, His appearance is not like that of my husband, yet how comes his voice to be so much like that of my husband? He then swallowed ashes to make himself hoarse, changing his voice . . .

And here is the end. Yẁ Ràng is caught in a later attempt to kill Syāngdž, but is allowed to fulfill his obligation symbolically by being given Syāngdž's cloak:

4:59 (JGT #232, excerpt, c0245). Yẁ Ràng drew his sword and thrice leaped up, shouting to Heaven as he struck at the cloak, Thus do I avenge the Lord of Jr̄. He then fell on his sword and died. And the day he died, when the knights of Jàu heard of it, they all shed tears for him.

Thus met in unequal combat the personal valor and honor of the old society and the collective loyalty and obedience of the new.

Chín now entered the escalation race in military theory. As it had done in the past, it turned to Ngwèi, and invited to Chín a Ngwèi military expert, who there extended his military manual, originally written to replace the Wú Chǐ:

> **Wèi Lyáudž** 尉繚子 (WLZ). A first stage (WLZ 1-10, c0238) was written in Ngwèi; the rest (WLZ 11-24, c0232) in Chín. The focus is organizational. The standard Confucian virtue words are mixed with notably ruthless advice for the conduct of war. Translated by Sawyer.

The Ngwèi part of this work already shows the iron discipline which was replacing the personal valor of Yẁ Ràng.

Here, as a pendant to Yw̌-ràng, is an emblematic story of the late 03c army:

4:60 (WLZ 8, excerpt, c0238). When Wú Chǐ fought with Chín, and before battle was joined, one man, unable to contain his ardor, went forward, took two heads, and returned. Wú Chǐ at once ordered him to be beheaded. The commander protested, This is a talented officer; he should not be beheaded. Wú Chǐ said, A talented officer he may be, but he opposed my orders. And he had him beheaded.

In Chín, this sort of discipline was systematically extended to the whole army, with rules about who, on the field of battle, could execute whom. Here are hints about how the desperate valor of Chín soldiers was produced:

4:61 (WLZ 14, 伍 制 令 "Orders for the Group," excerpt, c0232). Organization in the army: Five men are a group 伍; the group are mutually responsible. Ten men are a section 什 ; the section are mutually responsible. Fifty men are a team 屬; the team are mutually responsible. A hundred men are a company 閭; the company are mutually responsible.

If someone in the group resists an order or violates a prohibition, and others report it, they will be absolved of blame. If they know of it but do not report it, the entire group will be executed. If someone in the section resists an order or violates a prohibition . . .

4:62 (WLZ 16, 束伍 令 "Orders For Groups," excerpt, c0232). Orders concerning groups are: Five men make a group, and together they receive orders from the staff of the general. If they lose a group but get a group, it cancels out. If they get a group without loss, they are rewarded. If they lose a group without getting a group, they will die and their families will be extirpated.

If they lose their leader 長 but get a leader, it cancels out . . .

The rule for battlefield executions: The leader of a section 什 can execute the section. The leader of a platoon 伯 can execute the leader of a section. The general of a thousand can execute the leader of a hundred. The general 將 of a myriad can execute the general of a thousand. The Left and Right Generals of the Army 左右將軍 can execute the general of a myriad. The Generalissimo 大將軍 has no one he cannot execute.

Methodological Moment. These are the four classical military texts. Suppose their order is known to be Sūndž, Wú Chǐ, Szmǎ Fǎ, Wèi Lyáudž. There is a joint concordance to all four. What are the relations among them?

In the concordance (it is not necessary to know Chinese) we find sentences that recur in two or more of these texts. Such overlap occurs between Sūndž and Szmǎ Fǎ on the one hand, and Sūndž, Wú Chǐ, and Wèi Lyáudž on the other. Sūndž being the oldest, it seems to have led to two later developments: (1) in Chí, the Szmǎ Fǎ; and (2) in Ngwèi, the Wú Chǐ and the first half of Wèi Lyáudž, with the rest of the Wèi Lyáudž being written in Chín. It is then probable that there were not one but *two* sequences of military texts.

Defense. Offensive war hardened, and so did its defensive counterpart. Gates were covered, first with mud and later with metal, against fire arrows. Trenches outside the gates with a suspended bridge allowed only one person at a time to enter. At intervals along the walls were shields, fire screens, and crossbows to direct fire at enemy battering rams or movable observation and attack towers. These last were called "cloud ladders" (**#4:54**) because they did not need a wall, they were propped, as it were, against the sky.

On the attack side, here is how a mid 03c Chín city assault was organized, and how stringently it was encouraged to succeed:

> **4:63** (SJS 19, excerpt, c0256). In attacking or besieging a town, the Minister of Public Works examines and estimates the size and resources of the city. The military officials assign places, dividing the area according to the number of soldiers and officers available for the attack, and sets them a timetable . . .They dig out subterranean passages and pile up fuel, then set fire to the beams . . . For every man [of the enemy] killed, remission of taxes is granted, but for every man who cannot fight to the death, ten are torn to pieces by the chariots. Those who make critical remarks are branded or their noses are sliced off beneath the city wall.

But the Micians soon found countermoves. From the defending side, poison gas was piped into the attackers' tunnels. Houses were razed to contain fire attacks. The surrounding land was devastated to deny its use to the attacker:

> **4:64** (MZ 70:38, excerpt, c0242). For one hundred leagues beyond the outer wall, cut down and remove all walls, both high and low, and plants and trees both large and small. Fill in all the empty wells, so that water cannot be drawn from them. Outside, destroy all the empty buildings and chop down all the trees. Take into the city everything that could be used in attacking the city . . .

There was provision for medical leave, but also a procedure to detect fraud:

> **4:65** (MZ 70:25, excerpt, c0242). Let the wounded return home to heal their wound and be cared for. Provide a doctor who will give medicines . . . Have an officer go regularly to the village to see if the wound has healed . . . In the case of those who falsely wound themselves to avoid service, put the whole family to death.

And any sign of disaffection, or failure of morale, was brutally punished:

> **4:66** (MZ 70:11, excerpt, c0242). Extra prohibitions for a besieged city. When the enemy arrives unexpectedly, strictly order officers and people not to dare to make disturbances, gather in threes, go about together, look at each other, sit down and weep, raise their hands to touch each other, point to each other, call to each other, signal to each other . . . [Such persons] are to be executed. If the other members of the squads 伍 do not apprehend them, they too are to be executed; if they do apprehend them, they are to be pardoned . . .

Officer and citizen alike are subject to the group responsibility rule.

And thus it came about that in skill and resource, in discipline and ferocity, the attackers and the defenders in the end became virtually indistinguishable. Did it really matter, any longer, who won?

Offense. In the late 04c, the Sūndž had praised the general who preserved a conquered army to add it to his own force. This policy of appeasement and reuse (in effect, conciliating the conquered populace) was developed in the early 03c by the Wú Chǐ's emphasis on taking over intact the administrative and civil structures of the conquered states (**#4:43**). But as the wars went on, Chín preferred to devastate conquered cities and massacre surrendered armies (the Jàu soldiers who thus perished at Cháng-píng in 0260 numbered 400,000). This retaliation against resistance to Chín seems to have assisted, not retarded, the progress of Chín to final victory.

Nor did Chín spare its own resources. As the human cost of warfare rose, Chin proved willing to pay that cost. As supporting witness to SJS 19 (**#4:63**), here is a passage on generalship from the Chín portion of the Wèi Lyáudž:

> **4:67** (WLZ 24, excerpt, c0232). I have heard that in antiquity, those who excelled in using their troops could bear to kill half their officers and men. The next best could kill 30 percent, and the lowest, 10 percent. The awesomeness of one who could sacrifice half his troops affected all within the Four Seas . . . Thus I say that a mass of a hundred thousand that does not follow orders is not as good as ten thousand men who fight, and ten thousand men who fight are not as good as a hundred men who are truly aroused.

And Chín, in a passage already quoted, continued to hammer at its root idea: a state at war has room for nothing but farming and fighting:

> **4:68** (SJS 25:3, excerpt, c0236). And so my teaching is that if the people want profit, they cannot get it but by farming; if they want to avoid harm, they cannot do so but by fighting. If none of the people of the state but first engage in farming and fighting, then later they will get what they like. Thus, though the territory be small, the production will be large; though the populace be sparse, the army will be strong. If one can carry out these two principles in his own territory, then the Way of the Hegemon King lies open before him.

It did indeed. At that moment, seven states were still in contention. Hán was defeated in 0230 by a Chín army led by "Palace Official Tvng;" Chín generals Wáng Jyěn 王翦 and Wáng Bvn 王賁 were prominent in what followed. Jàu was destroyed in 0228; some Jàu forces escaped to Yēn. Ngwèi fell in 0225 and Chǔ in 0224. A Chǔ remnant under Syàng Yēn regrouped south of the Hwái River; they were wiped out in 0223. Yēn, with its Jàu refugees, fell in 0222. Chí surrendered without a battle in 0221.

The Six States were no more, and all the world belonged to Chín.

5. The Civilian Elite

We are at the beginning of the 05th century. The Spring and Autumn state is being refashioned and reorganized, and is readying itself for future conquest. What more does it need? We may let the war machine itself answer that:

5:1 (Sūndž 2, excerpt, c0311). The rule for using troops. Fast four-horse chariots, one thousand. Covered chariots, one thousand. Men in armor, ten myriad. Provisions for a thousand leagues 千里. Then what with the internal and external expenses, the necessities for visitors and guests,[1] materials like glue and lacquer and the readying of carriages and armor, the daily expense will run to a thousand of gold. After that [is in hand], the host of ten myriad can be raised.

Before war must come the wherewithal for war. This required an expanded civilian staff, managed by a civilian elite. Like the warriors, the civilian elite needed its own value system. Where was it to come from?

In part from experience of the new situation. But socially, from two sources. One was the followers of Confucius, the jyw̄ndž 君子 or "gentlemen," coming from the warrior tradition or otherwise familiar with palace ways. The other was people one step down socially: traders and wealthy landowners, eventually organized under the leadership of one Mwò Dí 墨翟 or Mwòdž. These we call the Micians.[2] They had a quite different view of the state, in some ways more enthusiastic (they viewed law, which the Confucians resented, as beneficial) and in other ways hostile (they opposed war, with which at first the Confucians had no problem). The two provide philosophical contrast throughout the period, though tending to come together toward its end.

There were issues for both. The Confucians felt that the duty of a ruler was to entrust the government to a wise minister. The problem of how to identify a wise minister was never solved, and no constitutional or other way of giving him executive power was ever found. The Micians sought in the concept of Heaven a higher power to which ruler and people would alike be subject. The Confucians made a similar attempt with the rules of ritual, or as we might say, due process, which ruler and minister would alike respect. None of this worked: the ritual system and the cosmos both supported the position of the ruler. This is a history without a Magna Carta, or the loss of sovereignty which in ancient Greece had forced the cities to reinvent government de novo. The state became conceptually separate from the ruler, but this did not undermine the ruler.

Protest was thus perilous; both Confucians and Micians showed courage.

---

[1] Diplomacy, both between states and between armies, was part of war.
[2] From the early Jesuit romanization of Mwòdž 墨子 (Master Mwò) as Micius.

The 05th Century

By the beginning of the 05c, a civil service tradition was already in being. In Lǔ, it consisted of admired figures from the past, somewhat re-envisioned as civil servants.[3] We can get a sense of them from some remarks, many of them disapproving, made in the Confucian school text, the Analects. For example:

5:2 (LY 5:18, excerpt, c0470). Dzāng Wýn-jùng had a Tsài tortoise in his house; he had mountain rafters and waterweed beams.

This is criticized by "Confucius" as inappropriate luxury. The implication is that at least current bureaucrats were earning big salaries, and liking it.

5:3 (LY 5:19a, excerpt, c0470). Director Intendant Dž-wýn 令尹子文 thrice took office as Director Intendant without showing pleasure, and thrice left it without showing resentment; of the former Director Intendant's acts he would always inform the new Director Intendant.

This shows fidelity to the needs of government, and in particular, to continuity in government operations, along with an admirable lack of personal feeling about the ups and downs of employment. Dedication to the job.

5:4 (LY 5:19b, excerpt, c0470). Master Tswēi assassinated the ruler of Chí. Chýn Wýndž had horses for ten chariots,[4] but he abandoned them and left him. Reaching another state, he said, They are as bad as our great officer Master Tswēi, and left them. Arriving at yet another state, he again said, They are as bad as our great officer Master Tswēi . . .

Notice the scruple about serving a bad ruler, but also the lack of scruple about taking office in another, necessarily a rival, state. Civic virtue was portable.

The Way. We have noticed these passages before (#3:3-4), as attesting a legal system, including imprisonment, by the early 05c. For the Confucians, this was not the right Way of government, and they do not accept its judgements:

5:5 (LY 5:1, c0470). The Master said of Gūngyě Cháng 公也長, He is marriageable. Though he has been in durance, it was not his fault. And he gave him his daughter to wife.

5:6 (LY 5:2, c0470). The Master said of Nán Rúng 南容, When the state has the Way 道, he will not be cast aside. When the state has not the Way, he will keep clear of penalties and punishments. And he gave him his elder brother's daughter to wife.

The surnames imply men of modest background (Confucius himself had only modest influence). Such men were eligible for office, but also vulnerable.

---

[3]Leading Spring and Autumn figures were of military background, and their careers included both military and civilian responsibilities. For the change, see Brooks **Lore**.

[4]That is, he was high enough in rank to be able to field a small army of his own. The Chýn or Tyén family later would usurp the throne of Chí. But all that lay in the future, and in this passage Chýn Wýndž appears as an exemplary figure.

Confucius, Kǔng Chyōu 孔丘 of Lǔ,[5] was born in 0549[6] and died in 0479. His father had earned a landholding by his valor in battle (page 33). Like other landed warriors, Confucius had a client circle: people of lower status than himself, for whom he was a patron and a possible career contact.[7]

He had served in the escort of Jāu-gūng when Jāu-gūng was exiled in 0517. The next Lǔ Prince, Dìng-gūng (r 0509-0495), proceeded with success against the Three Clans. By 0498, the position of the legitimate line had stabilized. Confucius served Dìng-gūng and his successor Āi-gūng (r 0494-0468) in modest but largely civilian ways,[8] as a provider of talent for the state.

Confucius advised his protégés by remarks. After his death, one of his protégés, probably Dž-gùng 子貢, recorded sixteen of those remarks. These became the nucleus of the Analects, the house text of the Lǔ Confucian school.

This, then, is the real Confucius, as his own protégés chose to remember him:

Rvn. Dž-gùng arranged the sayings in four groups. The first focuses on rvn 仁, "otherness" or "benevolence:" acting for others, not yourself.[9] To a warrior, it meant dedicated self-sacrifice. for civilians, it meant acting in the public interest. The seven rvn sayings suggest the stages of a career, from a young aspirant hoping to be noticed, to the senior person who does the noticing.

> **5:7** (LY 4:1, 0479). The Master said, It is best to dwell among the rvn. If he choose not to abide in rvn, how will he get to be known?

> **5:8** (LY 4:2, 0479). The Master said, He who is not rvn cannot long abide in privation, and neither can he forever abide in happiness. The rvn are content with rvn; the "knowing" turn rvn to their advantage.

"Knowing" here is sarcastic; it means the worldly-wise. The dedicated person wants to be noticed, not for advantage, but to serve the state, and the state's only method of recruitment at this early date was personal contact.

---

[5]"Confucius" is Latinized from Kǔng Fūdž, 孔夫子 "Our Respected Master Kǔng." His personal name Chyōu 丘 "hill" is related to his formal name Jùng-ní 仲尼 "Second Brother Ní." Since his older brother was crippled and could not inherit the father's position, his mother prayed on Ní-shān "Ní Mountain" for a second son. Chyōu "hill" is thus a synonym for "Ní [Mountain]."

[6]The usual birthdate 0551 (with a variant 0552) apparently involves a confusion between Confucius and his older brother; see Brooks **Analects** 264 and 269.

[7]There seem to have been more than sixty of these. For their names and probable social origins, see Brooks **Analects** 272-284.

[8]His military talents were scant. His one foreign assignment was a mission through Sùng to Chvn and Tsài. This failed disastrously; he and his party barely made it back alive (#**5:35**). The failure provided useful material for later opponents and satirists.

[9]Homophonous with rvn 人 "man, human," whence the translation "humane." In the 05c it refers to behavior toward others; in the 04c, it also comes to mean the ruler's "benevolence" toward the people, a vertical and not a horizontal relationship.

The next two (all these sayings are paired) show someone already in office:

5:9 (LY 4:3, 0479). The Master said, It is only the rv́n who can like others, or hate others.

5:10 (LY 4:4, 0479). The Master said, If he but set his mind on rv́n, he will have no hatreds.

One's associates should have the right qualities (**#5:9**), but hatred as such is not the gentleman's business (**#5:10**). "Hatred" is developed in the next pair:

5:11 (LY 4:5, 0479). The Master said, Wealth and honor: these are what men desire; but if he cannot do so in accord with his principles (dàu 道), he will not abide in them. Poverty and lowliness are what men hate; but if he cannot do so in accord with his principles, he will not avoid them. If a gentleman avoid rv́n, how shall he make a name? The gentleman does not for the space of a meal depart from rv́n. In direst straits he cleaves to this; in deepest distress he cleaves to this.

5:12 (LY 4:6, 0479). The Master said, I have never seen one who loved the rv́n and hated the not-rv́n. One who loved the rv́n would value nothing else above them; one who hated the not-rv́n would himself be already rv́n; he would not suffer the not-rv́n to come nigh his person. Is there anyone who for a single day can spend all his strength on rv́n? I for one have never seen anyone whose *strength* was not up to it. There may be such, but I for one have never seen them.

One's principles or Way (dàu 道) are the constant. To follow it may be difficult, but it is only will that is lacking. Everyone has the *capacity* to acquire rv́n.

This first section ends with an unpaired saying, giving advice to the senior civil servant about evaluating future candidates for office:

5:13 (LY 4:7, 0479). The Master said, People's faults run true to type. If we look at their faults, it is to discover their good qualities [rv́n].[10]

A shortcoming is definitely a shortcoming, but there may be associated virtues.

The Way. The individual's Way, his Dàu 道, his principles, we have met above. Here is the public Way, the way the political world should be ordered:

5:14 (LY 4:8, 0479). The Master said, If in the morning he hears that the Way obtains, and that evening he dies, it is enough.

5:15 (LY 4:9, 0479). The Master said, An officer who is dedicated to the Way, but ashamed of his poor clothes or poor food, is not worthy to be called into counsel.[11]

For one really dedicated to that Way, personal hardship does not matter.

---

[10]Confucius prepares his protégés to enter service, *and* to be effective at later stages of their careers. The same values apply, but the *way* they apply requires guidance.

[11]It is not only the well dressed who are qualified to discuss policy. Having the right principles (**#5:11**) is not enough; one must be ready to sacrifice all other advantages.

The section ends with a saying which has wider implications:

5:16 (LY 4:10, 0479). The Master said, The gentleman's relation to the larger world is like this: he has no predilections and no prohibitions. If he thinks something is right, he associates himself with it.

We might have expected a loyalty rule; instead, we get integrity: dedication to what is right (yì 義). This is not legal right, but what intuitively ought to be. It is another place where we see the detachment from particular states which also characterized the value system of the Lǔ civil servants at this time (#5:4).

The Narrow View. The next section contrasts the gentleman with the "little man," who is limited by his merely local outlook. This was a problem in recruiting palace personnel from those without a service background.

5:17 (LY 4:11, 0479). The Master said, The gentleman likes virtue 德; the little man likes his own place (tǔ 土). The gentleman likes justice [punishments; syíng 刑]; the little man likes mercy (hwèi 惠).

5:18 (LY 4:12, 0479). The Master said, He who conducts himself with an eye to profit will be much resented.

He is general, not local. In judging cases,[12] he does justice, not favors. Nor is he partial *to himself;* he does not take bribes or work for his own advancement.

The concluding saying in this group is about propriety in government.

5:19 (LY 4:13, 0479). The Master said, Can one run the country with propriety and deference (禮讓)? Then what is the obstacle? But if one *cannot* run it with propriety and deference, what good is propriety?

"Propriety" transmutes the old value of ritual appropriateness into something more nearly procedural: proper form and common principles in office.

The Self. The final group asks: How does one *acquire* the right qualities?

5:20 (LY 4:14, 0479). The Master said, He does not worry that he has no position; he worries how he is going to *perform* in the position. He does not worry that no one knows him;[13] he seeks to be *worth* knowing.

This is very important.[14] The gentleman is not responsible for results; he is only responsible for his own effort, and his own good qualities, which in part come from an unceasing effort to cultivate them. He is not required to be successful.

In this ethos, which is inherited from that of the warrior tradition, the subordinate dedicates himself wholly to the superior, without thought of reward (duty is not a transactional relationship), and with the understanding that duty is an open-ended obligation, which can never be entirely met.

---

[12]Notice the implied legal principle: justice is not justice unless it is uniform.

[13]Recognizes his merits; a standard nuance of "know."

[14]Variants of this saying were repeated three times in later layers of the Analects.

5:21 (LY 4:16,[15] 0479). The Master said, *The gentleman concentrates on*[16] right; the little man concentrates on advantage.

Here we see that "otherness" (page 123) is focused on right, not on the self.

The group ends with the technique for ethical self-improvement:

5:22 (LY 4:17, 0479). The Master said, When he sees a worthy man, let him think how to come up to him. When he sees an unworthy man, let him examine within himself.

Virtue is not learned in advance of experience, but *by* experience: observing one's reaction to what others do. One gets outside the self to realize the self.

This is the end of the original set of sayings: the authentic Confucius.

Methodological Moment. What about LY 4:15, which has been omitted? (1) Form: The pieces on both sides of it, LY 4:14 and 4:16, are part of a pair, so there is nothing left for 4:15 to pair with; it is formally intrusive. Also:

5:23 (LY 4:15, c0294). The Master said, Shv̄m 參![17] My Way 道: by one thing I link it together. Dzv̄ngdž said, Yes. The Master went out, and the disciples asked, What did he mean? Dzv̄ngdž said, Our Respected Master's Way is simply loyalty and empathy.

(2) Type: Other sayings in this set are quotes; this one is a dialogue. (3) Sense: The meaning of the others is obvious, but this one is cryptic; the disciples must ask. (4) Content: The others are wisdom sayings; 4:15 says that the Master's remarks *form a system*, an idea otherwise first seen in the late 04c (#**5:74-76**). The linking principle in this passage (empathy, shù 恕) was actually *rejected* in the 05c; see #**5:25** below. So LY 4:15 is not a plausible saying of Confucius.

––––––––––·•••·––––––––––

[15]For the gap in the Analects sequence, see the Methodological Moment, below.

[16]The words italicized in the translation (君子喻) appear in the above fragment of the Analects portion of the Hàn Stone Classics.

[17]The original final -m is retained to distinguish Dzv̄ngdž from his son Shv̄n 申. For Dzv̄ngdž as the mid 05c head of the Analects school, see below, 127f.

Others. Confucius was not the only preparer of talent for the state, not the only trainer of "gentlemen," as this remark makes clear:

> **5:24** (LY 5:3, c0470). The Master said of Dž-jyèn, A gentleman indeed is this man! If Lǔ indeed had no gentlemen, where did he get *that* from?

He obviously got it from his teacher, who (later tradition to the contrary) was not Confucius himself. There were others like Confucius in the same business.

Enter the Micians. We now hear from the people who would later be the highly organized Mician movement. They too, it seems, were in the business of training people in values appropriate to state service. One of their maxims (the one we now call the Golden Rule) had come to the attention of Dž-gùng, who was inclined to adopt it. Confucius, perhaps surprisingly to those coming from a modern European tradition, counsels caution:

> **5:25** (LY 5:12, c0470). Dž-gùng said, If I do not wish others to do something to me, I wish not to do it to them. The Master said, Sź, this is not something that you can come up to.

Confucius disapproves. But why? Because it contains nothing pertinent to state service; it is strictly interpersonal. It would have been useful to a farm village, as expressing the conventions by which people get along. It would have been useful to a trader, who meets people from a dozen tribes or states in his travels. A century later (#**5:68-70**), it would be accepted by the Confucians, but much had to happen before that acceptance could take place. Among other things, the Confucians had to acquire an interest in the doings of the lower populace.

Some of the upper populace, the palace circle and its secondary contacts, with whom the 05c Confucian school *were* concerned, were already socially marginal, and had to be defended as nevertheless worthy candidates for office:

> **5:26** (LY 6:6, c0460). The Master said of Jùng-gūng 仲弓, If the calf of a plough-ox is plain-colored and has horns, even though one might prefer not to use it, are the hills and streams really going to reject it?

Jùng-gūng was the formal name of Rǎn Yūng, of whom Confucius thought highly, though his surname suggests that he had come from a family of dyers. The passage is a strong expression of early Confucian social mobility.[18]

Dzvngdž 曾子 ("Master Dzvng"), the fourth leader of the Analects group, was a protégé of Confucius' disciple Dž-yóu, who had been Steward of Dzvngdž's native city Wǔ-chvng 武城, on the southern border of Lǔ, a town controlled by the Lǔ Prince and not the rival Three Clans. Dzvngdž marks the second generation of the Confucius movement. He had not known Confucius, and it is not surprising that his Confucius (preserved in LY 7, which he wrote) differs in several ways from the one implied in earlier Analects chapters.

---

[18]See later in this chapter. For populism from below, see Chapter 6, The People.

Under Dzv̄ngdž, the movement was organized as a school in the usual
sense, complete with tuition and an open admissions policy . . .

5:27 (LY 7:7, c0450). The Master said, From those who bring a bundle
of dried meat on up,[19] I have never been without a lesson to give them.

but there was a rigorous standard for students once admitted:

5:28 (LY 7:8, c0450). The Master said, If he is not eager, I don't
expound. If he is not urgent, I don't explain. If I give out one corner and
he doesn't come back with three corners,[20] I don't go on.

Dzv̄ngdž saw Confucius as content with his lack of political position . . .

5:29 (LY 7:16, c0450). The Master said, Eating coarse food, drinking
water, crooking one's arm and pillowing upon it – happiness may also be
found in these circumstances. To be unrighteous and so become wealthy
and even honored – to me this is like a drifting cloud.

and anxious to improve himself continually:

5:30 (LY 7:22, c0450). The Master said, When I am walking in a group
of three people, there will surely be a teacher for me among them. I pick
out the good parts and follow them; the bad parts, and change them.

5:31 (LY 7:17, c0450). The Master said, Give me several more years;
with fifty to study,[21] I might come to be without major faults.

What is remarkable is that, in these sayings, Confucius *has no teacher.* He
learns by circt observation (**#5:30**) and constant effort (**#5:31**). We are as far
as possible from the traditional view that Confucius taught the Classics.

Jōu. On the political side, Dzv̄ngdž's great innovation was to associate the
principles of Confucius with the culture of the Jōu Dynasty. This worked in Lǔ,
because Lǔ saw itself as the cultural and therefore the political heir of Jōu.

5:32 (LY 7:1, c0450). The Master said, In handing on and not inventing,
in being faithful to and loving antiquity, I may compare to our old Pv́ng.

5:33 (LY 7:20, c0450). The Master said, I am not one who knows things
from birth. I am one who loves antiquity and diligently seeks after it.

5:34 (LY 7:5, c0450). The Master said, Extreme has been my decline!
Long has it been since last I dreamed of Jōu-gūng.

Jōu-gūng 周公 ("The Prince of Jōu") had been regent for Jōu Wǔ-wáng's heir.

The Confucians are here reaching for a higher identity than just Confucius.
They claim that their value system preserves that of the revered Jōu Dynasty.
This move won for the Analects group a certain position at the Lǔ court.

---

[19] Apparently, the smallest acceptable gift of a prospective student to a teacher.

[20] The "one corner" is a teacher's maxim on which the student meditates; see **#7:3**.
For more on Dzv̄ngdž and the meditation art, see Chapter 7, Transcendence.

[21] Sywé 學 "study" is here not book-learning, but personal self-improvement.

Chv́n and Tsàı. The Jōu claim had its mystical side. Here is "Confucius" inspired by Jōu-gūng, and invulnerable (through the "virtue" or dv́ 德, almost a magical quality) that is in him, to perils encountered between Chv́n and Tsàı:

> **5:35** (LY 7:23, c0450). The Master said, Heaven begat virtue in me. What does Hwán Twéı expect to do to me?

Hwán Twéı was a minister of Sùng, by whom Confucius, on that dangerous mission for the Lǔ court, was supposed to have been threatened.

Dzv̄ngdž had his own sense of personal dedication:

> **5:36** (LY 8:3, 0436). When Master Dzv̄ng fell ill, he called the disciples at his gate, and said, Uncover my feet, uncover my hands.[22] The Shr̄ says,
>
>> Tremblingly and full of fear,
>> Like verging on the deep abyss,
>> Like treading on the thinnest ice –
>
> but now and hereafter, I know I have come through safely, my little ones.

The warrior's open-ended code (no one service fulfils the obligation of duty; duty always requires more) is here put in civilian terms: constant watchfulness.

Dzv̄ng Ywǽn 曾元 succeeded his father Dzv̄ngdž as head of the Analects school. Here is his version of the Dzv̄ngdž saying (#**5:35**) about Confucius' sense of personal invulnerability in his Jōu mission:

> **5:37** (LY 9:5, c0405). The Master was threatened in Kwáng. He said, Since King Wv́n passed away, does not culture survive here? If Heaven were going to destroy this culture, no one of later date could have managed to take part in this culture. And if Heaven is *not* going to destroy this culture, what can the men of Kwáng do to me?

Dzv̄ng Ywǽn also continued his father's ideal of constant moral effort:

> **5:38** (LY 9:17, c0405). The Master, standing by a stream, said, Its passing by is like this – it does not cease by day or night.

Like earlier Analects masters (#**5:26**), he could stand social conventions on their heads. Here, he reverses the idea of respect for age:

> **5:39** (LY 9:23, c0405). The Master said, The young are to be held in awe. How do we know that what is to come will not surpass the present day? But if someone is forty or fifty, and nothing has been heard from him, then indeed he is not worthy to be held in awe.

At this period, as earlier in the 05c (#**5:24**), there were many sources of education for those aspiring to a court position. These schools put out sayings, and by the end of the 05c the sayings had been gathered into texts which were known outside the schools which had produced them.

---

[22]The limbs of a dying man might be held down to prevent his assuming a ritually incorrect posture in death (Waley). For later variants of this story, see Eno **Sources**.

Here, "Confucius" comments on two of those sayings collections:

5:40 (LY 9:24, c0405). The Master said, The words of the Model Maxims (Fǎ Yǔ 法語): can one but assent to them? But the point is to change. The words of the Select Advices (Sywǎn Jyw̌ 選舉): can one but delight in them: But the point is to progress. Those who delight but do not progress, who assent but do not change; I don't know what is to be done with them!

To focus on maxims, and not do what they say, is the great educational mistake. This is an early protest against the textualization of traditions.

We take our leave of Dzēng Ywǎn by noticing a bit of career advice given out to the Confucian school under his leadership. We should bear in mind that the Confucian school was now in a strong position in the Lǔ capital, so that real advancement in the Lǔ civil service was possible. The problem arises: What to do with friends made at one stage in your career who do not fit in the next stage to which you have now advanced?

5:41 (LY 9:30, c0405). The Master said, One with whom one can study, one cannot always journey with. One with whom one can journey, one cannot always take one's stand with.[23] One with whom one can take one's stand, one cannot always consult with.

In short, you dump them.

The 04th Century

Textualization now went into high gear. The leadership of the Confucian school of Lǔ passed from disciples to members of the Kǔng family. These brought with them a new emphasis on lǐ 禮 or ritual, not rv́n 仁, as their central value. Probably due to this Kǔng connection with the Lǔ court, another group of Kǔngs gained access to the Lǔ chronicle, known to us as the Chūn/Chyōu, and began to annotate it from a ritual point of view. This grew into the Dzwǒ Jwàn; by the end of the century, it had become the largest Warring States text.

The Micians also began to issue their ideas in text form, beginning with a long argument against the state's war policy. This probably comes from the organizer of the movement: Mwò Dí himself.

5:42 (MZ 17:12, excerpt, c0390) . . . Killing one man they call wrong, and will surely judge it to be a capital crime. Extrapolating from this, killing ten men is ten times more wrong . . . With these things, the gentlemen of the world know to condemn them and call them wrong. But if we come to the case of making a great and wrongful attack on some state . . .[24]

On that critical note was ushered in the Golden Age of Chinese philosophy, when advocates addressed not only the rulers of the day (in remonstrance), but also sought a wider audience. Remonstrance had taken on a public character.

---

[23]That is, "cannot necessarily enter office with."

[24]For the whole of this remarkable public protest piece, see **#4:3**.

The Analects School was now led by Dž-sž, later said to be the grandson of Confucius.[25] Under him the school underwent a change in basic values, from Confucius' rv́n 仁 to lǐ 禮 or ritual propriety.[26] The first Kǔng addition to the Analects was a brief handbook of official behavior, describing such things as how to "takes one's stand" at court. Deportment is meticulously described, as though to instruct a newcomer to court service. Some of its prescriptions are:

> **5:43** (LY 10:2, c0380). When the ruler summons him to attend a visitor, his demeanor is severe and his strides are low. In genuflecting to those with whom he is to take his stand, he extends his hands left and right, letting his garment touch the ground before and behind; he is imposing. When he hastens forward it is as though he were on wings. When the visitor has withdrawn, he must return his charge, saying, The visitor is no longer looking back.

> **5:44** (LY 10:3, c0380). When approaching the Prince's gate, he bends his body low, as though it would not admit him; he does not assume an upright posture within the gateway, nor step on the sill. When passing by the Palace, his expression becomes severe and his strides become slow; his words are uttered as though they were insufficient. When gathering the skirt of his robe to ascend the hall, he bends low and holds his breath as though he were not breathing. When he emerges, as soon as he has descended one step, he relaxes his expression and appears more at ease. When he reaches the bottom of the stairs, he hastens forward as though on wings. On returning to his place, he shuffles restlessly.

> **5:45** (LY 10:13, c0380). When he is ill and the ruler comes to see him, he places his head to the east, covers himself with his court robe, and spreads out his sash.

So as to appear properly dressed for court, even though lying in bed.

> **5:46** (LY 10:14, c0380). When the ruler's command summons him, he does not wait for the horses to be yoked, but simply goes.

The position of the Confucians toward the supernatural was ambiguous, but they required respect for the sacrifices and for anything connected with death:

> **5:47** (LY 10:18, excerpt, c0380). On seeing one fasting or in mourning, even if it is an intimate, he changes expression. On seeing a [sacrificial] officiant or a blind man, even if it is an acquaintance, he assumes the proper attitude. Those in ill-omened garb[27] he bows to; he bows to one carrying planks . . .[28]

Nowhere in this handbook is there a hint of public policy, or personal ethics. Deportment is all.

---

[25]This is chronologically impossible; see Brooks **Analects** 263 and 59.

[26]For LY 9:1, later added to neutralize the 05c teachings, see Brooks **Word**.

[27]That is, mourning garb. Everything to do with death is "ill-omened."

[28]For a coffin, concerning the size of which there were precise ritual specifications.

Later, the Micians became candidates for office. In that role, they accepted more subordination in office than did the Confucians, though from what looks not unlike a meritocratic or social-contract conception of the social order:

5:48 (MZ 11:1-2, excerpts, c0372). When human life began, when there was no government; everyone had their own sense of right 義 . . . Each approved his own sense of right, and disapproved that of others.

. . . The disorder in the human world could be compared with that of birds and beasts. And all this disorder was due to the lack of a ruler. Thus they chose the most virtuous person in the world and made him the Son of Heaven.[29] Feeling his inadequacy, the Son of Heaven chose the most virtuous persons in the world and made them the Three Ministers. Seeing the vastness of the Empire and the difficulty of attending to matters of right and wrong or profit and harm among the people of far countries, the ministers divided the empire into feudal states and assigned them to feudal lords. Feeling their incapacity, the feudal lords in turn chose the most virtuous persons in their states and appointed them as their officials.

The first Micians had earlier argued from common experience. Now for the first time they employ an elite idea, one that the Spring and Autumn astrologers would have recognized: disasters come from the displeasure of Heaven:

5:49 (MZ 11:4, excerpt, c0372). How does it happen that order is brought about in the world? There is order in the world because the Son of Heaven can unify standards in the world. But if the people identify with the Son of Heaven and not with Heaven itself, then the complications are not removed. Now the frequent occurrence of storms and floods are nothing but the punishment of Heaven upon the people for not identifying their standards with those of Heaven . . .

This last point rescues the essay from being a mere counsel of subordination: in the end, it is Heaven, not any mere earthly superior, who must be obeyed. Like the 05c Confucians, the 04c Micians recognize a higher principle.

The Dzwǒ Jwàn Confucians, like the contemporary 04c Analects leaders, had seen things from a ritual viewpoint. They now ventured into Heaven theory, and held that Heaven rewards or punishes the deeds of individuals.

Here, the ruler of Lǔ has sent a message of sympathy for a flood in Sùng:

5:50 (DJ 3/11:2, excerpt, c0370) . . . [The ruler of Sùng] replied, This Lonely One was disrespectful, and Heaven has sent down this disaster.

The theory that good and ill events suffered by individuals are due to their own deeds is often refuted in practice. The Dzwǒ Jwàn people, noticing this, revised their Heaven theory, making success due to Heaven's arbitrary support:[30]

---

[29]One of the epithets of the Jōu King as a universal ruler; the Jōu royal ancestors were thought to reside in Heaven, and to be able to dispense blessings from there.

[30]For the third phase of DJ thinking about Heaven, see #**5:66-67**, below.

Thus, in one DJ story, Chúng-ăr (the future Jìn Wv́n-gūng) survives many perils, but then insults the Chǔ ruler. A Chǔ general asks that he be killed:

> **5:51** (DJ 5/23:6, excerpt, c0348) . . . [The ruler said], When Heaven intends to prosper a man, who can stop him? One who opposes Heaven must incur great guilt.

The Micians stuck to their theory that disaster came from personal failings:

> **5:52** (MZ 8, excerpts, c0338). Our Master Mwòdž said, This is because in conducting government, the kings, princes, and great men have been unable to exalt the worthy and employ the able . . . In administering government, the Sage Kings of old gave high rank to the virtuous and raised the worthy. Though they were farmers or artisans, if they had ability, they raised them, assigned them rank, awarded them salaries, entrusted them with affairs, and gave them rights of final decision.

Except that they now take a more radical view of meritocracy, holding that even a farmer or an artisan might qualify for office.[31]

Logic. Law, which was already highly developed by the 04c, does not like synonyms, and it tends to define its terms very closely. In the course of contact with Confucians in office, the Micians also had to do the same thing: to cope with the different senses of some common ethical terms that both sides used. Thus was born the Mician art of logic. That specialty seems to have been pursued by a group distinct from the Mician ethical theorists, since their position sometimes contradicted the views of the Mician ethical philosophers. (In particular, the *logical* Micians did not believe in ghosts and spirits).

The earliest of the logical canons show a tendency to appropriate, and to redefine, terms used by the Confucians. Here are the first few:

> **5:53** (MZ 40:7, c0335). Benevolence 仁 is collective love 體愛[32]

This turns a Confucian top-down virtue into a communal relationship.

> **5:54** (MZ 40:8, c0335). Right 義 is benefit 利

This turns Confucian duty into lateral good; the essence of utilitarianism.

> **5:55** (MZ 40:9, c0335). Propriety 禮 is respect 敬

This reduces elaborate Confucian ritual behavior to elemental human terms.

> **5:56** (MZ 40:10, c0335). Conduct 行 is action 爲

This removes the moral aspect, leaving only the fact of what one does.

It will be seen that these are subversive of the Confucian understanding of these terms, and attempt to standardize them instead in their Mician sense. There would be dialogue, but only (or so it was hoped) on Mician terms.

---

[31] For a fuller treatment of Mician and Confucian populism, see Chapter 6.

[32] We should note that this canon is often read the opposite way, thus "To be jen (benevolent/humane/kind) is to love individually (Graham **Later** 276).

The Legalists. In recruiting officials and judging performance, the Legalists wanted not merit, but competence. The Analects idea of official recruitment was recommendations from personal acquaintance (#5:7, **5:13**). They argued that in practice, any oversights would be automatically compensated:

> **5:57** (LY 13:2, c0322). Jùng-gūng was Steward of the Jì. He asked about government. The Master said, Lead the responsible officers, pardon small faults, advance worthy talents. He said, How shall I recognize the worthy talents so that I can advance them? He said, Advance the ones you know. The ones you do *not* know: will others reject them?

This deals with *omissions* in selection, but not with *errors* in selection. The Legalists envisioned a self-correcting method, specifying tasks and rewarding or penalizing success or failure in meeting those tasks. That is, the rewards and punishments used on the larger populace are here applied to the serving elite:

> **5:58** (GZ 4:5, c0315). Once a regulation has been made public, instances of noncompliance will be deemed disobedience to orders; the penalty is death without possibility of pardon. On examining the regulation, if it is contrary to the text in the palace archive, excesses will be deemed usurpation of authority, and deficiencies will be deemed failure to follow orders; the penalty is death without possibility of pardon.

The military ethos is encroaching on the civilian sphere: all crimes are treason.

This insistence on performing to specification angered the Analects people, who wanted more leeway, more room for personal judgement:

> **5:59** (LY 2:12, c0317). The Master said, The gentleman is not a tool 器.

Even the Micians, who preached subordination, wanted rights of final decision:

> **5:60** (MZ 9:3, excerpt, c0317). What are the three basics? If his position is not high, the people will not respect him. If his pay is not substantial, the people will have no confidence in him. If his official orders are not final, the people will not be in awe of him . . . And how can this be seen as a gift to the subordinate? It comes from wanting things to get done.

Expertise. One way to argue this is the metaphor of the specialist: a social inferior who nevertheless has expert knowledge, and is thus useful, in his way, to government. What if the expertise is precisely in government? The historian Xenophon (0487-c0354) reports Socrates as criticizing one Euthydemus for thinking that he can govern the state without studying:

> **5:61** (Xenophon: Memorabilia 4/2:2, excerpt, c0355). If in the minor arts great achievement is impossible without competent masters, surely it is absurd to imagine that the art of statesmanship, the greatest of all accomplishments, comes to a man of its own accord.

Xenophon's example of expertise in a person of low social standing is the musician. The idea of office gained by merit appealed to the Confucians, who probably learned this example from traders (perhaps Micians) who picked it up, along with other curious Greek ideas (page 78), in the taverns of Bactria.

Mencius, the second great Confucian figure, was in touch with the Dàuists (whose meditation technique he himself practiced), the Chí Legalists, and the egalitarian Micians.[33] He framed this exotic statecraft metaphor in terms of a jade cutter rather than a musician. Here is how he put it to use in practical life. The year is 0316, and Mencius is speaking to the King of Chí:

> **5:62** (MC 1B9, excerpt, c0316) . . . Suppose we have a piece of uncut jade. Even if it were worth a myriad yì of gold, you would still have to entrust its cutting to a jade-cutter. But when it comes to the government of your state, you say, "Just put aside what you have learned, and do as I tell you." How is this different from teaching the jade-cutter his job?

The Yēn Incident. In 0316, Mencius was made a minister in Chí. Then came the Yēn Incident. The principle of meritocratic rule was embodied in a tale of the ancient ruler Yáu abdicating in favor of virtuous Shùn, who in turn abdicated in favor of virtuous Yw, the supposed founder of the Syà dynasty. This appealing myth came to practical fruition in 0315, when the King of Yēn actually abdicated in favor of his virtuous minister Dž-jī 子之. The Heir Apparent of Yēn, deprived of his patrimony, rebelled. Civil disorder ensued. On Mencius' recommendation, Chí occupied Yēn and restored order. Should Chí then go further and *annex* Yēn? On this military question, as it turned out, the ministership of Mencius came to an abrupt and ignominious end:

> **5:63** (MC 1B10, c0314). The men of Chí attacked Yēn and conquered it. King Sywæn asked, Some say that This Solitary One[34] should not take it, others say that he should. When a state of a myriad chariots attacks a state of a myriad chariots, and in five weeks gets all of it, this is something that mere human strength cannot attain to. If I do not take it, there will surely be disasters from Heaven. How would it be if I take it?
>
> Mencius replied, If you can take it and have the people of Yēn be happy, then take it. Among the men of antiquity were some who did thus: King Wǔ was one. If you take it and the people of Yēn should not be happy, then do not take it. Among the men of antiquity were some who did thus: King Wvn was one.
>
> A state of a myriad chariots has attacked a state of a myriad chariots, and they welcomed the King's host with baskets of food and jugs of gruel. How can it be otherwise than that they were escaping from fire and water. If now the water should become deeper and the fire hotter, they will simply make another change.

Chí did annex Yēn. And a coalition of states, fearing that a Chí doubled in size would upset the balance of powers, invaded Yēn in 0314, expelled Chí, and installed a new King of Yēn. Mencius left Chí, and never again held a post in a major state.

---

[33]For his role in developing the concept of populism, see Chapter 6, The People.

[34]Conventional self-designation for a ruler; he is an orphan since his father has died.

The Micians, who had from the beginning opposed the war policies of the larger states,[35] picked up Mencius' "jade carver" version of the Xenophon expertise parable (#5:61-62) and used it to criticize a certain incompetent minister, one of the "gentlemen of the world" whose management of affairs the Micians regarded as wrong from beginning to end:

> **5:64** (MZ 47:8, c0310). Mwòdž said, As the gentlemen of the world cannot be butchers of dogs and pigs, they would refuse when asked to be such. Yet though they are not capable of being ministers in a state, they would accept such a position when asked. Is this not perverse?

Which in its witty way was unkind, but perhaps not entirely uncalled-for.

Jì-syà. The Yēn fiasco did not sour the Chí King on expert advice, but he did seek to put it on a firmer basis. After Mencius' departure in 0313, he set up a group of theorists at Jì-syà, headed by the naturalist philosopher Dzōu Yěn.[36]

Abandoning Heaven. The Dàu/Dv́ Jīng had earlier preached a similar naturalistic doctrine: All things change, and success is therefore temporary:

> **5:65** (DDJ 9, c0335).
>
> Than have it and add to it, better to stop.
> You may grind and polish, but you cannot keep long.
> Gold and jade may fill the hall, but none can ward them.
> The rich, high, and mighty but send themselves bane.
>> When the work is done, he then withdraws –
>> The Way 道 of Heaven.

The Dzwǒ Jwàn now dropped its earlier theories of a responsive Heaven, in favor of the view that stuff just happens. Says a wife to a sick ruler:

> **5:66** (DJ 3/4:1, excerpt, c0320). After fullness comes decline; this is the Way (Dàu 道) of Heaven.

Things come to an end, not as a penalty for our wrongdoing or miscalculation, but simply *because they come to an end.*[37] In another story, the wife of a Lǔ Prince, from the Chí house of Jyāng, is being returned to her home on his death, after her son, the heir, has been killed and a concubine's son set up as the ruler:

> **5:67** (DJ 6/18:6, excerpt, c0318) . . . She wailed as she passed the market, "Heaven! Jùng is wicked; he has killed the heir and set up a commoner." Those in the market all wailed. The men of Lǔ styled her "Doleful Jyāng."

A lot of good that did her. Heaven was silent, and the usurper ruled in peace.

---

[35]For the antiwar program of the Micians, see #4:3-6.

[36]For Chí naturalistic philosophy, see p83-85. Jì-syà was a neighborhood in the Chí capital. The six experts had no governmental responsibilities; they were told to investigate the causes of state success or failure (p75).

[37]Note that, in the spirit of the times, a *female* speaker expresses this truth. For the late, cynical DJ abandonment of Heaven, see also #3:31 and Brooks **Heaven**.

Affirming Man. The Golden Rule, dismissed by the 05c Confucians (#**5:25**), now turns up again, and this time it is accepted as a basic principle:

5:68 (LY 12:5, c0326). Szmǎ Nyóu, grieving, said, Other men all have brothers; I alone have none. Dž-syà said, Shāng has heard that death and life have their appointed limits, wealth and honor rest with Heaven. If a gentleman is assiduous and omits nothing, is respectful to others and displays decorum, then within the Four Seas, all men are his brothers. Why should a gentleman worry that he has no brothers?

5:69 (LY 12:22, c0326). Fán Chŕ asked about rŕn 仁. The Master said, Loving others [àı rŕn 愛人] . . .[38]

5:70 (LY 12:2, c0326). Jùng-gūng 仲弓 asked about rŕn. The Master said, He leaves the gate as though meeting an important visitor;[39] he uses the people as though assisting at a great sacrifice.[40] What he himself does not want, let him not do to others. In the state he will have no resentment; in the family he will have no resentment. Jùng-gūng said, Though Yūng is not quick, he begs leave to devote himself to this saying.[41]

The 04c Confucians have acquired a wider social sense of themselves.

Textualization continued. The Shr̄ repertoire was finalized at 300 poems:

5:71 (LY 13:5, c0322). The Master said, If he can recite the 300 Poems, but in applying them to government he gets nowhere, or if being sent to the Four Quarters he cannot make an apposite response, then many though they may be, what are they good for?

To the late 04c imagination, even the preservation of Confucius' remarks was seen as a process of writing them down, rather than remembering them:

5:72 (LY 15:6, excerpt, c0305). Dž-jāng asked about being successful. The Master said, If his words are loyal and faithful, and his actions sincere and respectful, then even among the [non-Sinitic] Mán and Mwò he will be successful . . . When he stands, he should see this [maxim] in front of him; when riding in his carriage, he should see it on his crossbar. If he does this, he will be successful. Dž-jāng wrote it on his sash.

The substitution of texts for teachers went hand in hand with the substitution of antiquity (in the Shr̄ and Shū) for present-day wisdom. Antiquity took wisdom out of contemporary arguments, and put it in the past, as shared wisdom. Texts did the same; they made possible comradeship among those who were not the literal followers of a specific teacher. This sense of solidarity across time and space gave a new dimension to the Confucian sense of duty.

---

[38]The term jyēn àı 兼愛 "universal love" is a primary Mician principle; see #**4:4**. There is a pun in #**5:69**: rŕn 仁 and rŕn 人 "people, others" are pronounced identically.

[39]He approaches his public service with due gravity and ceremony.

[40]That is, with the utmost care, so as not to overwork the people.

[41]A conventional remark after one has received instruction.

.ere is a parable of duty: a duty to set the record straight.

ͻJ 9/25:2, excerpt, c0318). The Grand Historian[42] had written, ɪ϶ᴠᴠ϶. Jù assassinated his ruler. Master Tswēi had him killed. His younger brother took his place, and wrote it, and so the dead now numbered two. *His* younger brother also wrote it, and [Master Tswēi] then desisted. A historian of the south, hearing that the Grand Historians [of Chí] had all died, took up his bamboo strips and set out [for Chí], but heard that the record had been made, and so returned.

This envisions a whole fraternity of professionals, all dedicated to the truth.

System. With textualization came systematization; the idea that wisdom is more than just a lot of sayings, and has a structure of its own. We have met the second of these as an interpolation (#**5:23**); here is where it fits chronologically:

5:74 (LY 15:3, c0301). The Master said, Sż, you regard me as one who has studied and remembers it, do you not? He replied, Yes. Is that wrong? He said, It is wrong. I have one thing by which I string it together.

5:75 (LY 4:15, c0294). The Master said, Shv̄m 參! My Way 道: by one thing I link it together. Dzv̄ngdž said, Yes. The Master went out, and the disciples asked, What did he mean? Dzv̄ngdž said, Our Respected Master's Way is simply loyalty and empathy.[43]

The notion of a principal concept which explains all the specifics was new. So was predicting the unknown from the known, as was being done at this time in calculating eclipses. That idea is here applied to the history of ritual:

5:76 (LY 2:23, c0317). Dž-jāng asked whether things ten generations hence could be foreknown. The Master said, In the Yīn's continuing with the Syà rituals, what they subtracted and added can be known. In the Jōu's continuing with the Yīn rituals, what they subtracted and added can be known. And if someone should carry on after the Jōu, even though it were a hundred generations, it can be known.

Up to now, we have had Chinese thought. From this point on, with the new ideal of internal consistency, we are beginning to have Chinese philosophy.

Peace. By the late 04c, the Lǔ Confucians refused even to *discuss* war:

5:77 (LY 15:1, c0305). Wèi Líng-gūng asked Confucius about tactics. Confucius replied, If it is a matter of stem dish and stand,[44] I have heard of them. If it is a matter of armies and campaigns, I have never studied them. Next day he resumed his travels.

This put them closer to the Micians. It also ended their political influence in Lǔ.

---

[42]Tài-shř 太史 is in origin the "Grand Astrologer," but here clearly a Historian.

[43]Loyalty 忠 is a traditional warrior-ethos virtue (p116). Empathy 恕 is new; it is the civilian Golden Rule quality (see #**5:25**). Confucian philosophy is here being redefined, and in partly civilian terms. For the 04c Analects rejection of war, see #**5:77**.

[44]Sacrificial vessels, symbolizing ritual knowledge in general.

The 03rd Century

Being thus limited to private life, they attempted to justify private life:

5:78 (LY 1:1, c0294). The Master said, To learn something and in due time rehearse it: is this not pleasurable? To have friends coming from far places: is this not delightful? If others do not recognize him but he is not disheartened: is he not a gentleman?

In private life, women too can display virtues:

5:79 (LY 1:13, c0294). Yŏudž said, If his promises are close to what is right, his word can be relied on. If his respect is close to what is proper, he will avoid shame and disgrace. If he marries one who has not wronged her own kin, she can be part of his clan.

Virtue in one context is the best predictor of virtue in another context.

A Canon of six texts began to emerge at this time. Its first hint is in . . .

> **The Gwōdyèn** 郭店 **Texts**, from Tomb 1 (c0282) at a site near the old Chǔ capital. They were used by the tutor of the Chǔ prince who became King of Chǔ in 0262. They include several tracts on human nature, and three sets of excerpts from the Dàu/Dv́ Jīng.

. . . an early 03c text called the Six Virtues 六德. The virtues define proper relations between husband and wife, father and son, and ruler and minister:

5:80 (Gwōdyèn, "Six Virtues," excerpt, c0290). If we observe the Shī and Shū, they are present; if we observe the Lǐ and Ywè, they are present; if we observe the Yì and the Chūn/Chyōu, they are present . . . [45]

Remonstrance was seen in another text as the highest function of ministers:

5:81 (Gwōdyèn, "Lǔ Mù-gūng," c0290). Lǔ Mù-gūng asked Dž-sz̄, What sort of person can be called a loyal minister? Dž-sz̄ said, One who always points out his ruler's evils can be called a loyal minister. Mù-gūng was displeased, and motioned Dž-sz̄ to withdraw. Chv́ngsūn Yì had an audience, and Mù-gūng said, Just now, I asked Dž-sz̄ about loyal ministers, and he said, One who always points out his ruler's evils can be called a loyal minister. This Solitary One is confused, and does not understand. Chv́ngsūn Yì said, Ah; excellent, this saying! Those who have risked death for their ruler's sake: there have been such. But there have never been any who always pointed out their ruler's evils. Those who risk death for their ruler's sake do it for salary and position. But those who always point out their ruler's evils do it out of their sense of right, and have no thought of salary or position. Were it not for Dž-sz̄, how could I ever have heard this?

But we may notice that it is the colleague, not the ruler, who is impressed.

---

[45]This is the first mention of the six-text canon. The Shī and the Yì were complete by c0320, the DJ ("Chūn/Chyōu") by c0312; Shū and the Lǐ were still being written.

The Chín Legalists rejected the whole idea of attaching authority to the words of the ancient sages, simply because the times themselves change:

5:82 (SJS 7:2c, excerpt, c0288). The Sage neither imitates the ancient nor cultivates the modern. If he imitates the ancient, he falls behind the times; if he cultivates the modern, he blocks his position (shr̀ 勢) . . .

This is a military metaphor: any fixed position inhibits later maneuverability.

They also had doubts about what the Confucians and Micians were pushing. Quite apart from their being obsolete, these things were positively pernicious:

5:83 (SJS 4:2, excerpt, c0270). Farming 農, trade 商, and office 官 are the three permanent functions 官 in the state. These three functions produce six parasitic functions: concern for age and concern for nourishment, amusements and desires, and emphasis on intention and conduct.[46] If concern for these six becomes general, then the state is certain to be dismembered . . .

5:84 (SJS 4:3, excerpt, c0270). If a state has ritual 禮 and music 樂; if it has the Shr̄ 詩 and Shū 書, if it has the good 善 and the cultivated 修, if it has the filial 孝 and the fraternal 悌, if it has integrity 廉 and discrimination 辯[47] – if a state has these ten, the superiors will not be able to order the people to war, and the state is certain to be dismembered, and even to disappear altogether. But if the state has not these ten, then the superiors will be able to order the people to war, and the state is certain to flourish, and may become King.

The last comment is especially pointed: the Confucians held that only with respect for age and antiquity, and an emphasis on cultivating personal virtue, could the ruler of a state become a true King.

The Micians, despite many disagreements on points of doctrine, later on came to be not unwilling to overlap strategically with the Confucians:

5:85 (MZ 48:16, c0275). Master Mwòdž was disputing 辯 with Chv́ngdž, and made reference to Confucius. Chv́ngdž said, You oppose the Rú;[48] why do you then refer to Confucius? Master Mwòdž said, This is something which is right, and cannot be altered. If a bird senses heat and drought, it will fly high; if a fish senses heat and drought it will swim low. On this, even if Yw̌ and Tāng were to discuss it, they could not reach a different conclusion. Birds and fish are stupid, but Yw̌ and Tāng must still go along with them. Should Dí then never refer to Confucius?

By this date the assimilation of Micianism to Confucianism was well advanced.

---

[46]These, by pairs, are the faults of the three classes: the filial piety of the village, the extravagances of the rich, and the dedication of the serving elite.

[47]Not the fine discriminations of the sophists, but any claim of the individual to discern and distinguish: to exercise private judgement. The state alone will judge.

[48]A sly reference to the Mician chapters called 非儒, "Against the Confucians."

Demoralization. The Mencians might feel isolated from their own time, but their textual self-identity now gave them some internal consolation:

> **5:86** (MC 5B8, c0275). Mencius said to Wàn Jāng, A good officer in a county will befriend the good officers in that county; a good officer in a state will befriend the good officers in that state . . . [And if that is not sufficient] he will also hold converse with the men of antiquity: he intones their poems, he recites their writings; can he then remain ignorant of what kind of men they were? On this basis he can discourse about their era. This is making friends in antiquity.

Sywndž was beginning to be heard from at this time. His way of making himself known was to attack the other philosophers:

> **5:87** (SZ 6:2, c0269). They give rein to their nature, are comfortable with their desires. Their conduct is bestial; unworthy to be joined with the elegant or associated with the orderly. But what they propose has its reasons, what they say has its logic; it is sufficient to fool and mislead the stupid many – such are Twō Syāu and Ngwèi Móu.[49]

. . . and so on for five other pairs of wrong thinkers: Chv́n Jùng and Shǐ Chyōu (excess scruple), Mwò Dí and Sùng Kv̄ng (egalitarians), Shv̀n Dàu and Tyén Pyén (Legalism and innovation), Hwèi Shī̄ and Dv̀ng Syī (sophists), and worst of all, Dž-sz̄ and Mencius (that is, the Analects and the Mencian schools).

The Mencians were having little discernible effect on the rulers of the time:

> **5:88** (MC 6A9, excerpt, c0273). Mencius said, Do not wonder that the King is not wise. Though it be the easiest plant in the world to grow, if for one day you warm it and for ten days chill it, it will never be able to grow. My audiences are also few, and then I withdraw, and in come others to chill it. Even if I should get some sprouts, what then? . . .

But they had courage:

> **5:89** (MC 6A10, excerpt, c0273). Mencius said, "Fish is what I want, and bear's paw is also what I want. Of the two, if I cannot have both, I will let the fish go and take the bear's paw. Life is what I want, and righteousness is also what I want. Of the two, if I cannot have both, I will let life go and take righteousness. Life is indeed what I want, but there are things I want more than life, and so I will not keep it at all costs . . .

And they saw hardship as toughening them for future achievement:

> **5:90** (MC 6B15, excerpt, c0270) . . . When Heaven is about to place a great burden on a man, it first tests his resolution, exhausts his frame and subjects him to starvation and want, frustrates his efforts to free him from his mental torpor, toughens his nature and supplies his deficiencies.

---

[49]Twó Syāu is now entirely forgotten. Ngwèi Móu figures in Jwāngdž 28:14 (Watson **Complete** 317f) as unable to restrain his desires.

As a rule, a man can mend his ways only after he has made mistakes, and it is only when a man is frustrated in mind that in his deliberations he is able to innovate . . . As a rule, states without orderly families and trustworthy gentleman, and without threat of foreign invasion, will perish. Only then do we learn that we survive in adversity and perish in ease and comfort.

Service. Those who avoided service in dangerous times clashed with those who accepted the risk. Thus did the dropout Jwāngdž people attack Confucius:

5:91 (JZ 4:7, c0264). Confucius went to Chǔ, and Jyé-yẃ, the Madman of Chǔ, wandered past his gate, saying

> Phoenix, oh! Phoenix, oh!
> How is your virtue now brought low.
> A future age, you'll never live to see;
> Back to a former age, you cannot go.
> When All Under Heaven has the Way,
> The Sage spreads virtue far and wide;
> When All Under Heaven lacks the Way,
> The Sage in private does reside.
> And now, in the world of the present day,
> From punishment he tries to hide . . .
> Have done, oh! Have done, oh!
> With ruling by virtue those below . . .

The Analects people rewrote the Madman's jibe in this way:

5:92 (LY 18:5, c0264). Jyé-yẃ, the Madman of Chǔ, sang as he passed Confucius' gate:

> Phoenix, oh! Phoenix, oh!
> How is your virtue now brought low!
> No point to criticize what's past and done;
> You may perhaps escape a future woe.
> Have done, oh! Have done, oh!
> Those who now serve, at their own risk do so.

Confucius came down to speak with him, but the Madman quickened his steps and got away, and Confucius was not able to speak with him.

Here, *Confucius* wins: it is now the cowardly Madman will not stand and argue.

The Analects also answered a primitivist challenge by parodying their story:

5:93 (LY 18:6, c0264). Tall-in-the-Mud and Bold-in-the-Mire were ploughing as a team. Confucius passed by, and sent Dž-lù to ask where the ford was. Tall-in-the-Mud said, Who are you driving? Dž-lù said, Kǔng Chyōu. Tall-in-the-Mud said, Would that be Kǔng Chyōu of Lǔ? He replied, Yes. Tall-in-the-Mud said, Oh, *he* knows where the ford is.[50]

---

[50]Sarcastic; Confucius thinks he knows how to get the world out of its evil state.

Dž-lù asked Bold-in-the-Mire. Bold-in-the-Mire said, Who are you? He said, Jùng-yóu. Bold-in-the-Mire said, Would that be the follower of Kǔng Chyōu of Lǔ? He replied, Yes. Bold-in-the-Mire said, A thing overflowing torrentially – All Under Heaven is like this everywhere, and who is going to change it? And besides, rather than follow one who only withdraws from this or that man, why not follow one who withdraws from the entire age? And he went on ploughing without further pause.

Dž-lù returned and reported this. The Master said, consolingly, One cannot flock together with birds and beasts. If I did not take part with other men, such as they are, with whom *should* I take part? If the world possessed the Way, Chyōu would not be doing his part to change it.

So ashamed were the Jwāngdž people at this imputation of cowardice that they *accepted* the duty of service, and added advice on how to minimize its dangers. In the third such piece, Confucius praises Yén Hwéı in meditational terms:

5:94 (JZ 4:1, excerpt, c0256) Confucius said, You have got it. I will tell you about it:
> You can now go wander in the ruler's little cage
> and not be confused by thoughts of fame.
> If you are received, then sing for him.
> If you are not received, then be still.
> Have no gateway, have no aperture,
> Make Unity your abode, dwell in what can't be helped,
> and then you will be there.

Methodological Moment. Is the Analects from the time of Confucius? Answer: See how it and the Jwāngdž here *respond to each other*, and how it and the Mwòdž (#6:44-46) *argue back and forth*. This cannot be explained as one text reacting to the other; the two texts *must occupy the same time period*. No one claims that Jwāngdž and Mwòdž were contemporaries of Confucius. Then much of the Analects must be *at least a century later* than Confucius.

———————•••••———————

Sywńdž was now the chief Confucian. He called the Confucians Rú 儒, and within the Rú, he downranked Dž-sz̄ and Mencius. He himself was a Great Rú:

5:95 (SZ 8:9, excerpt, c0268) . . . Such a Great Rú, though he dwell hidden in a poor alley in a leaky house, with not a pinpoint of territory, kings and princes cannot rival him in fame. When he has the use of territory a hundred leagues square, no state of a thousand leagues can challenge his superiority. He will beat down and crush aggressive states, and unify and unite the world . . . When poor and out of office, vulgar Rú scorn him. But when successful in office, the belligerent and aggressive change, the conceited and petty avoid him, evil persuaders dread him, and the mass of the people are made to have a sense of shame. If he can obtain office, he will unify the world . . .

Not less sharp were the enmities between different schools. The Confucians, or Rú, with their idea of service, were open to the charge that they were merely in it for the salary, like so many robbers. The Jwāngdž pounces on this idea:

5:96 (JZ 26:4, c0260). The Rú use the Shr̄ and Shū in robbing graves. The Great Rú announces to his henchmen,

> It's growing lighter in the skies,
> How goes our little enterprise?

and the Little Rú answer,

> The grave-clothes we have not unwound,
> But in his mouth a pearl we've found.

The Shr̄ indeed tell us,

> Green, green stands the wheat,
> Growing on that hilly slope;
> In life, you were not generous,
> In death, what are you doing with a pearl?

Pushing back his whiskers and pulling down on his beard, the Rú insert their metal bar into his mouth, and gently pry apart his jaws, so as not to hurt the pearl inside.

The uncertainty of outward success led to an emphasis on inner success:

5:97 (MC 7A1, excerpt, c0269). Mencius said, For a man to develop his heart fully is to know his own nature, and one who knows nature will know Heaven. By retaining his heart and nurturing his nature, he is serving Heaven. Whether he is going to die young or live long makes no difference to his firmness of purpose. It is by awaiting what will befall with a perfected character that he stands firm on his proper destiny.

Emphasis is now being placed on the inner qualities of the Mencian sage.

Sincerity (chv́ng 誠) was the name found at this time for the situation where one's inner feeling and outer expression coincide. That word is sometimes only an adverb ("really"), but it acquires a special sense in this text:

> **Jūng Yūng** 中庸 (JY) "The Doctrine of the Mean," a treatise attributed to [Kǔng] Dž-sz̄ 子思, but actually compiled between 03c and Hàn. It takes a mystical but Confucian view. It was a central text in the Neo-Confucianism of the 12th century. Translated by Legge.

The early Confucians (#**6:1-2**) had already emphasized reflection on basic principles. This is taken up in mystical terms in a key section of the Jūng Yūng:

5:98 (JY 20:18, c0270). Sincerity 誠 is the Way of Heaven; being sincere toward things 誠之 is the Way of Man. Sincerity is hitting the target without effort, achieving the result without conscious thought. He who can effortlessly reach the Way is a Sage. To be sincere toward things is to pick out the good and firmly hold onto it.

The one who has so internalized virtue that it becomes reflexive is a Sage:

5:99 (JY 20:19, c0270). Study it widely, inquire into it deeply, think of it carefully, analyze it perceptively, carry it out diligently.

When the Mencians wrote JY 20:17-18 into their own text, they duplicated JY 20:17 (c0270) almost exactly, but changed JY 20:18 (here *italicized*):

5:100 (MC *4A12, excerpt, c0268). Mencius said, If those in subordinate position do not evoke confidence from their superiors, the people cannot be governed. There is a way 道 to gain the confidence of one's superiors: If one is not trusted by his friends, he will not get the confidence of his superiors. There is a way to be trusted by friends: If in serving one's parents one does not please them, he will not be trusted by his friends. There is a way to please one's parents: If on turning to look at himself, he finds that he is not sincere 誠, he will not evoke pleasure in his parents. There is a way to make the self sincere: If one is not clear about the good, he will be unable to make his self sincere. *So "Sincerity is the Way of Heaven; being sincere toward things is the Way of Man." There was never one who was wholly sincere yet did not move others. But if one is insincere, one will not be able to move others.*

The Mencians also added this parable of sincerity to the end of MC 4:

5:101 (MC *4B33, c0264). A man of Chí had a wife and a concubine, who lived with him in the same house. When their goodman[51] went out, he would get his fill of wine and meat before returning. When the wife asked who he was eating and drinking with, it was always someone rich and honored. The wife said to the concubine, When our goodman goes out, he gets his fill of wine and meat before returning. When I ask who he ate and drank with, it is always someone rich and honored, but no distinguished person ever comes here. I will see where our goodman goes. She got up early, and followed unobserved where the goodman went. All through the city there was no one he stopped and talked with. At last he came to some people who were sacrificing at the tombs beyond the city wall, and begged their leftovers. When that was not enough, he turned around and went to another. This was the way 道 he filled himself. The wife returned and told the concubine, Our goodman is the one we look up to and spend our lives with, and now it is like this. With the concubine she cursed the goodman, and they wept together in the middle of the hall. And the goodman, knowing nothing of this, came swaggering in from outside, ready to brag to his wife and concubine.

Methodological Moment: Is this a true story? It involves difficulties: how could wife and concubine not know that they were living with a beggar? But like all parables, it emblematizes an issue, and packs a literary punch at the end. That is what it is there for: to emblematize a lesson and to be literarily effective. The question of historicity does not matter.

---

[51]Lyáng-rźn 良人, literally "goodman," here (as in older English) "husband."

Sywndž Again. In 0258, the King of Chí invited Sywndž to be the senior figure at Jì-syà. Sywndž proceeded to argue against Chí cosmology (#3:79-81), but misjudged his mandate, and had to leave. He took a post at Lán-líng, in territory recently conquered from Sùng and Lŭ only months earlier by Chŭ.

The southern Mencians resented the need to argue against "Yáng" (the Dàuists)[52] and "Mwò:"

> **5:102** (MC 3B9, excerpt, c0251). Gūngdūdž said, The outsiders say that you, Master, are fond of arguing. I venture to ask why. Mencius said, How should I be fond of arguing? But I cannot do otherwise . . . Sage Kings do not appear; the Lords give rein to their lusts; hermits put forth cranky theories, and the teachings of Yáng and Mwò fill the world . . .

Their northern Mencian colleagues (who, be it noted, here call themselves Rú) added this advice on how to handle an argument after you have won it:

> **5:103** (MC 7B26, c0251). Those who escape from Mwò go to Yáng, and those who escape from Yáng will come to the Rú. When they come, we should simply accept them. Those who in these days dispute with Yáng and Mwò are like chasing an escaped pig; once they have got it in the pen, they proceed to tie its feet.

The above remarks, which show Warring States advocacy groups opposing each other by name, go far to refute the modern superstition that there were no "schools of thought" in Warring States times.

Words. The Dàuists had denied that wisdom could be conveyed in words:

> **5:104** (DDJ 2, excerpt, c0315). Therefore the Sage abides in Affairs Without Action; practices the Teaching Without Words.

> **5:105** (DDJ 1, excerpt, c0310). The Dàu that can be spoken of is not the Constant Dàu.

The rival Legalists of Chí, on the contrary, claimed to possess the secrets by which Gwăn Jùng had made Chí Hwán-gūng (page 27) first among 07c rulers. The Jwāngdž people attacked this claim, in a story about Hwán-gūng himself:

> **5:106** (JZ 13:7, c0250). Hwán-gūng was reading a book in his hall of state. Wheelwright Byĕn was making a wheel in the courtyard below. He put aside his mallet and chisel, went up the steps, and asked Hwán-gūng, I venture to ask, what sort of book is it that the Prince is reading? The Prince said, The words of the Sages. He said, Are the sages living? The Prince said, They are dead. He said, Then what the Sovereign is reading is only the dregs and leavings of the men of old. Hwán-gūng said, I am reading a book; how should a mere wheelwright have an opinion about it? If you can explain yourself, very well. If you cannot, you die.

---

[52]Pejoratively so called, in allusion to the hedonist philosopher Yáng Jū 楊朱.

Wheelwright Byĕn said, Your servant will consider it from the point of view of your servant's own trade. When making a wheel, if I go too slow, the stroke is easy and infirm; if I go too fast, the stroke is hard and shallow. If it is neither too slow nor too fast, I get it in my hand, and respond to it with my heart. It cannot be explained in words, but there is a certain skill to it. Your servant cannot teach it to his son, and the son cannot receive it from your servant. Thus it is that now, at seventy years, I am still making wheels. The relation of the men of old to what they could transmit has likewise perished, and so what the Sovereign is reading is merely the dregs and leavings of the men of old.

Not even the Confucians could accept everything in the canonical writings. The Mencians challenged the authenticity of one current Shū text in this way:

5:107 (MC 7B3, c0255). Mencius said, If one were to believe everything in the Shū, it would be better not to have the Shū at all. Of the Wŭ Chv́ng, I accept only two or three strips. A benevolent man has no enemy in the world; how could it be that "the blood spilled was enough to float staves," when the most benevolent made war against the most cruel?[53]

In 0254, Syẃndž, who had been unsuccessful in Chí, gained a more potent authority when he was made Governor of Chŭ-occupied Lŭ. This area was the home base of both Mencian groups, the Analects group, and the DDJ school.

Syẃndž described his policy toward the rival thinkers in this way:

5:108 (SZ 5:10b, excerpt, c0254) . . . If one attends to their words, they are mere rhetoric with no guiding principle; if one employs them, they are deceitful or achieve nothing. Above, they cannot follow the lead of a Wise King; below, they cannot bring order to the masses . . . If a Sage King should arise, these would be the first people he would put to death, only afterward proceeding to the mere robbers and thieves. Robbers and thieves can reform, but people like these cannot reform.

The last Mician ethical chapter takes up the danger of remonstrance, but also stresses the need of contrary opinion to the health of the state:

5:109 (MZ 1, excerpt, c0250). Rulers need contrary ministers; superiors need candid inferiors. If those who publicly dispute persist, and if those who privately advise carry on, [a ruler] can prolong his life and protect his state. If ministers and inferiors, fearing for their position, do not speak; if nearby ministers fall silent and distant ministers hum, if resentment knots up in the hearts of the people, if groveling and flattery are at one's side and good advice is kept away, then the state is in danger.

This could have been a Confucian statement: Protest is not at all irregular; *it is what keeps things working*. This sentiment shows how far the Micians had come toward merging with their rivals in office, the Confucians.

---

[53]So effective was this complaint that the Wŭ Chv́ng was later suppressed.

All very well. But true to his earlier threat, in 0249 Sywndž shut down all these text-producing operations, not excluding the Mencians, the "Small Rú." It was his way of winning the human nature argument of twenty years before.

After 0249. Together with the more or less simultaneous Chín conquest of the Jōu King's small domain, the end of Lǔ brought about a major redrawing of the map. The prestige centers had vanished: Jōu, the survival of the once powerful Jōu Dynasty of old, and Lǔ, descended from the first minister of Jōu. But neither Jōu tradition nor Lǔ literature was now going to count for anything. In their stead, there loomed Chín and Chǔ.

It is perhaps not to be wondered at if, at about this time, groups of Micians established themselves in both Chín and Chǔ. Those Mician branches were still remembered in Hàn.[54] There was not much they or anyone else could achieve in the real world by way of further text production, and except for some Chí continuations of the Analects and the Mencius, text production now languished. But there was still ample scope for the display of courage in lost causes.

Conspicuous rigor like that of the desperado Yw̌ Ràng (#4:58-59) was now forthcoming from the Micians. These stories are from the Lw̌-shr̀ Chūn/Chyōu, a late Warring States and Chín work. Each stage of that text has its agenda, but all drew on a doctrinally diverse group of contributors, some of whom did have Mician affinities. The stories may not be true, but they are probably Mician.

Here is a story from the time when the Micians among the followers of Lw̌ Bù-wéi were hoping to recommend themselves in their new Chín home:

> **5:110** (LSCC 1/5:5, c0241). Among the Micians was Grandmaster Fù Tūn. He dwelt in Chín. His son killed a man, but Chín Hwèi-wáng said, Your Excellency's years are advanced, and he will not have another son. This Solitary One has already ordered the officials not to execute him. Let Your Excellency heed the Solitary One.
>
> Fù Tūn replied, The law of the Micians says, He who kills shall die, he who injures shall be punished.[55] This is in order to forbid the killing and injuring of others. Now, to forbid the killing and injuring of others is the most righteous thing in the world. Though the King has made me this gift, and ordered the officials not to execute him, Fù Tūn cannot but follow the law of the Micians. So he declined Hwèi-wáng's [generosity], and subsequently did kill him.

No Legalist state could ask for greater rigor. But we may notice that Fù Tūn follows not Chín law, but Mician law – he inhabits a state within a state.

---

[54]For the Hàn evidence, which is from c0140, see HFZ 50 (Liao **Han** 2/298).

[55]This is reminiscent of the three-article lawcode proclaimed by the Hàn founder Lyóu Bāng on abolishing the harsh Chín laws. "He who kills shall die, he who injures or steals, according to the gravity of the offense" (**SJ 8**, 1/362; Watson **Records** 1/62).

From a generation later, here is a story of Mician dedication in Chŭ:

5:111 (LSCC 19/3:4, excerpt, c0212). The Mician Grandmaster Mv̀ng Shv̄ng was friendly with the Lord of Yáng-chv́ng in Jīng.[56] The ruler of Yáng-chv́ng ordered him to mount guard in his city. He broke a jade ring as a tally. The oath went, "When the halves of the tally match, I shall heed [the order]." When the King of Jīng died, the officials attacked Wú Chī, drawing their swords in the place of mourning;[57] the Lord of Yáng-chv́ng took part with them. Jīng found him guilty. The Lord of Yáng-chv́ng fled, and Jīng moved to confiscate his state. Mv̀ng Shv̄ng said, I have received in care another's state, with the gift of a tally. Now, I see not the tally, and yet my strength is not sufficient to resist. If I cannot die, it will not be right. His disciple Syv́ Rwò remonstrated with Mv̀ng Shv̄ng, saying, If your death would benefit the Lord of Yáng-chv́ng, then dying for him would be right. But if it will be of no benefit, and if moreover it would cut off the Micians in this age, then it would not be right. Mv̀ng Shv̄ng said, Not so. I am to the Lord of Yáng-chv́ng not a leader, but a friend; not a friend, but a servant. If I do not die, then from now on, those who seek a strict leader will surely not do so among the Micians; those who seek a worthy friend will surely not do so among the Micians; those who seek a faithful servant will surely not do so among the Micians. To die for him is to carry out Mician principles and to perpetuate the Mician enterprise. I will convey the Grandmastership to Tyén Syāngdž of Sùng. Tyén Syāngdž is a worthy man; what worry is there that the Micians will be cut off in this age?

Syv́ Rwò said, Be it as the Master has said. Rwò asks permission to die first, to prepare the way for him. And he cut off his own head, in [Mv̀ng Shv̄ng's] presence. Mv̀ng Shv̄ng accordingly sent two men to transmit the Grandmastership to Tyén Syāngdž. When Mv̀ng Shv̄ng died, those disciples who died with him numbered 180 men. When the two men had delivered the order to Tyén Syāngdž, they wished to go back to die for Mv̀ng Shv̄ng in Jīng. Tyén Syāngdž sought to stop them, saying, Master Mv̀ng has conferred the Grandmastership on me; you must heed me. But they afterward went back and died for him.[58]

As a way of winning, this sacrificial rigor does not commend itself. But for those who *have* no way of winning, as Mencius told the ruler of tiny Tv́ng,

5:112 (MC 1B14, excerpt, c0311) . . . If a man but do good, then of his descendants in a later age, there will surely be one who will be a King. A gentleman in making a beginning starts a tradition that can be carried on.

Micians and Confucians, like the early Christians with their cult of martyrdom, could see that one's own death is not necessarily the end of the affair.

---

[56]The older name for Chŭ; used here because of a Chín taboo on the word Chŭ.

[57]The tale of Wú Chĭ's death is an invention, and so therefore is this story.

[58]We omit the concluding comment of the LSCC compilers.

The End. Thus did the learned squabble over whether to serve the state, counter each other's theories, impugn each other's texts, examine their inner lives, and display their outer dedication. Meanwhile, the state needed officials. The Chín law official Syǐ shows how Chín got them. Among his texts was his diary. It is mostly terse entries about state events: battles and court intrigues. The few personal entries suggest how he learned his trade and advanced in it:

5:113 (Shwèihǔdì plates 50-54, excerpts covering the years 0262-0217).

- 0262. Syǐ is born
- 0257. [Chín] attacked Hándān
- 0250. Wv́n-wáng succeeds as King of Chín; dies the same year
- 0249. Jwāng-wáng succeeds as King of Chín
- 0246. "Present" King succeeds;[59] Syǐ [in his 17th year] has a tutor
- 0244. Syǐ [at 19] is appointed recorder 史
- 0243. Syǐ [at 20] is appointed senior recorder 令史 at Añ-lù
- 0241. Syǐ [at 22] is appointed senior recorder at Yēn
- 0235. Syǐ [at 28] is appointed hearing officer 治獄
- 0234. With the army
- 0232. With the Píng-yáng Army
- 0231. Father dies; Syǐ [at 32] divines about his own future life
- 0217. "30th year" [There is no entry after this year; Syǐ has died]

After two years with a tutor, Syǐ was functionally literate. He became a lower officer at 19,[60] was promoted to hearing officer at 28, and remained at that rank for the rest of his life. He died aged 46, after 27 years of service to Chín, in the 30th year of the reign. He was buried where he fell, crammed into a cheap coffin with his official and personal bamboo-strip files piled about his body. Time would reduce them from neat bundles to disordered single strips.

It is not a terribly romantic story. It is merely the kind of story out of which the administrative success of Chín was built, piece by piece and man by man.

---

[59]The future First Emperor. Syǐ would not have known his later sacrificial name.
[60]That is, in the 19th year of his life (Chinese swèi 歲).

6. The People

Who were the people? Some were Sinitic, and some were not. The meeting of the two gave a rich cultural mixture, and we will look at some details of it.

As the new army came into being, the people, Sinitic or not, became soldiers and thus citizens: subject to the state's laws and able to earn rank and reward in its wars.[1] The importance of the people led the state to worry about revolutions. It also led some thinkers to define the state *in terms of* its people; this we call populism. They held that the people had an interest in government, that some were able to serve in government, and that all were entitled to express opinions about government, or even to influence the choice of a ruler.

The 04c state had a theory of human nature: people can be controlled by rewards and punishments. This developed into the 03c human nature debate, which has proved to be an important contribution to Chinese philosophy.

The 05th Century

At the beginning of the Jōu Dynasty, Lǔ was relocated to non-Sinitic territory east of the Shāng enclave at Sùng, to guard against future rebellions. Around Lǔ were several non-Sinitic states or settlements, some of them close to its capital Chyw̄-fù. It was not until Lǔ suppressed the nonstate Rúng people (**#1:22-1:34**) that it acquired boundaries, and became at last a territorial state. Other interactions with the non-Sinitic peoples were less drastic.

Words. In 0632, the Lǔ Prince's brother Mǎi was executed for failing to defend Wèi (**#1:11**). Mǎi 買 means "buy;" its derivative mài 賣 means "sell." But when grain was bought from Chí in 0666 (**#1:9**), a different word, dí 糴, was used. So what exactly is the Chinese word for "buy?"

Methodological Moment. An idea introduced from one culture into another tends to have connections in its home setting, but to be isolated in the new one. The chariot had a long history in West Asia, but it appears suddenly in Shāng, implying the directionality West Asia > Shāng. Similarly, the Sinitic word pair mǎi 買 "buy" / mài 賣 "sell" has a counterpart, two words distinguished by tone, in the Myáu language. Which has borrowed from which? In Chinese, "buy/sell" is a word family by itself, but the Myáu pair have cousins: they are related to the word for "have." The implied directionality is Myáu > Sinitic.[2]

---

[1] For the creation of citizenship through military service, see Weber **Peasants** 292f.

[2] Haudricourt **Hmong** 304. For other Myáu words, see Schuessler **Etymological**.

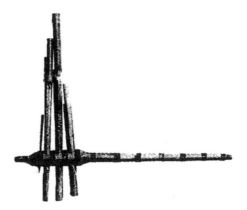

Objects. Among the instruments in the classical Sinitic court orchestra was the shvng 笙, a windchest base with many tuned tubes rising from it; it can play chords as well as single notes. Its role in Chinese music is limited. By contrast, in Southeast Asia the shvng is found in many forms and varieties. It is the instrument most commonly mentioned in stories told by modern Myáu.[3] The implication is that the shvng arose in a substrate culture whose descendants (among them the modern Myáu) can still be observed in and near south China.[4]

The Shr, the canonical collection of 305 poems, began as a collection of popular songs. The person responsible was probably the disciple Dž-syà, whom "Confucius" reproves in the following terms:

> **6:1** (LY 6:3, c0460). The Master said to Dž-syà, You should work on the rú 儒 of the gentleman, not the rú of the little people.

That is, the gentleman's concern is with elite values, not popular values. The poems against which Confucian disapproval has been consistently expressed are especially numerous in the section of the Shr devoted to Jvng.

---

[3] Among the Myáu of Sżchwān, as recorded by Graham, the shvng, typically used with a drum at ceremonies, has six pipes and is called the lyòu-shvng 六笙 "Six-[pipe] shvng" (Graham **Miao** 93). There is an origin myth for it, involving six brothers who play single flutes at their father's funeral: ". . . After three years the sons thought . . . it will be best if we can take these tubes and bind them together and make a hole in each as we did in the tubes we were blowing, and use a hollow tube to put them in, and peach-tree bark to bind them together, and let one person play it . . . This custom we can pass on to later generations as a memorial service. The length of the [lyòu-shvng] tubes differs because the ages and heights of the sons differ. The drum's shape is long and round because it illustrates the fact that the family will never desert the ancestors" (Graham **Miao** 21). Peach wood is credited by the Myáu with magical properties, and this association is also made in a number of what are now "Chinese" tales and customs.

[4] By no means all Sinitic borrowings from the substrate cultures are this peaceful. For the Myáu origin of the crossbow, and its modern Myáu tradition, see p106 n25.

Here is a late expression of that disapproval:

6:2 (LY 17:15, excerpt, c0270). The Master said, I hate the purple encroaching on the crimson. I hate the Songs of Jv̀ng disturbing the classical music . . .

Some of those songs are indeed outrageous, from a conventional Sinitic point of view. They feature female sexual initiative, and even sexual promiscuity:

6:3 (Shr 86, Jv̀ng #12, early 05c).

    86A   Yonder madcap boy, ah,
          Won't consent with me to meet, ah;
              It is all because of you
              That my food I cannot even eat, ah

    86B   Yonder madcap boy, ah,
          Won't consent with me to share a bite, ah;
              It is all because of you
              That my rest I cannot get at night, ah

. . . in which a girl unsuccessfully tries to attract a mate. Even worse is:

6:4 (Shī 87, Jv̀ng #12, early 05c).

    87A   If you fondly think of me,
          Lift your robe and cross the Dzv̄n.
          If of me you do not think,
          Are you then the only one?
            – The craziest of crazy boys, is all you are!

    87B   If you fondly think of me,
          Lift your robe and cross the Wăı.
          If of me you do not think,
          Are you then the only guy?
            – The craziest of crazy boys, is all you are!

. . . where the girl threatens to go elsewhere if the boy is not interested, thus adding the threat of promiscuity to the confession of desire. None of this is proper in a Sinitic household. Nor is Jv̀ng the only place such things turn up. Here is a piece from Chv́n, in which a boy teases a girl about her lack of social standing (Jyāng and Dž are the ruling clans of Chí and Sùng, respectively):

6:5 (Shr 138, Chv́n #3, excerpt, early 05c).

    138B   Why must the fish one eats
           have to be a River fāng?
           Why must the wife one weds
           have to be a Chí Jyāng?

    138C   Why must the fish one eats
           have to be a River lĭ?
           Why must the wife one weds
           have to be a Sùng Dž?

These are not poems, but templates for a song process; the song can go on as long as the singer can find rhymes to substitute in the otherwise identical frame.

It is characteristic of these template songs[5] that they are sung by a member of one sex to members of the other sex: they are invitations in real time. That songs *were* sung back and forth, as incidents in choosing a mate from across the river, or perhaps just for fun, comes from the next of the Chv́n poems, which praises girls for their skill at this sort of poetic repartee:

6:6 (Shī 139, excerpt, early 05c).

139A   The pond by the Eastern Gate
is good for steeping hemp.
That beautiful Shú-jī
Is good at answering songs . . .

This describes a culture of repartee without itself participating in that culture, but at least this stanza does seem to describe it. What do we do with it?

Granet, who visited China in the early 20c, discovered songs like these, implying gatherings of maidens and youths, which were responsive or literally antiphonal, and often sung in the vicinity of a river. Since the reports he cites mention similar customs among the modern Lolo and the modern Myáu, we probably have an area trait rather than a Sinitic trait.[6] Then the songs in our Shī are products of contact between Dž-syà's elite culture (which, as we have seen, disapproved of them) and one or another of these local cultures.

Chv́n was destroyed by Chǔ in 0479. In that confusion or shortly before, the Confucian disciple Dž-jāng had come to Lǔ. With such an informant at hand, Dž-syà will have had no difficulty in obtaining material from Chv́n. As for Jv̀ng, the storm center of Spring and Autumn diplomacy, Lǔ remained in contact with it throughout the early 05c. There is no problem with sources.

So what was Dž-syà up to? He too probably disapproved of these songs, and gathered them precisely to show the cultural depravity of the states, on the theory that only culturally virtuous states could be strong enough to survive the wars of conquest that were already beginning.[7] This view of the Shī was still current in some circles late in the 04c, as witness comments made in a Dzwǒ Jwàn story by a visitor observing a complete performance of the Shī:

6:7 (DJ 9/29:13, excerpt, c0315) . . . They sang for him the [airs of] Jv̀ng. He said, "Very beautiful. But the detail is excessive; the people will not be able to bear it. Will not [Jv̀ng] be first to perish?" They sang for him the [airs of] Chí. He said, "Very beautiful. And what a great wind it is! The one who plants his staff on the Eastern Sea, was it not [Chí ancestor] Tàι-gūng? The future of this state is immeasurable . . ."

This might be called the elite political reading of the Shī.

---

[5]For the term and further examples, see Brooks **Template**.

[6]Granet **Festivals**, Appendix III.

[7]For the geographical aspects, see Brooks **Political**.

This had its uses as political propaganda, but the wider culture was scandalized. The Shr̄ poems were publicly performed by the court orchestras, and perhaps at wealthy private residences. In that context, they were felt to glamorize improper conduct to the more impressionable among the audience. Soon, new stanzas were added to the bantering poems, and new poems were written to stand beside the indecent poems, as better models for the elite young.

Thus, to the two-stanza teasing song **#6:5**, there was added a first stanza setting a tone of unworldly retreat and resignation, and removing the situation as far as possible from any suggestion of young love:

6:8 (Shr̄ 138, excerpt, late 05c).

> 138A   Beneath my simple doorway
> I can be at ease;
> From the flow of the spring
> I can cure hunger.[8]

To further draw attention away from the indecent invitations of the floozies of Jv̀ng, poems like this one were added to the Jv̀ng section. It depicts a girl eager to devote herself to cooking and mending as the wife of a nobleman:

6:9 (Shr̄ 75, Jv̀ng #1, excerpt, late 05c).

> 75A   Your black robe, how well it fits, ah!
> When it is worn out, another I will stitch, ah!
> I will go to your residence, ah!
> and there I will serve you delicacies, ah!
>
> 75B   Your black robe, it hangs just so, ah!
> When it is worn out, another I will sew, ah!
> I will go to your residence, ah!
> and there I will serve you delicacies, ah! . . .

And this they put at the head of the whole Jv̀ng section, where the modest and beautiful girl could have her maximum effect as a positive cultural example.

Rural Economy. The people on the land were grouped in villages and connected by larger-area arrangements called dǎng 黨[9] or associations. These were mutual-aid arrangements, as may be seen in a passage previously read:

6:10 (LY 6:5, c0460). Ywæn Sz̀[10] was the Steward [of the Jì clan]. They were going to give him nine hundred measures of grain, but he declined. The Master said, Was there no way you could have given it to the neighboring village 鄰里 or the county association 鄉黨?

The association would then distribute it for him to those who could use it.

---

[8]More logically "thirst," but that would not rhyme.

[9]The modern term for a political party. In our period, it meant a political faction, and was a term of disapproval: people who together hold political opinions are subversive.

[10]Another Chv́n disciple? The Ywæn were, or had been, a prominent Chv́n family.

Here is another aspect of the duty of the elite toward the commoners:

6:11 (LY 6:22, c0460). Fán Chŕ asked about knowledge. The Master said,
Concern yourself with what is due the people 民, and be assiduous toward
the ghosts and spirits so as to keep them at a distance – this can be called
knowledge.

The mín 民, as here, are usually the common people.[11] Both parts of the answer
involve participation at a distance: the "ghosts and spirits" were not the gods
of the elite, who were chiefly the ancestors of the elite, but the local gods of the
common people. Knowing how to manage such things, outside one's own
culture, is knowledge needed by officers of the new society.

A later glimpse of the elite engaging with local ceremonies comes in these
lines from an early 04c Analects chapter describing the basics of court protocol:

6:12 (LY 10:7b, c0380). When the country folk 鄉人 are drinking wine
and the elders have left, he also takes his leave.

6:13 (LY 10:8, c0380). When the country folk are performing an
exorcism, he takes his stand in his court dress on the formal stairs.

Here again are the religious observances of the lower populace, which the local
elite watch over, but do not themselves perform.

Rural Welfare. The role of the association in distributing resources,[12] as
above, and also responsibilities, comes through in a late Gwăndž passage,
where an ideal welfare system is described. This part of it is about orphans:

6:14 (GZ 54:4, excerpt, 03c). "Pitying orphans" means that in the capital
and all metropolitan areas there shall be officers in charge of orphans.
When an officer or commoner dies and his orphan child is young, without
parents to care for him and unable to provide his own livelihood, they
shall assign him to the county association 鄉黨 or to acquaintances or
friends. [Families] supporting one orphan shall have one son exempt from
service; those supporting two orphans shall have two sons exempt from
service; those supporting three orphans shall have the whole family
exempt from service. The one in charge of orphans shall regularly inquire
about them, and ascertain that they have adequate food and drink . . .

The unit of caring is a foster family. Costs are met, not by payment of state
money, but by remission of state obligations. If no friend or acquaintance offers
to provide foster care, the county association presumably assigns it. This is the
county association in something like its original function, though by this time
it has been absorbed into the structure of government, and works from above.

---

[11]The contrast is with rýn 人: freemen or officeholders. The verbal distinction is not
consistent throughout the literature, but the social contrast is important.

[12]Such arrangements are very common. For mutual benefit associations among
commoners in ancient Greece, especially in hard times, see Gallant **Risk** 143f, 171f.

The 04th Century

The Micians, though not themselves exactly commoners (they were the entrepreneurial sub-elite who later entered public service, and finally became assimilated to the Confucians), were near to ordinary life. Much of the impetus for what we call populism comes from them. Their influence as a movement, in this and other areas, begins to be felt in the 04c, and on the populism issue they are presently joined by the Dzwǒ Jwàn group.

Populism is the theory that the people are part of the state; that the state in fact exists for the people. First we need a model of the state in which the people have a secure and recognized place. This is provided by the Micians, at the time when they themselves began to enter state service, and were concerned to emphasize their own subordination to authority. But they also emphasize the requirements in the other direction. If the state is going to run by something other than total compulsion, there must be a ground of participation for those below. The Micians here transport the old military virtues jūng 忠 "loyalty" and syìn 信 "fidelity" into the social sphere. The people's loyalty must be earned by benefitting the people, and their trust must be gained by concern for their welfare, not sporadically, but consistently:

> **6:15** (MZ 21:1, excerpt, c0367). The reason wise kings and sages of antiquity could possess the world and bring order to the feudal lords, was that their love for the people was very loyal, and their benefits toward the people were very substantial. Loyalty 忠 led to trust 信, and was made manifest by benefit. Thus it was that the people all their lives did not flag, and til the end of the age they did not weary.

Rebellion. Minor incidents of popular unrest might be imagined by a nervous elite . . .

> **6:16** (DJ 9/23:2, excerpt, c0358). The people were repairing the walls [of the Chvn capital], and a plank fell down and killed someone. The workmen took cause together 相命 and each killed his overseer . . .

. . . but there were no popular rebellions. The people lacked the essentials for rebellion – organization, unity over distance, ideology, theoretical spokesmen.[13]

But populist theory did make a place for action from below against an evil ruler. Here is a Dzwǒ Jwàn story which turns on the idea that the ruler is liable to the judgement of the people, and that a ruler who fails that test is not properly a ruler at all. Such a theory was dangerous to express in direct terms, and the DJ makes its suggestion as a story about the past.[14]

---

[13] For these factors, see the German Peasant War of 1258 (Pirenne **Europe** 2/283f). When these factors came to exist in China, there followed the Yellow Turban Rebellion, which in effect brought the Latter Han Dynasty to an end (Levy **Yellow**).

[14] The sometimes populist Shū are of course stories about an even more remote past.

6:17 (DJ 9/14:6, excerpt, c0350). Master Kwàng was attending on the Lord of Jìn. The Lord of Jìn said, The people of Wèi have expelled their ruler, is this not too much? He replied, Perhaps it was the Wèi ruler who was too much. A good ruler will reward the good and punish the profligate; he will nourish the people as his own children, covering them like Heaven and supporting them like Earth. Then the people will uphold their ruler, loving him as their father and mother, looking up to him as to the sun and moon, reverencing him as the gods and spirits, fearing him as the thunder and lightning – how should they expel him? The ruler is the chief of the Spirits, the hope of the people . . .

This follows from the basic idea that the people are constitutive for the state, and that their welfare is the test of good government in the state.

Now appears the idea that the people are capable of advising government:

6:18 (DJ 8/5:4, excerpt, c0356). Lyáng-shān collapsed.[15] The Lord of Jìn sent word of it and summoned [Jìn noble] Bwó-dzūng. Bwó-dzūng found his path blocked by a heavy cart, and said, Make way. The carter said, Rather than wait for me, it would be faster to take a shortcut. Bwó-dzūng asked where he was from; he said, "I am from Jyàng [near Lyáng-shān]." He asked him about the affairs of Jyàng. The man said, "Lyáng-shān has collapsed, and they are summoning Bwó-dzūng to consult about what should be done."[16] He asked what should be done. He said, "When a mountain has a fault and collapses, what *can* be done? Mountains and rivers are the state's major concern, so when a mountain collapses or a river runs dry, the ruler accordingly has leaner repast, plainer robes, and slighter music; leaves his residence for a temporary one, makes prayers and invocations, and has the Astrologer write out a text for a ceremony. That is all. Even were there a Bwó-dzūng, what else could be done?" Bwó-dzūng asked permission to present him at court, but he would not permit it. Subsequently he reported all this, and the court followed it.

. . . or (add the Micians), even being in sole charge of the government:

6:19 (MZ 8, excerpt, c0340). Tāng [the founder of Shāng] raised Yī Yǐn from the kitchen and gave him charge of the government, and his plans were successful. Wv́n-wáng [the moral founder of Jōu] raised Húng Yāu and Tài-dyěn from their snares and nets and gave them charge of the government, and the Western Regions submitted . . .

There can be no argument against success. Especially legendary success.

---

[15]This much is given in the CC entry for 0586. Bv̄ng 崩 "collapse" is the term for a mountain landslide. It is also the polite way to refer to the death of the King, and in the CC it is reserved for that situation; deaths of lesser persons have other verbs.

[16]The carter's insolence, and his uncanny knowledge of Bwó-dzūng's errand, are typical of these stories: humble persons are brash, and know more than elite persons. See also the Tsáu Gwèi story, **#6:25**, where the low character gives his counsel directly.

Non-Sinitic Persons could be sympathetically portrayed. In this story, a Jìn leader has accused his Rúng ally of leaking information; he excludes the Rúng chieftain from a meeting. The Rúng chieftain cites the fidelity of the Rúng in the Battle of Yáu (#**1:43**), and then notes the cultural gulf between them:

> **6:20** (DJ 9/14:1 excerpt, c0350). He replied, Of old, the men of Chín, relying on their greater numbers and being covetous of our territory, drove out us Rúng. [The former Jìn ruler] Hwèi-gūng, displaying his great virtue, and saying that, as we were the descendants of the Four Peaks and should not be thus cut off, bestowed on us lands on his southern border, where foxes dwelt and wolves howled. We Rúng cut down thorn and bramble, drove out fox and wolf, and became peaceable and loyal subjects of your former ruler, and until the present day we have remained faithful.
>
> Of old, Wín-gūng and Chín attacked Jvng. The men of Chín secretly covenanted with Jvng, and left guards behind, whence came the encounter at Yáu. Jìn engaged them from above, the Rúng beset them from below, and that the Chín host did not return was in truth due to us Rúng. As in catching a deer: the men of Jìn took it by the horns, the Rúng took it by the feet; together they laid it low. Why then have we not escaped [these accusations]? From that time on, the doings of Jìn, one after another through the ages, have always been in concert with us Rúng; we have followed its leaders, as in the time of Yáu; how should we have dared to keep apart? Now, the hosts under the leadership of your officers have made mistakes and antagonized the Lords, and yet you blame us Rúng.
>
> We Rúng differ in our food and clothing from the Sinitic 華 peoples, our fabrics and other products are not exchangeable, and our languages are not mutually intelligible – what evil, then, could we have committed?[17]
> If I do not take part in this meeting, it will be no disgrace to me.

Like Cooper's romanticized Mohicans,[18] or the speech of Logan,[19] this piece probably comes from a time when the Rúng were no longer a serious threat.

---

[17]That is, it is not possible for us to have had communication with other states.

[18]The last Mohican Indians began to leave the Hudson River Valley for Wisconsin in the early 1820's; Cooper's first "Leatherstocking" novel appeared in 1823.

[19]"I appeal to any white man to say, if ever he entered Logan's cabin hungry and he gave him not meat; if ever he came cold and naked and he clothed him not. During the course of the last long and bloody war, Logan remained idle in his cabin, an advocate for peace. Such was my love for the whites, that my countryman pointed as they passed, and said, Logan is the friend of the white men. I had even thought to have lived with you, but for the injuries of one man. Colonel Cresap, last spring, in cold blood and unprovoked, murdered all the relations of Logan, not even sparing my women and children. There runs not a drop of my blood in the veins of any living creature. This called on me for revenge. I have sought it; I have killed many; I have fully satisfied my vengeance. For my country, I rejoice at the beams of peace. But do not harbor the thought that mine is the joy of fear. Logan never felt fear. He will not turn on his heel to save his life. Who is there to mourn for Logan? Not one."

We should not think that the Micians sympathized with non-Sinitic peoples. On the contrary, they deplored the cruel ways of the ancient Myáu, on which MZ 12 (c0322) quotes this account of legal history from the Shū:

> **6:21** (Shū 55:3, excerpt, c0330). The Myáu people did not use persuasion, but kept order by punishments. They made a penal code of Five Cruelties and called it Law . . .

Elsewhere, the Micians report with equal disapproval the savage customs of other clearly non-Sinitic peoples:

> **6:22** (MZ 25:14, excerpt, c0330). Now those who advocate lavish funerals and extended mourning say, If lavish funerals and extended mourning are really not the Way of the Sage Kings, why do the gentlemen of the Central States constantly practice them and unvaryingly follow them? Master Mwòdž said, This is what one calls "finding convenient what one is used to, and finding right what one is accustomed to." Long ago, to the east of Ywè, there was the Country of the Kaimuk 輆沐. When the first son was born, they dismembered and ate him, calling it "appropriate for his younger brothers." When the grandfather died, they carried away the grandmother and abandoned her, saying that the wife of a ghost could not be dwelt with.[20] This, the superiors regard as standard practice and the inferiors consider customary, to be done and not ceased; chosen and not discarded. But how is it truly the Way of Humanity and Justice? It is what one calls "finding convenient what one is used to, and finding right what one is accustomed to."

The Lord of the River (Hv́-bwó 河伯). Local gods sometimes turn up in elite texts. This tale explains the defeat of the Chǔ general Dž-yẁ at the Battle of Chv́ng-pú (#**1:40**). Probably the original story showed that this was due to the general's refusing the God's request. It is here overlaid by a populist moral:

> **6:23** (DJ 5/28:4, excerpt, c0330). Before this, Dž-yẁ of Chǔ had made himself a carnelian cap with jade capstrings, but had never worn it. Before the battle, he dreamed that the River Spirit said to him, Give it to me, and I will give you the marsh of Mv̀ng-jū. But he would not do it.[21]
>
> Dà-syīn and Dž-syī had [their father] Rúng Hwáng remonstrate with him, but he would not listen. Rúng Jì said, If by your death you could profit the state, you would do it, how much more these bits of jade? They are dirt, and if by them you could bring the army through safely, why would you grudge them? But he would not listen. He came out and told his two sons, It is not this Spirit who will defeat the Director Intendant. He is not assiduous for the people, and in truth, he will defeat himself.

The people's gods and their political interest get all mixed up in these tales.

---

[20]A custom of exposing old women (not old men!) is remembered in Japan, and is the background for the Hokkaido writer Inoue Yasushi's story Obasute 姨拾 (1956).

[21]For the custom of offerings to the Lord of the River, see Waley **Nine** 48-52.

Methodological Moment. Another Dzwŏ Jwàn story includes both popular and elite versions *of the same incident* (the death of a Lord of Jìn in 0581). This time the two can be separated by observing a discontinuity in the DJ text. The elite version [here indented] shows the Lord nobly accepting his coming death and rewarding the doctor who predicted it. The popular version shows the Lord killing the sorcerer who had predicted it, and then meeting his own death in the most humiliating way imaginable. The element of rude humor is unmistakable:

6:24 (DJ 8/10:4a, excerpt, c0350). The Lord of Jìn dreamed he saw a great spectre, with its hair hanging down its back to the ground. It beat its breast, leaped up, and said, You have wrongfully killed my descendants, and I have been able to make my request to God. It broke through the great gate, went as far as the sleeping quarters, and entered. The Prince was afraid, and entered his private chamber, but it broke through the door. The Prince awoke, and summoned the Medium of the Mulberry Field. The Medium told him what had occurred in his dream. The Prince said, What will happen? He said, You will not eat of the new harvest.

(DJ 8/10:4b, c0330) The Prince fell ill, and sought a doctor from Chín. The Elder of Chín sent Doctor Hwǎn to treat him. He had not yet arrived when the Prince dreamed that his illness was two boys. One said, That is a good doctor; I am afraid that he will harm us. Where can we hide from him? The other said, If we go above the diaphragm and below the heart, what can he do to us? When the doctor arrived, he said, The illness cannot be treated. It is above the diaphragm and below the heart, and I cannot attack it. Probing would not reach it; medicine would have no effect on it. I cannot treat it. The Prince said, You are a good doctor, showed him great courtesy, and sent him back.

In the sixth month, on day #43, the Lord of Jìn wanted wheat, and sent his bailiff to present some. His cook prepared it. He called the Medium of the Mulberry Field, showed it to him, and killed him. As he was about to eat it, he had to go to relieve himself, fell into the privy, and died . . .

The separation is easy, but what does it tell us about the formation history of the Dzwŏ Jwàn text? Since the elite story is an intrusion, it must be later, and so, for a certain length of time, this story consisted *only of its popular element:* a tale of revenge which was taken into the DJ with very little change.

Other DJ stories contain popular *elements;*[22] this is a complete specimen. But for these tales, we would not suspect that popular literature even existed.

————————————••••••————————

[22]The most celebrated case is a suspected saga of the wanderings of the future Jìn Wv́n-gūng; see Maspero **China** 358. We may notice, before leaving the subject, that all the tales so far mentioned have to do in one way or another with Jìn, and especially with the Jàu clan. Later literature continues to show strong sympathies with the Jàu clan.

Tsáu Gwèı. Here is a populist rather than a popular story, expressing sympathy from above with the common people. The point is that the people's gratitude for justice under the laws is their motive for serving the state in war:

> **6:25** (DJ 3/10:1, excerpt, c0328). The army of Chí invaded us, and the Prince was about to do battle. Tsáu Gwèı asked to be received. A fellow-countryman of his said to him, The meat-eaters[23] are discussing it, why should you intrude? Gwèı said, The meat-eaters are too limited; they are incapable of planning for the long term. He went in, and was received. He asked, On what basis do you propose to do battle? The Prince said, Such food and clothing as conduce to comfort, I dare not to monopolize; I always share them with others. He replied, That is a small kindness, and not yet general. The people will not follow you for that. The Prince said, Sacrificial animals, and offerings of jade and silk, I dare not to multiply, but I always keep my word [about promised sacrifices]. He replied, that is only a small sincerity, and not true candor; the spirits will not bless you for that. The Prince said, In criminal cases small or large, though I am not able to investigate fully, I always render my decision based on the facts. He replied, That is something like fidelity; you may undertake one battle. If you should do battle, I beg leave to follow you . . .

The Prince granted this favor, and Tsáu Gwèı's directions led to victory. We may notice that this story rejects frugality and spirit piety (both basic to Mician populism), and makes justice the basis of the relation between ruler and people.

Confucian populism held that the people could advise government, criticize government, or even replace a government. Shū 32 tells how conflicting advice (from the ruler, his advisors, the people, bone divination, and Yì divination) is to be resolved. In sum, two divinations plus one human opinion are favorable, *even if the human opinion is that of the people:*

> **6:26** (Shū 32:29, excerpt, c0322) . . . If the common people are favorable and the turtle oracle is favorable and the stalk oracle is favorable, while you are opposed and the nobles and officers are opposed, it is fortunate.

Popular criticism of policy was sanctioned in this Dzwǒ Jwàn story:

> **6:27** (DJ 9/31:11, excerpt, c0322). Some people of Jv̀ng had gone to a county school and were discussing the administration. Rán Míng said to [Jv̀ng minister] Dž-chǎn, How about eliminating these county schools? Dž-chǎn said, What for? If people morning and evening go there to discuss the pros and cons of the administration, what they approve I will put into effect, and what they dislike I will change.[24] They are my teachers. How should I eliminate them? . . .

And the story ends in a word of approval from "Confucius."

---

[23]That is, the nobles, who alone (compare **#2:43**) regularly had meat in their diet.

[24]This near repeat of an Analects saying (**#5:30**) gives it a new political meaning.

Light Love. Along with these efforts to recognize a popular interest in the workings of government, elite wealth and leisure continued to grow. The old indecent poems of solicitation (**#6:3-5**) continued to be in the Shr̄, and though they offended some people, they amused others. For that amused public, a final poem was added to the already long Jv̀ng section. It picked up on the Dzv̄n and Wăı Rivers from Shr̄ 87 (**#6:4**), and on that basis constructed – yes, a two stanza poem, but one of sophisticated urban dalliance, rather than of rural seduction. It recreates the sexual potency, but in a more sophisticated guise:

6:28 (Shr̄ 95, Jv̀ng #21, 04c).

95A The Dzv̄n and eke the Wăı
Are now at floodtime height, ah
The gallants and the girls
With sweetgrass are bedight, ah
A girl says, "Have you seen the sight?"
A gallant says, "I have indeed.
But shall we see again the sight?"
Out beyond the Wăı
One may roam delightfully.
And so the gallant and the girl
Exchange a bit of pleasantry
And she presents him with a peony

95B The Dzv̄n and eke the Wăı
Are flowing very clear, ah
The gallants and the girls
In multitudes appear, ah
A girl says, "Have you seen the sight?"
A gallant says, "I have indeed.
But shall we see again the sight?"
Out beyond the Wăı
One may roam delightfully.
And so the gallant and the girl
Exchange a bit of pleasantry
And she presents him with a peony

This must have maddened the moralists.

Dog. More primary as a popular influence on elite culture was continued input into basic vocabulary (compare page 151). Readers of this Dàu/Dv́ Jīng passage will probably guess, and most commentators remark . . .

6:29 (DDJ 5, excerpt, c0320).
Heaven and Earth are unkind:
they treat the Myriad Creatures like straw dogs;
The Sage is unkind:
he treats the common people like straw dogs . . .

. . . that the "straw dogs" are substitutes used in sacrifice and then discarded. Such a practice is confirmed by a Jwāngdž passage (JZ 14:4). So far so good.

That practice is unknown to the elite ritual texts, and probably belonged to popular culture "Straw" and "dog" (chú-gŏu 芻狗) have Austro-Asiatic affinities (the Myáu word for "dog" is related to gŏu). The Sinitic word for dog, chywăn 犬, was being replaced by gŏu 狗 already in classical times.[25]

The lure of wealth also operated in the area of public policy. In in the effort to attract and retain population, the state offered livelihood advantages:

6:30 (GZ 1:1, excerpt, c0322).

If the state has much wealth,	A
the distant will come;	A
If open land is plentiful,	B
the people will remain.	B

We have already (**#2:28**) met a piece of poetic propaganda for that idea, in which the supposed singers are those valuable specialists, the jade carvers:

6:31 (Shr̄ 184, Syău Yă 24; c0325).

184A In ninefold marsh the crane-bird trills,
      Its voice is heard upon the moor;
      Fishes hide in watery lair,
      Or they linger by the shore.
          Pleasant is that garden there,
          With timber trees all planted fair,
          But all beneath the deadwood fills,
          And the stones of other hills
          Would suffice for making drills

184B In ninefold marsh the crane-bird trills,
      Its voice is heard upon the air;
      Fishes linger by the shore,
      Or they hide in watery lair.
          Pleasant is that garden there,
          With timber trees all planted fair,
          But all beneath the thornwood fills,
          And the stones of other hills
          Would suffice to show our skills

Methodological Moment. Having read Shr̄ 95 (**#6:28**), we now see that a sophisticated poet is using the old two-stanza form to evoke a folk atmosphere. The methodological moral is that it helps to read the texts more than once.

———————•••••———————

[25]Chywăn 犬 "dog" is now obsolete, except in modern Fùjōu. In classical times, the Shr̄, the Analects, and Mencius and his northern successor school, use older chywăn. The southern Mencians and Sýwndż use popular gŏu 狗. In mixed texts, gŏu is later or tends to imply a vulgar context. Synonyms were a problem for legal language, and the lexicographers assigned the meaning "puppy" to the newer word. That artificial distinction is already made in the Mician logical writings (Graham **Later** 218f).

Mencius held that rulers get the people's loyalty by benevolence, not by social engineering. He left Lǔ in 0320 to visit the King of Ngwèi:[26]

6:32 (MC 1A1, 0320). Mencius saw King Hwèi of Lyáng. The King said, Since the aged one[27] has not thought a thousand leagues too far to come, he will surely have something to benefit my state?

Mencius replied, Why must the King speak of "benefit?" There is surely no more to it than rvn 仁 and right 義. If the King says, Wherewith shall I benefit my state, the great dignitaries will say, Wherewith shall I benefit my family, and the officers and common people will say, Wherewith shall I benefit my self? When high and low compete in the search for benefit, the state will be in danger. In a myriad-chariot state, it will be the thousand-chariot families who will assassinate the ruler; in a thousand-chariot state, it will be the hundred-chariot families who will assassinate the ruler. A thousand in a myriad, or a hundred in a thousand, are not a small proportion, but if you put right last and benefit first, they will not be satisfied until they have snatched it all. There was never one who was rvn but neglected his parents; never one who was rightful but put his ruler last. If the King would only speak of "rvn and right," what need would he have to speak of "benefit?

The King says he has been using his "heart," by which he means his attention:

6:33 (MC 1A3a, 0320[28]). King Hwèi of Lyáng said, The way the Solitary One[29] deals with the state is to give it his full attention 心. If things are bad inside the River, I move people east of the River, and move grain inside the River. If things are bad east of the River, I do likewise. If I observe the governments of the neighbor states, none is as assiduous as the Solitary One. But the neighbor states' population does not decrease, and the Solitary One's population does not increase. Why is this?

The King is following a materialist version of populism, given in #**6:30**, above.

Mencius said, The King is fond of war, and I ask leave to take an illustration from war. The drum rumbles, the swords cross – and then they cast off their armor and flee, trailing their weapons behind them. Some run a hundred paces before they stop, others fifty paces. If because he had run only fifty paces, someone should laugh at one who had run a hundred, how would that be? He said, It would not be right. It's just that he didn't run a hundred paces, but he too ran away.

[26]Or "King of Lyáng," from the city where his capital was located.

[27]A formula of respect. Mencius at this time was 65: younger than the King.

[28]We give only the original 0320 part of this text. An accusatory section was added later, emphasizing the hardships suffered by Hwèi-wáng's people. We omit MC 1A2 and 1A4, they too are later compositions (Brooks **Nature**). The followers of Mencius were not philosophically content with his actual speeches, and soon augmented them.

[29]A modest third-person self-reference, proper for this formal occasion.

He said, Since the King understands this, he need not expect that his people will become more numerous than those of the neighbor states. If one does not miss the planting season, the grain will be more than can be eaten. If fine nets do not enter the pools and ponds, the fish and turtles will be more than can be eaten. If axes and hatchets enter the mountain forests only at the proper season, the timber will be more than can be used. When grain and fish and turtles are more than can be eaten, and timber is more than can be used, this will let the people nourish their living and mourn their dead without reproach [to their superiors].[30] When the people nourish their living and mourn their dead without reproach, this is the beginning of the Kingly Way.

The King, in effect, is taking too much from the people, and thus is causing the very hardships he is trying to relieve. This will not earn the people's gratitude, and only the people's gratitude can be the basis for true Kingship.

The hard question, in a hard world, was approximately this: What is the people's gratitude *worth*, in practical military terms? Mencius did not shrink from answering this. His answer was given at the last of the three interviews:

6:34 (MC 1A5, 0320). Lyáng Hwèi-wáng said, Than the state of Jìn, none in the world was stronger, as the aged one is aware. But since it came to my humble self, on the east we were defeated by Chí and my eldest son died there; in the west we lost 700 leagues to Chín; in the south we have been humiliated by Chǔ. My humble self is ashamed of this, and wishes at one stroke to wipe it all out before he dies. How can this be done?

Mencius replied, With a territory only 100 leagues square, one can still be a true King. If the King gives the people a benevolent government, being sparing of punishments and fines and frugal in imposing taxes and levies, they will plough deep and weed carefully, and their able-bodied in days of leisure will cultivate filiality, fraternity, loyalty and good faith. At home, they will thus be able to serve their fathers and older brothers; outside the home, they will be able to serve their elders and superiors. With nothing but sharpened sticks, one can use them to oppose the strong armor and sharp weapons of Chín and Chǔ.[31]

Lyáng Hwèi-wáng inquired no further of Mencius; he died shortly after this third interview. Given his long and not altogether successful experience of war, he might have wondered whether a grateful population armed with sharpened sticks could resist a well-equipped invading army, let alone invade other states. The defensive-war pacifism which lay at the root of Mencian political theory did not augur well for the effectiveness of that theory in practice.

---

[30]They do not lack food to feed their living, or coffin timber to bury their dead.

[31]The strong armor and sharp lances of Chǔ are noted by Syẃndž (SZ 15:4, c0250), in connection with the battle of 0300 (see p109), in which Chín defeated Chǔ.

The core of Mencian populism is a common (túng 同) interest, and feeling, between ruler and people. Here is Mencius' first meeting with the King of Chí:

> **6:35** (MC 1B1, excerpt, 0318). Jwāng Bàu saw Mencius, and said, When I saw the King, the King told me that he liked music, and I had nothing to say in return. He said, What about liking music? Mencius said, If the King liked music enough, would not the state of Chí be almost there? Another day, he was given an audience by the King, and said, The King once spoke to Master Jwāng about liking music. Was this true? The King blushed and said, This humble one is unable to appreciate the music of the Former Kings, he just likes the popular music of the present day.
>
> He said, If the King liked music enough, would not the state of Chí be almost there? The music of the present day is as good as the music of antiquity. He said, May I hear about this? [Mencius] said, To enjoy music alone, or to enjoy it with others, which is more enjoyable? He said, It is better with others. He said, With a few others or with many others; which is more enjoyable? He said, It is better with many.
>
> Your servant begs to speak to the King about music. Suppose the King is having a music performance, and the common people hear the sound of the King's bells and drums, the tones of his pipes and flutes; they all with aching heads wrinkle their brows and say to one another, Our King likes to perform music; how then can he bring us to this extremity, where father and son cannot meet, where elder and younger brother, wife and child, are separated and scattered? . . . This is for no other reason than that the King does not share his pleasure 同樂 with the people.
>
> But now suppose the King is having a music performance, and the common people hear the sound of the King's bells and drums, the tones of his pipes and flutes; they all are pleased, and with happy countenances say to one another, Our King must be in pretty good health, or how could he have a music performance? . . . This is for no other reason than that the King shares his pleasure with the people. If the King would share his pleasure with the common people, he would truly be a King.

To the tiny and militarily hopeless state of Tv́ng, at the end of his career, Mencius stressed this same ideal of togetherness between ruler and people:

> **6:36** (MC 1B13, c0312). Tv́ng Wv́n-gūng asked, Tv́ng is a small state, between [the large states of] Chí and Chǔ. Should I serve Chí? Should I serve Chǔ? Mencius replied, That kind calculation is not something I am capable of. But if I must reply, there is one thing. Deepen these moats, heighten these walls, and stand guard over them with the people 與民. If at the point of death the people have not left you, then this is something that can be done.

Another possibility was later offered by Mencius to the Tv́ng ruler: the Jōu ancestor who left his city under pressure from enemies, and went elsewhere:

> **6:37** (MC 1B15, excerpt, c0310) . . . The people said, This is a benevolent man. We cannot lose him. And they followed him like crowds to market.

The 03rd Century

After Mencius, benevolence theory focused on the disposition, the "heart," of the ruler: his capacity to be concerned for others. This was first embodied in a later piece based on MC 1B1 (**#6:35**) and added to the genuine interviews:

> **6:38** (MC *1A7a, excerpt, c0302) . . . The King said, What must my virtue be like, so that I can be a true King? He said, Protect the people, and none can prevent you from being a true King. He said, Can such as this Solitary One really protect the people? He said, You can. He said, How do you know that I can?
>
> Your subject heard from Hú Hv́ that the King was sitting in his hall, and someone led an ox past in the lower part of the hall, and when the King saw it, he said, Where is the ox going? The reply was, It is going [to be sacrificed] to consecrate a bell. The King said, Let it go; I cannot bear its fearful look, like an innocent man going to the execution ground. The reply was, Shall we cancel the consecration of the bell? The King said, How can the consecration be canceled? Substitute a sheep for it. I don't know if this happened or not.
>
> The King said, It did.
>
> Mencius said, This feeling 心 is enough to make one a true King. The common people all thought that the King grudged it, but his subject is sure that it was because the King could not bear it.
>
> The King said, Yes. But did the people really 誠 think that? Cramped and small though the state of Chí may be, how should I grudge one ox? It was just that I could not bear its fearful look, like an innocent man going to the execution ground, so I substituted a sheep for it.
>
> Let the King not wonder that the people thought he grudged it. When he exchanged small for large, how should they understand? If the King felt it was like an innocent going to the execution ground, what was there to choose between an ox and a sheep?
>
> The King laughed and said, What really 誠 *was* my feeling 心? I did not substitute a sheep for it because I grudged its value. It was only fitting that the common people should have thought I grudged it.
>
> No harm. This is the way benevolence works: you had seen the ox and not seen the sheep. The gentleman's relation to animals is that if he has seen them living, he cannot bear to see them dead; if he has heard their cries, he cannot bear to eat their flesh . . .

"Mencius" goes on to argue that an empathy reaching as far as animals needs only to be employed on the common people, and the Way to Kingship is open.

Methodological Moment. Why is **#6:38** a "later" passage? Answer: The concordance (it is not necessary to know Chinese) tells us that it is several times longer than any other MC 1 interview, and only it uses the term 心, which is common in higher-numbered Mencius chapters. The anomalies coincide.

Vengeance. There are grateful people and there are resentful people, and the latter have their theory too. The Micians, aware of popular resentment of injustice, had insisted on the reality of avenging ghosts and spirits. In their third essay on that subject, they claimed support from official chronicles (there were no official chronicles, but the newly public Chūn/Chyōu plus certain tales in the associated Dzwǒ Jwàn had implied their existence). These imaginary chronicles the Micians promptly quoted for their own purposes:

> **6:39** (MZ 31:4, excerpt, c0298). Those who hold that there are no ghosts and spirits say, Those who have heard or seen such things as ghosts and spirits are innumerable, but who of them have really heard and seen whether ghosts and spirits exist? Our master Mwòdž says, If we want an instance where many have seen and many have heard, then in antiquity there is Dù Bwó. Jōu Sywæn-wáng killed his minister Dù Bwó, though he was innocent. Dù Bwó said, My sovereign is going to kill me, though I am innocent. If the dead have no consciousness, there is an end. But if the dead *have* consciousness, then before three years, I will surely let my sovereign know about it. Three years later, Jōu Sywæn-wáng was hunting in Pú-tyén with his feudal lords. Their carriages numbered in the hundreds; their escort, several thousand; the men filled the hunting fields. At noon, Dù Bwó, in a plain carriage drawn by white horses, wearing scarlet clothes and cap, holding a scarlet bow and carrying scarlet arrows, pursued Jōu Sywæn-wáng; his shot went into the chariot, pierced his heart and split his spine, and spent itself in the chariot;[32] he slumped over his bow case and died. At that time, none of the Jōu escort party but saw it, and none of those further away but heard of it.
>
> It was written in the Jōu chronicle, for rulers to teach their ministers and for fathers to instruct their sons, with these words: "Be cautious, be careful: whoever kills the innocent will reap misfortune, so swift is the vengeance of the ghosts and spirits." If we consider what is written in this book, how can it be doubted that ghosts and spirits exist?

This popular proof of supernatural sanctions against wrongdoing (with claimed support from elite documentation) made no impression on elite thought.

Summoning the Soul. Funerals are one occasion where the everyday world comes into contact with whatever other world there may be. The Micians had always objected to the lavish funerals of the elite, but other factors are involved. If we look into the Confucians' rules for mourning . . .

> **Yí Lǐ** 儀禮 (YL) "Ceremonial Usages." Those for the gentleman are from the 03c; those for higher ranks are later. Translated by Steele.

. . . we find a seemingly anomalous feature, a "summoning:" Where could that be coming from? First, here is what it looks like:

---

[32]The King's body was entirely transfixed; a supernaturally mighty shot.

6:40 (YL 12, excerpt, c0290?). When he dies in his chamber, for a shroud they use a simple coverlet. The summoner (復者) takes his official cap and clothing and pins the skirt to the jacket. Throwing them over his left shoulder, he joins the collar to the sash and ascends from the east end of the house front. In the middle of the roof, he faces north and beckons to the garments, saying, I beg [name] to return. This he does thrice, then throws down the clothes, where they are received in a basket; they ascend by the eastern steps, and use them to clothe the corpse. The summoner descends by way of the back end of the west wall . . .

It was thought that the soul leaves the body in dreaming or when in a coma; calling it back was a sensible precaution against too early burial. Sentimentally, it avoided the impression that the family were hurrying to get the deceased into the ground. But the procedure was open to ridicule, and ridicule is what it got:

6:41 (MZ 39:1, excerpt, c0287). . . When a parent dies, they lay out the body but do not dress it for burial. They go up on top of the house, they climb down the well, they poke into ratholes and peek into washbasins, seeking for the person in them. If the person is really alive, then this is surely very stupid. If he has died, to insist on seeking him in these places is the greatest imaginable artificiality.

Whence this "summoning?" Summoning is used by the modern Myáu to convey the soul of an infant to earth, or see the soul of a deceased adult safe to the other world.[33] In our period, it was also characteristic of non-Sinitic Chǔ. In 0263, the Chǔ King fell ill. A crisis occurred: the heir was a hostage in Chín. Efforts were made to cure the King, among them this poetic one:

> **Chǔ Tsź** 楚辭 (CT) "Poetry of Chǔ," a Latter Hàn anthology of 03c Chǔ court poetry and Hàn poems in Chǔ style. Translated by Hawkes.

6:42 (Chǔ Tsź, Jàu Hún, "Summoning the Soul," excerpt, 0263).
> O Soul, come back!
> Why have you left your wonted abode, for the Four Quarters, oh?
> Abandoning your delightful place, to go to the ill-omened, oh?
>
> O soul, come back! In the east you cannot sojourn, oh.
> Giants a thousand fathoms tall, and it is for souls they seek, oh.
> Ten suns rise in succession, liquefying metal and melting stone, oh.
> They are used to it, soul, but if you went there, you would perish, oh.
> O come back! In the east you cannot sojourn, oh . . .

The King died that autumn, but at least they had done what they could for him. His heir escaped from Chín and succeeded him as King.

---

[33]Symonds **Calling**; for a modern medical context, see NYT 20 Sept 2009 p21.

Replacing the Ruler. Can a subject kill his ruler? Quite apart from populist theory, that problem arose with the elite theory of dynastic transitions, when a former vassal kills an evil ruler and himself becomes the first ruler of a new dynasty. This violates the duty of the vassal to his lord. Is it then permissible? The Mencians solved this by redefining what we mean by "ruler:"

> **6:43** (MC *1B8, c0285). King Sywǣn of Chí asked, Tāng deposed Jyé 傑 and King Wǔ attacked Jòu 紂 – did these things actually happen? Mencius replied, It is there in the record. He said, For a subject to assassinate his ruler – is this permissible? [Mencius] said, He who steals benevolence [as a cloak for his evil acts] we call a "thief;" he who steals righteousness we call a "ruffian;" one who is both a ruffian and a thief we call a mere "fellow." I have heard of someone executing the "*fellow*" Jòu; I have not heard of anyone assassinating a *ruler*.

This makes the atrocities of the ruler an effective self-abdication by the ruler. The ruler is not defined by his having succeeded a previous ruler; he is defined by correctly representing the qualities that define him as a ruler, which are closely related to the ruler's duty to his people. *Duty is now reciprocal.*

The Three-Year Mourning. We now come to a case of culture conflict. Since the 04c, the Confucians had recommended an extended mourning period, since they felt that a true sincerity of feeling took years to be fully expressed. The Lǔ Micians argued for a more "natural" one-year mourning period:

> **6:44** (MZ 48:8, c0272). Our master Mwòdž said to Gūngmv̀ngdž, According to the rituals for mourning, when a ruler or parent, a wife, or an eldest son dies, mourning garments are to be worn for three years; for an uncle, a brother, or a clan member, five months; for an aunt, a sister, a cousin, or a nephew, several months. Some, during the mourning period, recite the 300 Shī, they play on instruments the 300 Shī, they sing the 300 Shī, they dance the 300 Shī. If we put your words into practice, when will the gentlemen ever attend to the business of government? When will the common people ever do their work?

This practical objection got a feeling-based response from the Lǔ Confucians:

> **6:45** (LY 17:19, c0270). Dzǎı Wǒ asked, Is not the three-year mourning period too long? If gentlemen for three years perform no ceremonies, ceremonies will be lost. If gentlemen for three years perform no music, music will vanish. When the old grain is gone and the new is piled high, when bow and tinder have changed the fire – that should suffice.
>
> The Master said, If you were to eat your rice and wear your brocades, would you feel comfortable with yourself? He said, I would. [The Master] said, If you would feel comfortable, then do it. But as to the gentleman's way of mourning: if he ate dainties, he would not find them sweet; if he heard music, he would not find it enjoyable; if he abode in his usual place, he would not be comfortable; therefore he does not do these things. But if you would be comfortable, then do them.

Dzǎı Wǒ went out. The Master said, Such is Yẃ's lack of humane feeling (仁). Only when Yẃ had been alive for three years did he finally leave the bosom of his father and mother. Now, a three-year mourning is the universal custom of the world. Did not Yẃ receive three years of love from his father and mother?

This argument from emotion was promptly ridiculed by the Micians:

6:46 (MZ 48:13, c0272). Gūngmv̀ngdž said, I mourn for three years in imitation of the affection that a son shows his parents. Our master Mwòdž said, All an infant knows is to want its parents. When its parents cannot be found, it cries endlessly. And why? It is the ultimate stupidity. In what way is the wisdom of the Confucians any better than that of a baby?

Nice touch. But the elite side won this cultural war. It was ultimately about standardization, of individuals within a culture as well as between cultures. Here is Syẃndž, on the effort to produce standard results in the individual:

6:47 (SZ 8:11b, excerpt, c0279). Setting a goal and repeating it as a custom transforms one's nature 性. It becomes one thing and not two, and thus constitutes a personal resource 積.[34] Repetition of custom redirects the will, and if long continued, it can modify the inner reality 質.

Human Nature. The Jwāngdž Primitivists made a strong response to this, in the process setting off a long philosophical debate about the nature of man, in which it becomes obvious that the participants are focusing on elite man, and on the process of self-improvement by which he fully realizes his potential.

6:48 (JZ 8:4, excerpt, c0278). A minor confusion alters one's sense of direction; a major confusion alters one's nature . . . From the Three Dynasties on down, no one in the world but has altered their nature because of some external thing. The petty man will risk his life for profit; the officer will risk his life for reputation, the noble will risk his life for family advantage, the sage will risk his life for the world. So these several people have different intentions, and are known by various names, but in disfiguring their nature and risking their lives, they are the same . . .

Syẃndž appealed to a universally recognized standard of correctness:

6:49 (SZ 19:2d, excerpt, c0278). Compass and square are the perfection of square and round, as ritual is the ridgepole of the Way of Man . . .

He was again answered, from one corner in terms of a human argument:

6:50 (JZ 8:3, excerpt, c0277). And to rely on curve and plumbline, or compass and square, to make something right, is to scrape away its nature . . . to violate its character. So to use the bendings and bowings of Ritual and Music, the smiles and simperings of Benevolence and Righteousness, to comfort the hearts of the world, is to lose what is always so . . .

---

[34]Jī 積 "stored grain" is a technical term for what is accumulated by moral effort.

From another corner of the Jwāngdž came a more inclusive answer:

6:51 (JZ 9:2, excerpt, c0276). When horses live on the plain, they can drink from the stream. If pleased, they twine their necks and rub; if angry, they turn their backs and kick. This is all horses know how to do. But if you pile poles and yokes on them, and line them up in crossbars and shafts, they will learn to snap the crossbars, break the pole, and chew the reins . . . In the time of Hv̀ Syẁ, people stayed home but didn't know what they were doing; went out but didn't know where they were going . . . Then the Sage came along with the bendings and bowings of Ritual and Music to reshape the form of the world, with the reachings and strivings of Benevolence and Righteousness to comfort the hearts of the world, and the people for the first time went on tiptoe for love of wisdom, fought and struggled with a view to profit, and they could not be stopped. This was all the fault of the Sage.

But for Syẃndž, only ritual standards can show the way to the ideal:

6:52 (SZ 19:5b, excerpt, c0276). Ritual trims what is too long and extends what is too short, eliminates excess and remedies deficiency . . .

This was less desirable to others differently situated, who accepted even the irregular as natural and therefore good:

6:53 (JZ 8:2, excerpt, c0275). He who makes Normality 正 his norm 正 does not lose sight of the conditions of his original nature. What is joined is not for him "webbed," what branches off is not "extra." What is long does not seem excessive; what is short does not seem deficient. Thus, the duck's legs are short, but to stretch them would hurt him; the crane's legs are long, but to cut them would pain him. So what is naturally long is not to be cut, what is naturally short is not to be stretched . . . I wonder if Benevolence 仁 and Righteousness 義 are really the nature of man?

Syẃndž finally had to directly insist that artifice (wèi 僞) is desirable:

6:54 (SZ 19:6, excerpt, c0275). And so I say, nature is the basic initial material; artifice 僞 is the elegant realization. If there were no nature, artifice would have nothing to augment. And if there were no artifice, nature would not be able to become beautiful of itself . . .

In Syẃndž's world, individual self-improvement needs guidance from outside. In the social realm, outside compulsion had long been the order of the day.

The Mencian theory of human nature went back to this early statement:

6:55 (MC 2A6, excerpt, c0300) . . . The reason I say that men all have a heart that cannot bear the ills of others [the psychological basis of the virtue of benevolence] is this: Suppose a man suddenly sees a baby about to fall into a well, he will inevitably experience feelings of concern and distress. This is not to get on good terms with the child's parents; it is not to be praised by neighbors and friends; it is not that he does it because he would hate the reputation of not doing it. Seen thus, if one lacks feelings of compassion he is not a man . . .

In the final Mencian view, virtue is instinctive. It includes an innate respect for parents and an innate fellow-feeling; the latter ultimately owes much to the Mician idea of universal love (#4:4). The Sage not only preserves intact this instinctual endowment, but develops it until it includes all humanity. Only the Sage has sympathies which can include all the people of a state, or the world; the All Under Heaven (Tyēn-syà 天下).

Sywndž disagreed. For him, human nature is fundamentally bad, and must be schooled into a human condition. Effort is necessary:

> **6:56** (SZ 23:4a, excerpt, c0274). The Sage's relation to ritual principles is just like that of the potter molding clay. How indeed could the principles of morality, resource, and acquired abilities be part of man's original nature? . . . This being the case, the Sage's relation to Ritual and Righteousness . . . is like that of the potter to his pots . . . Thus it is plain that human nature is bad, and any good is acquired by artifice 偽.

Sywndž was still living, and the Mencians referred to him under another name:

> **6:57** (MC 6A1, excerpt, c0274). Gàudž said, Nature is like the willow wood; Righteousness is like cups and bowls. To make man's nature into Benevolence and Righteousness is like making cups and bowls out of willow wood. Mencius said, Can you make cups and bowls out of willow wood by following the nature of the wood? You must do violence to the wood and only then can you make cups and bowls . . . Will you also have to do violence to men to produce Benevolence and Righteousness? What will lead the people of the world to see Benevolence and Righteousness as a calamity will surely be your words.

That is, the public reaction to philosophical statements must also be considered.

Sywndž restated his position:

> **6:58** (SZ 23:2a, excerpt, c0274) . . . Ritual and Righteousness come from the Sage's artifice, and not from man's nature. When the potter shapes clay to make the vessel, this is the creation of the potter's artifice, and not inherent in its nature . . .

And the Mencians recast it for purposes of discussion in this form:

> **6:59** (MC 6A2, excerpt, c0274). Gàudž said, Man's nature is like water whirling around: open a passage for it to the east, and it will flow to the east; open a passage for it to the west, and it will flow west. Man's nature is indifferent to good and bad. Mencius said, Water will flow indifferently east or west, but will it flow up or down? Man's nature is good, just as water tends to flow downward . . . by damming and directing, you can force it up a hill, but is that movement according to the nature of water? . . . When men are forced to do wrong, their nature is being dealt with in this way.

This introduces the factor of external conditioning, as an explanation of the seeming bad nature of some persons.

Sywndž grants the point, but makes the circumstances themselves very early:

> **6:60** (SZ 23:1d, excerpt, c0274). Mencius says the nature of men is good, but that they are made to lose or destroy their original nature. I say that portraying men's nature like this goes beyond the truth. . . As soon as he is born, man begins to diverge from his original simplicity and childhood innocence, so that necessarily these are lost or destroyed.

We seem to have agreement about the *loss* of natural feelings. But then comes:

> **6:61** (SZ 23:1e, excerpt, c0274). It is the nature of men that when hungry they want something to eat, when cold he they want warm clothing, and when tired they want rest: these qualities are inherent in his nature . . . A son's deference to his father and a younger brother's deference to his elder brother, a son relieving his father of labor . . . these are contrary to men's nature. If we consider the implication of the facts, it is plain that human nature is bad, and any goodness is acquired by artifice.

Many theories of human nature were being proposed at this time. Here "Mencius" clarifies his own position:

> **6:62** (MC 6A6, excerpt, c0274). Gūngdūdž said, Gàudž says man's nature is neither good nor bad. Others say that nature can be either good or bad [as the people are good under good rulers and vice versa] . . . Still others say that the nature of some people is good, and that of other people is bad [as witness good people appearing under the reigns of bad rulers] . . . And now you say, Nature is good. Are all the others then wrong?
>
> Mencius said, The condition of men is that they can become good; this is what I mean by "good." If they do wrong, it is not the fault of their endowment. The capacity for compassion, all men have; the capacity for shame, all men have; the capacity for respect, all men have; the capacity for distinguishing true from false, all men have . . .

Sywndž was not to be convinced. He sees the Sage not as resonating with the people, but as prescribing for them out of his superior ritual knowledge, a knowledge which also includes the fundamentals of the legal system:

> **6:63** (SZ 23:3a, excerpt, c0274). Mencius says that nature is good. I say it is not . . . Were that the case, what use would there be for the Sage Kings, and what need for ritual and moral principles? . . . The nature of man is bad. Thus in antiquity the Sages . . . established the authority of lords and superiors to supervise men, elucidated ritual and morality to transform them, set up laws and standards to make them orderly, and added penalties and punishments to restrain them . . .

Here the world of law and the world of lǐ (ritual) have come together. It is an argument from the status quo, and on behalf of those who serve the status quo or propose to do so, a group which included Sywndž himself.

The argument climaxed on the nature of the people: political man at large. Yes, there are bad people in the world, is this really the deep nature of men?

The Mencians preferred to account for bad men by external circumstances, a view they expressed in this, the most beautiful passage in the Mencius:

6:64 (MC 6A8, c0274). Mencius said, The trees on Bull Mountain were once beautiful. But because it adjoins a great state, axes and hatchets assailed it, and could it remain beautiful? To be sure, what with the winds of day and night, and the moistening of rain and dew, shoots and sprouts did appear on it. But oxen and sheep came along and grazed on them, and thus it came to be bare. Men see how bare it is, and think there never were any timber trees 材 on it, but how is this the nature of the mountain?

And if we consider men, how can they be without feelings of kindness and justice? The way they lose these better feelings is like the axes and hatchets and the trees: morning after morning they hack at them, and can they remain beautiful? With the winds of day and night, and in the air of dawn, their loves and hates are near to those of other men, but these feelings are only faint, and with what happens during the day, they are fettered and destroyed. And when they are fettered again and again, the air of night is not strong enough to preserve them, and when the air of night is not strong enough to preserve them, they become little different from animals. People see that they are like animals, and think there never was any potential 才[35] there, but how is this the condition of man?

And so, if it gets its nourishment, there is no creature but grows; if it loses its nourishment, there is no creature but declines. Confucius said,

> Hold it and it remains;
> Release it, and it is gone.
> Its coming and going have no season;
> No one knows its home.

Was he not speaking about the heart?

Thus did the Mencians explain the inhumane. The theory of innate goodness is saved – but not as a description of the world in which we live.

The Analects people, watching this from the sidelines, allowed themselves a comment on the issue. After all, if new Confucius sayings are going to be invented, who more qualified than themselves?

6:65 (LY 17:2a, c0270). The Master said, By nature 性 they are near each other; by habitual action 習 they become further apart.

And they added this comment on the malleability of human nature in general:

6:66 (LY 17:2b, c0270). The Master said, It is the highest wisdom and the lowest stupidity that do not change.

The Analects school had always emphasized an effort at self-improvement, and they here attribute the possibility of change (that is, betterment) to most men. However, they reserve a place for the Sage, who is outside that process.

---

[35]Note the echo between tsái 材 "timber trees" and tsái 才 "talent, human potential."

Gods. If non-Sinitic Chǔ should conquer the world, what religion would it impose on its northern subjects? Chǔ gods were summoned by a shaman; what if northern gods were included in a mixed shamanic pantheon? Some Chǔ poet wrote nine hymns to show how this would go. At the head of the set came the principal god of the Chǔ people. The part here italicized is where the shaman's wooing is successful, and the spirit, drawn by food and music, actually comes:

6:67 (Chǔ Tsź, Nine Songs #1, 太一 "The Great Unity," c0260).

A lucky day, ah; the stars are auspicious;
Solemn we come to please, ah, the August on High.
I grasp the long sword, ah, by its hilt of jade,
My sash pendants sound, ah, they clink and chime.
The jeweled mat, ah, is weighted with jade,
Why not now take up, ah, the rare incense?
Meats cooked in lotus, ah, on a bed of orchid,
I lay out cassia wine, ah, and pepper sauce.
Raise the drumsticks, ah, and strike the drums –
To a stately measure, ah, the song is quiet,
Add the pipes and strings, ah, the melody rises –
The Spirit moves, ah, in rich apparel,
A pungent fragrance, ah, fills the hall.
The Five Notes mingle, ah, in rich concord,
The Lord is happy, and shows his pleasure.

The eighth Song is in the words of a girl who is being sacrificed to the northern Lord of the River (page 160) by setting her adrift on a raft. She drowns as the raft is overturned, and her search (she is her own shaman) is consummated:

6:68 (Chǔ Tsź, Nine Songs #8, 河伯 "The Lord of the River," c0260).

With you I wander, ah, the Nine Rivers.
A wind rises, ah, and whips up waves;
I ride a water chariot, ah, with lotus canopy;
I drive a pair of dragons, ah, with water-serpents.
I ascend Kūnlún, ah, and look in all directions,
My heart takes wing, ah, in anticipation.
The sun is about to set, ah; I am sad, with no thought of return:
Only for that far shore, ah, do I sleeplessly long.
Fish-scale chamber, ah, and dragon hall;
Purple shell gates, ah; a palace of pearl.
What is the Sprit doing, ah, amid the waters?
Astride a white turtle, ah, he pursues spotted fishes.
With you shall I wander, ah, the river isles,
The current swells, ah; I now come below.
She folds her hands, ah, as she journeys east;
We send off the lovely one, ah, to the southern cove.
The waves come surging up, ah, to be my welcome;
Fishes in shoals, ah, accompany me.

These songs are part of a Chǔ-centered Chinese history that never happened.

Again Replacing the Ruler. Ruler abuses are denounced by the Mencians in one imaginary interview (**#2:48**, c0273); a justification for killing rulers had been stated in another (**#6:43**, c0282). At about the same time, we have this:

> **6:69** (MC 5B9, excerpt, c0275) . . . [Mencius] said, If the ruler has a great fault, [the ministers who are his kinsmen] will remonstrate. If they do so repeatedly and he does not listen, they will make a change in the position. The King looked uncomfortable; his countenance changed. Mencius said, Let the King not take it amiss: the King asked about ministers, and his subject did not dare but answer truthfully . . .

Such passages would later cause the Mencius text to be banned or expurgated in China, Japan, and Korea. In the mid 03c, this concept was again expressed, in an almost casual way. So unimportant is the ruler in the populist scheme of things that his replacement seems little more than routine normal maintenance:

> **6:70** (MC *7B14, excerpts, c0253). Mencius said, The people are the most honorable, the altars of soil and harvest are the next, and the ruler is the least . . . When a prince endangers the altars of soil and harvest, he is changed, and another is put in his place . . .

Commoners might be honorable in theory, but there were limits to how high commoners could reach; thus, the wise but humble carter of **#6:18** refused to appear at court. This late Mencian anecdote reveals disdain for the officer of common origins who cannot really escape his common way of doing things:

> **6:71** (MC *7B23, excerpt, c0252) . . . In Jìn there was a man, Fv́ng Fù, who was good at taking on tigers barehanded. In the end, he became a good officer 善士. But once when he went to the wild country, there was a crowd pursuing a tiger which had holed up in a cranny. Nobody dared approach it. Seeing Fv́ng Fù, they hurried to welcome him. Fv́ng Fù, baring his shoulders, got down from his chariot. The crowd were pleased, but those who were really officers 爲士者 laughed at him.

Theory is all very well, but do we *really* want these people as colleagues?

Non-Sinitic Persons are especially unlikely to be envisioned as leading the government. Some, in real life, reached a level of *cultural* authority . . .

- Chún'yẃ Kūn 淳于髡, whose surname comes from a non-Sinitic town on the western end of Chí, was one of the six given stipends by the King of Chí, with a mandate to investigate the rise and fall of states.[36]
- Gv̄nmóudž 根牟子, or "the Master from [non-Sinitic] Gv̄nmóu," is listed before Syẃndž in the transmission genealogy of the Shī; he was probably the music master of Lǔ with whom Syẃndž studied.

. . . but there was a difference between intellectual prestige and political power.

---

[36]SJ 74, our best source, specifies that the Jì-syà stipendiaries (c0313, p136) had no role in administration, but were limited to the task of producing new political theory. There was a clear divide between the merely professional and the fully governmental.

When the main Confucian and Mician centers, and the DDJ group, were shut down by Sywndž in 0249 (page 114), some of their members went to Chí, where they continued to produce text. Others went to Chín, where they were welcomed by Lw Bù-wéi, the Chín minister whose merchant background inclined him toward mild government policies. The Lw-shr Chūn/Chyōu, compiled under his patronage, thus came to have, especially in some chapters, a distinctly Mencian or Mician tinge. At the beginning, we find the Mencian idea of attracting the people and winning their loyalty: Here LSCC advises the future Emperor how to proceed in his contest with the rulers of rival states:

> **6:72** (LSCC 2/5:4, excerpt, c0241). When the Great Cold has come, the people value warmth; when the Great Heat is ascendant, the people flock to the cool. For this reason, the people have no permanent location: when they see a benefit, they gather, and when it there is none, they leave. If one would be Son of Heaven, where the people go must be studied. In the present age, when it turns cold or hot the people do not move, because if they chose something it would be no different. If one would be Son of Heaven, what is displayed to the people must be different . . .

Lw Bù-wéi died in exile not long afterward. But some of his team stayed on, and under the unified Chín Empire, they put out an extension of the LSCC:

> **Lw-shr Chūn/Chyōu: Lǎn** 覽 (LSCC 13-20). Added to the LSCC in the First Emperor's reign, probably by some of those who had worked under Lw Bù-wéi in the 0240's. Translated by Knoblock and Riegel.

This continuation of the work confronts an entirely different world. There is no longer an interest in attracting people; Chín already possesses all the people of the world. The only theoretical issue is how to use them correctly.

> **6:73** (LSCC 19/4:4, c0211). In the time of Yw [Syà], there were a myriad states in the world. When it came to Tāng [Shāng], there were more than three thousand. All those that have not survived to the present time were unable to use their people. That the people were not used is because rewards and penalties were not adequate. Tāng and Wǔ merely took over the people of Syà and Shāng, but they had discovered how to use them. Gwǎn [Jùng] and [Lord] Shāng likewise merely took over the people of Chí and Chín, but they had discovered how to use them. There is a secret to using the people, and if one finds that secret, the people can always be used . . . What do the people want and not want? They want honor and profit, and they hate disgrace and injury. So disgrace and injury are how one makes penalties adequate, and honor and profit are how one makes rewards functional. If rewards and penalties are adequate and functional, then among the people there will be none who cannot be used.

This is the reward-and-punishment theory, the core idea of 04c Chí statecraft. By those classic Pavlovian means, the people can be controlled in ordinary life, to the point where they can be used in military service. Dependably.

Still later, under the incompetent Second Emperor, when the Chín Empire was rapidly unraveling, populist ideas have still further diminished.

Lǔ-shř Chūn/Chyōu: Lùn 論 "Essays" (LSCC 21-26). These six chapters were probably written during the Second Emperor's reign (0209-0207). The taboo on the personal name of the First Emperor is rigidly observed (it was only *sporadically* observed during his lifetime, in the Jì and Lǎn). Translated by Knoblock and Riegel.

First comes the establishment of social fixity. An old Gwǎndž rule, briefly echoed by the 04c Analects, reappears, as much as to say that there shall be no more ministers arising from the ranks:

6:74 (LSCC 25/5:1, excerpt, c0207). In governing, the first thing is to establish social distinctions 定分. The ruler being a ruler and the minister a minister; the father being a father and the son a son, the husband being a husband and the wife a wife – when these six occupy their proper places, the lowly do not overstep limits and the high do not act wrongly. The young are not fractious and the adults are not arrogant . . .

There shall be no such thing as personal initiative, however virtuous:

6:75 (LSCC 25/5:5, c0207). Suppose someone acts on his own arrogant authority and saves his native state. He had taken account of possible consequences with complete accuracy, he had laid out his lines as though with a compass and straightedge. This would be skillful; it would even be artful. But it would not be enough to make it lawful. Law is that under which all are equal, that to which worthy and base alike devote their efforts. If some plan arises from what cannot be generally used, or if some action comes from what cannot be a common rule; this is what the Former Kings would have discarded.

And there shall be no personal ideas about what is virtuous in the first place:

6:76 (LSCC 26/3:1, excerpt, c0206). That in which the Sage Kings of antiquity led their people was a primary concern with agriculture. When commoners farm, they not only work to realize the potential benefits of the earth, they set store by having this as their goal. When commoners farm, they are simple, and when they are simple, they are easy to use. When they are easy to use, the borders are secure and the ruler's position is honored. When the commoners farm, they are solid, and when they are solid, they rarely hold private ideas of what is right 私義. When they rarely hold private ideas of what is right, then the universal law 公法 is established, and all efforts are as one . . .

That about covers it. Populism, the idea that the people should have a role in government, or even the right to an *opinion about* government, is now dead. What lives on is the state.

Though as it turned out, in the specific case of Chín, not for very long.

7. Transcendence

One 05c Warring States person, Yén Hwéı, seems to have possessed a kind of breath control technique, most likely derived from Northeast India by trade contact via Burma, Assam, and the lower Brahmaputra River.[1] It involved mental concentration and reduced sensory input; it gave its adepts calm within and insight without. By the 04c, this proto-Dàuism was cultivated for its own sake and taught in schools; the Dàu/Dv́ Jīng is the record of one such school. This special knowledge gradually spread. In the middle 03c, it was adopted by several primitivist movements, whose textual record is in the Jwāngdž. Out of this came, first, a statecraft theory of strength based on weakness, which we have met in earlier chapters, then a philosophy of resignation and acceptance, and finally, a hope to transcend worldly dangers.

The 05th Century

Yén Hwéı. Among the disciples of Confucius, Yén Hwéı 顏回 stands out as unique, celebrated for his poverty and for his equanimity. These are standard attributes of the meditation adept, who schools himself in ignoring externals:

> 7:1 (LY 6:11, c0460). The Master said, Able[2] indeed was Hwéı! One dish of food, one dipper of drink, living in a narrow alley – others could not have borne their sorrow, but Hwéı did not waver in his happiness. Able indeed was Hwéı!

Meditation involves emptying the mind of all else and focusing on one subject. Yén Hwéı had this ability to an unsurpassed degree:

> 7:2 (LY 6:7, c0460). The Master said, Hwéı: he could go three months without in his heart departing from rv́n. The others: they can manage it for a day or a month, but that is all.[3]

Confucius taught by gnomic maxims and cryptic precepts; students were expected to work out their implications by reflection. With his unparalleled mental ability, Yén Hwéı outperformed the other disciples in this task:

> 7:3 (LY 5:9, c0470). The Master said to Dž-gùng, Of you and Hwéı, who is abler? He answered, How dare Sž even *look* at Hwéı? If Hwéı hears one thing, he gets ten; if Sž hears one thing, he gets two. The Master said, Not as good as him: you and me *both* are not as good as him.

This modesty of Confucius will presently be reversed.

---

[1]One difficult but negotiable route was traced in 1905-1906; see Young **Journey**. In Hàn, an effort was made to develop the southwest route for use by caravans. It failed.

[2]賢哉. The word syén 賢 is usually given a moralized sense "worthy," but its basic meaning is "capable."

[3]Here too, note the emphasis, not on Hwéı's moral qualities, but on what he can *do.*

Dzv̄ngdž, the fourth head of the Confucian school, was from Wŭ-chv́ng, in southern Lŭ, and seems to have been in contact with Indian traditions. In the Analects school, he found a special friend in Yén Hwéı:

> **7:4** (LY 8:5, 0436). Dzv̄ngdž said, Able yet inquiring of the less able; versatile yet inquiring of the limited; having yet seeming to lack; full yet seemingly empty; wronged yet not retaliating – long ago a friend of mine used to devote himself to these.

Seemingly lacking, yet possessing; seemingly empty, yet in a mystical sense full – these are ways in which the meditation adept is often described.

The portrait of Confucius in LY 7, the chapter Dzv̄ngdž wrote, is sometimes reminiscent of the oldest record of the Buddha: the Mahâ-Parinibbâna Sutta (MPnS). In LY 7, and only there, Confucius is a wandering sage:[4]

> **7:5** (LY 7:29, c0450). In Hù County[5] it was hard to find anyone to talk with. A youth presented himself. The disciples had their doubts, but the Master said, We are involved with his coming forward, but not with his going away. Why be so fastidious? If someone purifies himself and comes to us, we accept his purification; we do not guarantee his future conduct.

The Confucius of LY 7 speaks of fifty years for self-cultivation:[6]

> **7:6** (LY 7:17, c0450). The Master said, Give me several more years; with fifty to study,[7] I might come to be without great faults.

And he keeps nothing back from his students:[8]

> **7:7** (LY 7:24, excerpt, c0450) . . . Do you disciples take me as concealing something? I conceal nothing from you . . .

The Analects school had not previously been interested in Confucius' death. But LY 7, which is arranged as a description of his life, ends with his death, and with his renunciation of the consolations of conventional religion:

> **7:8** (LY 7:35, c0450). The Master was very ill. Dž-lù asked to offer a prayer. The Master said, Is this done? Dž-lù replied, It is. The Elegy says, "We prayed for you to the higher and lower divinities." The Master said, Chyōu's praying was done long ago.

Some of these MPnS-like details in LY 7 were to become part of the later picture of Confucius. Others remain eccentric to this day: a development of the Confucius persona that was not taken into the Confucian mainstream..

---

[4]The beginning of the MPnS shows Buddha and his disciples wandering from town to town. (Later texts anachronistically picture him as the abbot of a monastery).

[5]Location unknown, but probably near to modern Tv́ng; south of the Lŭ capital area.

[6]In MPnS 5:27, the Buddha speaks instead of fifty-*one* years for self-cultivation.

[7]Sywé 學 "study," which in the next century will mean book-learning, is here a more personal effort of self-improvement: not in memorization, but in moral progress.

[8]MPnS 2:32.

Dzv̄ng Ywæn, the elder son of Dzv̄ngdž, succeeded him in 0435 as head of the Analects school; his small collection of his father's sayings makes up the LY 8 core. His own writings, in LY 9, develop some of Dzv̄ngdž's themes.

In a developing tradition, traits characteristic of minor figures are often later reassigned to the tradition's central figure. In LY 9, the superiority which Confucius had conceded to Yén Hwéı in LY 5 (#**7:3**) was transferred to Confucius himself, with Yén Hwéı being now the admirer from below:

> **7:9** (LY 9:11, c0405). Yén Ywæn sighed deeply, and said, I look up at it and find it lofty; I try to bore into it and find it hard; I behold it in front of me, and then suddenly it is behind. Our Master in his solicitude is good at guiding people. He broadens me with culture, limits me with propriety. I want to desist, but I cannot, and when I seem to have utterly exhausted my capacity, it still seems that there is something there, towering up majestically. Though I want to go toward it, there is no path to follow.

Another Indianate touch is seen in Dzv̄ng Ywæn's remake of his father's version of the Confucius death scene (#**7:8**). The emotional point of the remake is Confucius' embarrassingly low rank at the time of his death:

> **7:10** (LY 9:12, c0405). The Master was very ill, and Dž-lù had the disciples act as attendants. When the illness moderated, he said, Of long standing indeed are Yóu's dissemblings! I have no attendants, but you act as though I had attendants. Who will I deceive? Will I deceive Heaven? And besides, for my own part, than die in the arms of attendants, would I not rather die in the arms of you disciples? And even if I cannot have a grand funeral, will I be dying by the roadside?

This is very appealing: the affection of Confucius' disciples is enough for him.[9] But we may also note that it echoes the MPnS description of Buddha's death.[10]

Methodological Moment. Not only so, but that detail of Buddha's death in MPnS is a *late addition* to MPnS. How can we tell? Because that paragraph (a disciple's complaint that Buddha should not be dying in some minor town) interrupts the narrative, and because the location of Buddha's death suggests the later cult of relics and pilgrimages. Then LY 9 (c0405) knew a *later stratum* of MPnS. Since legends take time to accumulate around a revered figure, and since the cult of relics is a second, legendary growth, the first MPnS stratum, and the event it describes, must be earlier. We have just taken a step toward confirming the validity of the traditional early 05c date for Buddha's death, against recent arguments that it was more than a century later.

———————··•··———————

[9]Affection between the Buddha and his disciples is emphasized in the MPnS.

[10]In MPnS 5:17-18, the disciple Ânanda's complaint is that Buddha is dying in an inappropriately unimportant town; compare the "roadside" of the preceding passage.

The 04th Century

In the 06c,[11] as India urbanized and trade prospered, there appeared the first of the Upanishads. These are popular, not priestly texts: they show outsiders teaching the priestly Brahmins or besting them in argument. Of them, the early Brhad-Âranyaka (BrA) and the later Îśâ Upanishad (IsU) were written in Videha, which was near the lower Ganges Valley, the homeland of Buddhism.[12] Both these Upanishads are echoed in several Chinese meditation texts.

Breath control is basic to the Upanishadic worldview. Thus:

7:11 (BrA 3:9, excerpt, 06c?).

> On what are you and your self (âtman) founded?
> On the out-breath.
> On what is the out-breath founded?
> On the in-breath.
> On what is the in-breath founded?
> On the inter-breath.
> On what is the inter-breath founded?
> On the up-breath.
> On what is the up-breath founded?
> On the link-breath.
>
> Of this self (âtman), one can only say "Not . . . not . . ." He is ungraspable, for he cannot be grasped. He is undecaying, for he is not subject to decay. He has nothing sticking to him, for he does not stick to anything. He is not bound; yet he neither fears nor suffers injury . . .

Breath control typically involves the suppression of desires:

7:12 (BrA 4:4, excerpt, 06c?).

> When they are all banished,
> those desires lurking in one's heart,
> then a mortal becomes immortal
> and attains Brahman in this world.

Considerably later comes the Îśâ Upanishad, named for the Lord (variously Îśâ or Îśvara) Âtman, a concept of breath or the self as filling the universe:

7:13 (IsU, excerpts, 04c?).

> This whole world is to be dwelt in by the Lord (Îśâ),
> Whatever living being there is in the world . . .
>
> Although unmoving, the One is swifter than the mind,
> The gods cannot catch it, as it speeds on ahead,
> Standing, it outpaces all others who run . . .

---

[11]Precision is impossible; we here follow Olivelle **Upanisads** xxiv and following, except that we doubt that a long lull occurred in the middle of the Upanishadic period.

[12]Michael Witzel, cited in Olivelle **Upanisads** xxxix.

It moves – yet does not move.
It is distant – yet near at hand . . .
When a man sees all beings
within his very self,
and his self within all beings,[13]
It will not seek to hide from him . . .

An Analects reference to Yén Hwéı in c0360 calls him "empty" (kūng 空), a common term for one whose mind has been emptied of distractions by breath control. He is contrasted with Dž-gùng, who was seen as a successful merchant:

7:14 (LY 11:18a, c0360). The Master said, Hwéı is almost there, is he not? He is often empty 空. Sż does not accept his fate, and has traded to advantage. If we reckon up his results, then he is often on the mark.

There is "empty" success and "full" success, and the former is the better.

The Dàu/Dv́ Jīng we have met as a statecraft text of mystical type. Its oldest chapter treats meditation in the paradoxical style of the Îśâ Upanishad:

7:15 (DDJ 14, c0346).

Look but cannot see it:
  its name is Yí 夷.
Hearken but cannot hear it:
  its name is Syī 希.
Feel but cannot find it:
  its name is Wēı 微.
These three are inexplicable,
So we put them together into One.

If we combine "these three" into one, we get approximately phonetic Ishvaı.[14]

Its top is not bright,
Its bottom is not dark,
Continuous, it cannot be named,
And it returns to where there are no creatures.
This is called the Form that has no form,
the Image of what has no substance;
This is called the ineffable.
If you go to meet it, you do not see its head;
if you follow after it, you do not see its back.

[13]This theme is precisely echoed in the late Mencian writings; see #7:25.

[14]The suggestion that these three lines are an esoteric way of spelling out Îśvara, Lord Âtman, is due to Liebenthal **Lord**. Against it is the fact that two of these lines are reversed in the 02c Măwángdwēı text of the DDJ, the oldest text of this passage. But MWD reverses other things too, up to and including the "Dàu" and "Dv́" sections of the text itself, so its evidence against the received order is not necessarily conclusive

> Hold to the ancient Way
> to master modern situations.
> To be able to know the ancient Beginning:
> This is called the main thread of the Way.

So a knowledge of an ancient and powerful entity, the Dàu 道 which cannot be directly apprehended, but is something like the Way the universe works, is here to be applied to contemporary problems. A further claim is that others, in ancient times, were already skilled in this application:

7:16 (DDJ 15, c0344).

> Those who of old were good at being officers
> Were exquisite 微, subtle 妙, mysterious 玄, profound 通;
> So deep they cannot be known.
> For them, I therefore make this ode 頌:
>> "Cautious, like crossing a stream in winter,
>> Hesitant, like fearing neighbors on all sides,
>> Unassertive, like one who is a guest,
>> Reticent, like something dissolving,
>> Simple, like uncarved wood,
>> Turbid, like muddy water."
> He who, though muddy, can be still, will gradually come clear.
> He who, though calm, can yet move, will gradually come alive.
> One who keeps to this Way does not wish to be full.[15]

The goal is to be part of a process, and not its final stage. The image of crossing a stream in winter (over uncertainly firm ice) may remind us of the last words of Dzv̄ngdž in 0436; they quote a poem which is now part of the Shr̄:

7:17 (LY 8:3, 0436). When Dzv̄ngdž fell ill, he summoned the disciples at his gate, and said, Uncover my feet, uncover my hands. The Poem says:

> Tremblingly and full of fear,
> As though I verged the deep abyss,
> As though I trod the thinnest ice —[16]

but now and hereafter, I know I have come through safely, my little ones.

Dzv̄ngdž seems to have been the inventor of the Last Words topos in Chinese literature; this he did in his portrait of Confucius' death in LY 7:35 (#7:8). Here, he stars in his own script, and sounds the same note as did "Confucius:" a difficult crossing safely negotiated. Did the language of the meditation texts – a personal peace difficultly achieved – affect this summary of his life?

---

[15]We here follow the Gwōdyèn text. The later standard text has several additional lines, which add little to the thought of the passage.

[16]These lines match our Shr̄ 195, but *almost* match Shr̄ 196, whose sense is more appropriate to Dzv̄ngdž's statement. The text, and undoubtedly the inventory, of the Shr̄ seem to have been still in a somewhat fluid condition at the time of Dzv̄ngdž's death.

The DDJ school founder died in 0336 and was succeeded by the person who was later always associated with the text: Lǐ Dān or Lǎudž. He moved quickly to develop the statecraft side of the school's teachings. The Indian concepts of oneness and wholeness (#7:13, #7:16) now recur in a paradoxical form:

7:18 (DDJ 22, c0336).

> Be crooked, and you will be whole 全.
> Be bent, and you will be straight 直.
> Be exhausted, and you will be filled 盈.
> Be worn, and you will be renewed 新.
>
> Have little, and you will gain.
> Have much, and you will be troubled.
> Thus the Sage holds to the One
>   and is the pattern for the world:
>
> Does not show himself,
>   and so is famed.
> Does not assert himself,
>   and so is known.
> Does not obtrude himself,
>   and so succeeds.
> Does not flaunt himself,
>   and so endures.
> It is just because he does not contend
> that no one in the world can contend with him.
>
> What of old they said, "Be crooked and you will be whole" –
> How can it be mere words?
> If you are truly whole 全,
>   then you will cause others to give you their loyalty.

Here is the new promise of a practical statecraft ("give you their loyalty") and a new kind of ruler: reticent rather than assertive, and yet wholly successful.

At the end of the 04c, as the DDJ school under Lǎudž's leadership developed its meditationist model for the ruler, the position of the meditative Yén Hwéi in the increasingly ritualized Analects tradition became untenable. The Analects proprietors first tried to ritualize him:

7:19 (LY 12:1, c0326). Yén Ywæn [the formal name of Yén Hwéi] asked about rˇvn. The Master said, To overcome the self and turn to propriety is rˇvn. If one day he can overcome himself and turn to rˇvn, the world will turn to rˇvn along with him. To be rˇvn comes from the self; does it then come from others? Yén Ywæn said, I beg to ask for the details. The Master said, If it is improper, do not look at it. If it is improper, do not speak of it. If it is improper, do not do it. Yén Ywæn said, Though Hwéi is not quick, he begs leave to devote himself to this saying.

To see Yén Hwēi, who in an earlier century (#7:3) was praised as unequaled among the disciples for his perception and his grasp of Confucius' maxims, here reduced to begging for clarification like a novice, is a painful spectacle.

The meditative Way was also practiced in Chí, and a group associated with the statecraft text Gwǎndž constitute a third Dàuist tradition. The earliest of the Gwǎndž meditation chapters is the Nèi Yè 內業 or "Inner Project." Here is a selection from the end of its first stratum:

7:20 (GZ 49:15, first half, c0333).

> If your Essence abides, you will be naturally vital 自生,
> externally, there will be calm and prosperity.
> Store it within, to make a source 泉原,
> and, boundless (hàu-rán 浩然), it will confer peace.
> Take it as the deep well of Breath.
> If that deep well runs not dry,
> the Four Limbs will be firm.
> If that spring is not spent,
> the Nine Apertures will connect.
> You can then reach the limits of Heaven and Earth,
> and encompass the Four Seas.

In a later stratum, this text would claim meditation as a way of knowledge:

7:21 (GZ 49:20, c0305).

> To ponder deeply 思索 produces wisdom,
> idleness and carelessness produce worry.
> Cruelty and arrogance produce resentment,
> sorrow and trouble produce illness,
>   and when illness becomes acute, you die.
> If you meditate but do not put it aside,
> you will be ill within and weak without.
> Do not make plans in advance,
> or your vitality will lose its dwelling.
> In eating, it is best not to be full;
> and in meditating, it is best not to go all the way.
> Do it with moderation,
> and the thing will come to pass of itself.

This sort of claim seems to have produced a final break in the Analects school, between intuitive and acquired knowledge:

7:22 (LY 15:31, c0300). The Master said, I once went all day without eating, and all night without sleeping, in order to meditate [sź 思 "think"]. I gained nothing. It is not as good as studying [sywé 學 "reading texts"].

Mencius in his early days had practiced meditation, probably under Lǎudž's master Shāng Rúng. During his first visit to Chí, in c0332, he made contact with the Chí meditation group, and from them picked up the term "boundless" (hàu-rán 浩然), which does not occur in the Lǔ text DDJ. The Analects school's rejection of meditation had not yet occurred, and for Mencius, as for Yén Hwéi before him, meditation usefully sharpened the mind. It also, as the early Nèi Yè said, could be "stored within," to confer a sort of personal peace.

This comes out in a private conversation of c0316:

7:23 (MC 2A2a, excerpt, c0316).

>. . . I venture to ask wherein the Master is superior [to Gàudž].
>
>I know words. I am good at nourishing my boundless 浩然 breath.
>
>I venture to ask, what is the boundless breath?
>
>It is difficult to say. As breath, it is very great and very firm. If it is nourished straightforwardly and is not injured, it fills up all between Heaven and Earth. As breath, it accompanies righteousness 義 and the Way 道 ; without these, it is starved. It is something that arises when righteousness accumulates; it is not something one can capture with a sudden rush of righteousness. If one's conduct produces discontent in the heart, then it will starve. It was for this reason that I said that Gàudž has never understood righteousness – it is because he makes it external. There must be some effort toward it, but do not correct it. Let the heart not forget it, but do not try to help it grow. Do not be like the man of Sùng.
>
>In Sùng, there was a man who was worried that his rice plants were not growing, so he pulled them longer. After doing this for a long time, he came home and said to his people, I am really tired out today; I have been helping the rice plants to grow. His son hurried out to look, and the rice plants were all withered . . .

Mencius's concluding joke would nicely illustrate the practical advice given in GZ 49:20 (#**7:21**): don't push too hard.

By the end of the 04th century, there appeared another meditation group. Its leader carried a staff topped by a twelve-sided jade finial, on which was engraved the above text describing stages of breath control:

7:24 (Jade inscription text "行氣," c0310). "Circulating the Breath"

>Once it is intaken, let it accumulate 畜
>Once it has accumulated, let it spread 神[17]
>Once it has spread, let it descend 下
>Once it has descended, let it stabilize 定

---

[17]Reading shv́n 神 "spirit" as shv̄n 伸 "spread out."

> Once it has stabilized, let it be firm 固
> Once it has become firm, let it grow 明[18]
> Once it has grown, let it mature 長
> Once it has matured, let it return 復
> Once it has returned, let it ascend to Heaven 天
>
> Heaven: its roots are on high 上
> Earth: its roots are below 下
> When this is followed, one lives 生
> When it is violated, one dies 死

Meditation is here said to assure a long life for the practitioner. Letting the breath fill Heaven (as in #**7:13**) is the key to this result. The later Mencians imagined Mencius as making an equally comprehensive mystical statement:

7:25 (MC 7A4, excerpt, c0268). All things are complete in me . . .

Mencius died in c0303, before the Analects break with meditation. But that break caused problems for his successors. They added a section to the MC 2A2 conversation, to deal with it. The questioner sets a trap for him . . .

7:26 (MC 2A2b, excerpt, c0297). Long ago, I heard that Dž-syà, Dž-yóu, and Dž-jāng each had one aspect of the Sage, while Rǎn Nyóu, Mǐndž, and Yén Ywǣn had all of him in miniature. I venture to ask, with which are you more comfortable?

[He said] We will let that one go.

. . . which he simply dodges. Yén Hwéi had become an undiscussable topic.

We are here witnessing a major intellectual realignment. The DDJ had taken over the Confucian terms Dàu and Dv́. The Analects school then renounced meditation, which meanwhile had been taken up by the Gwǎndž people in Chí. The Mencians were caught in this crossfire of shifting orthodoxies.

For his part, the Nèi Yè author moved in the opposite direction, combining his Way with Confucian elements: the Shr̄ poems and ritual and music.

7:27 (GZ 49:22, excerpt, c0305).
> The vitality of all human beings
> must be based on tranquility 平正.
> And the way you lose it
> will always be happiness and anger, sorrow and worry.
> And so, to stop anger, nothing is as good as the Shr̄,
>   to banish sorrow, nothing is as good as Music,
>   to set a limit to Music, nothing is as good as Ritual,
>   to conserve Ritual, nothing is as good as respect . . .

---

[18]Reading míng 明 "bright" [an attribute of spirits] as mv́ng 萌 "sprout."

The 03rd Century

Magic. In India, feats of magic such as levitation were ascribed to the Buddha, at first only in a symbolic sense:

> **7:28** (MPnS 1:33-34, mid 05c). But the Blessed One went on to the river. At that time, the River Ganges was brimful and overflowing, and wishing to cross to the opposite bank, some began to seek for boats, some for rafts of wood, while some made rafts of basket-work. Then the Blessed One as instantaneously as a strong man would stretch forth his arm, or draw it back again when he had stretched it forth, vanished from this side of the river, and stood on the further bank with the company of the brethren.
>
> [34] And the Blessed One beheld the people looking for boats and rafts, and as he beheld them he brake forth at that time into this song:
>
>> They who cross the ocean drear
>> Making a solid path across the pools –
>> Whilst the vain world ties its basket rafts –
>> These are the wise, these are the saved indeed![19]

The lesson is that only by exceptional means (the magical crossing of the river), not by conventional ones such as this-worldly boats or rafts, can one be saved.

Protection from dangers is explicit in the Upanishad texts:

> **7:29** (BrA 3:7, 06c?) . . . He is undecaying, for he is not subject to decay. He has nothing sticking to him, for he does not stick to anything. He is not bound; yet he neither fears nor suffers injury . . .

and also in the Chinese jade inscription which we met earlier:

> **7:30** (Jade Inscription text "行氣," excerpt, c0310).
>
>> When this is followed, one lives 生
>> When it is violated, one dies 死

But the theme is less common on the Chinese side of the mountains. Here is the only instance of invulnerability in the DDJ:

> **7:31** (DDJ 50, excerpt, c0297). We go forth to life, and go in to death. The companions of life are thirteen; the companions of death are thirteen.[20] The danger spots for a man during his lifetime are also thirteen. And why? Because he is trying to get too much out of life.
>
> I have heard it said that for him who is skillful at living: on land, he will never meet a tiger or a rhinoceros; in the army, he will never be harmed by arms and armor. The rhinoceros has nothing to stick his horn into; the tiger has nothing to lay his claws on; the weapon has nothing to stab at. Why is this? Because he has no "death ground."

Here, a medical analogy is used to make a mystical point.

---

[19]The translation is by Rhys Davids.

[20]The vital points are also the vulnerable points. Life contains the risk of death.

A wish to avoid injury was natural enough in these times. Chí Sywæn-wáng, who dismissed his minister Mencius after the Yēn military disaster of 0315, did not abandon war; but he proceeded deliberately, by setting the six Jì-syà philosophers to first work out the theory of the rise and fall of states (page 75). His successor, Mǐn-wáng, was notably more impatient for conquest, and his Chí advisors had all they could do to restrain him. That concern also affected the Lǔ meditation center from which the DDJ was giving advice to the world. This piece acknowledges that the final goal of government is world conquest, but advises that the way to conquer the world is by leaving it alone.

> **7:32** (DDJ 57, excerpt, c0291).
>
>> Govern the state by the regular 正
>> Deploy troops by the unexpected 奇 [21]
>> Capture the world 取天下 by nondoing 無事
>
> How do I know that this is so?
>
>> If Heaven requires many abstinences, the people will be fractious
>> If the commoners use clever devices, there will be confusion
>> If people multiply knowledge, strange things will emerge
>
> And thus the Sage says,
>
>> I have no doing, and the people of themselves become rich;
>> I have no actions, and the people of themselves are transformed;
>> I love quiet, and the people of themselves are orderly 正;
>> I desire to not desire, and the people of themselves are simple.

A critic might note that the only advice the text has for conquering other states is based on its doctrine about ruling the state one already possesses.

Despite many warnings, Chí Mǐn-wáng in 0287 prepared to invade Sùng. The aged Lǎudž issued a reminder about a better and milder policy:

> **7:33** (DDJ 66, excerpt, c0287).
>
>> The Sage who would be in front of the people
>>> will take his place behind them;
>> [the one] who would be above the people
>>> will take his place below them.

In 0286, Chí invaded and annexed Sùng. In 0285, much as in 0314, Chí was driven out by a coalition of powers who feared its sudden doubling of territory, and was almost destroyed. The Chí King died in exile, and it was several years before the next King and his generals could expel Yēn from Chí territory.

Lǎudž's successor, his grandson Lǐ Jù 李注, took over the DDJ school at this time, and from this point on, the DDJ no longer has a meditationist basis. Lǐ Jù's first effort was a warning against this sort of rash aggression.

---

[21]There is here an allusion to the basic military terms 正 "frontal attack" and 奇 "flank attack;" see Sūndž 5 (**#4:25**).

Remarkably, the warning is based on three principles of the early Micians: love for others (#**4:4**), frugality (#**4:5-6**), and renunciation of war (#**4:3**):

7:34 (DDJ 67, c0285).

> All the world say my Way is great, but it seems not to be useful.
> Yet it is just because it is great that it seems not to be useful.
> If it were "useful," it would long ago have become small.
> I always have three treasures; I protect and guard them.
>> The first is Kindness,
>> The second is Frugality,
>> The third is Not Daring to Be First in the World.
> I am kind, and thus I can be bold.
> I am frugal, and thus I can be magnanimous.
> I do not dare to be first in the world,
>> and thus I can become Steward of the Sacrificial Vessels.
> If one abandons kindness and yet is bold,
> If one abandons frugality and yet is magnanimous,
> If one abandons humility and yet takes first place,
>> he will die.
> So one who goes to war with kindness will be victorious,
> and one who mounts guard with frugality will be secure.
> Heaven will establish him,
> and with its Kindness will safeguard him.

Responding to the same situation, and perhaps addressing the new Chí ruler (Syāng-wáng, r 0283-0265), the Gwǎndž meditationists started a new text, the Syīn Shù 心術 or Mental Technique, to follow and summarize the old Nèi Yè. The first two paragraphs, no more meditationist than Lǐ Jù's new-style DDJ, are essentially administrative advice:

7:35 (GZ 36:1, c0283). The heart within the body occupies the position of the ruler. The Nine Apertures have their duties, like the assignments of the officials.

> If the heart is set upon the Way,
>> the Nine Apertures will be obedient.
> If likes and desires fill and overflow,
>> the eye will not see colors,
>> the ear will not hear sounds.
> Therefore it is said:
>> If the superior departs from the Way,
>> the inferiors will fail in their tasks.

7:36 (GZ 36:2, c0283).

> Do not run for the horse;
>> let it use its own strength.
> Do not fly for the bird;
>> let it work its own wings.

The third parallels the DDJ 67 position on caution in foreign policy:

> **7:37** (GZ 36:3, c0283).
>
> Do not move ahead of things,
> so as to observe their tendency
> If you move 動, you will lose your position;
> If you are still 靜, you will succeed naturally 自得.

Somewhat later, DDJ entered a protest against increasing state executions:

> **7:38** (DDJ 74, excerpt, c0267). If the people do not fear death, why frighten them with death? If I put the people in constant fear of death, and they still do irregular things, I might then arrest and kill them, but who would dare? There is always the Executioner[22] to kill. Now, to do the killing for the Executioner may be called cutting for the Master Carpenter. And who cuts for the Master Carpenter will rarely but hurt his hand.

The Jwāngdž Primitivists. Governmental severity also got a response from the Jwāngdž Primitivists, JZ 8-10. We have seen how the government's wish for standardization, as expressed by Syẃndž in terms of lǐ . . .

> **7:39** (SZ 19:5b, excerpt, c0276). Ritual trims what is too long, stretches out what is too short, eliminates excess, and remedies deficiencies . . .

. . . was met by the Primitivists, who accepted even extra fingers as natural:[23]

> **7:40** (JZ 8:2, excerpt, c0275). He who makes Normality 正 his norm 正 does not lose sight of the conditions of his original nature. What is joined is not for him "webbed;" what branches off is not "extra." What is long does not seem excessive; what is short does not seem deficient . . . So what is naturally long is not to be cut; what is naturally short is not to be stretched . . .

The Mencian school did not go that far in opposing the idea of standardization; for them, there were reasonable biological and social norms:

> **7:41** (MC 6A12, excerpt, c0273). Suppose your nameless finger[24] were bent and could not be straightened. It is not an illness, and it is not painful, but if there were someone who could straighten it, you would not think the road to Chín or Chǔ too long to travel, because your finger is not like those of other people . . .

Like Syẃndž's argument for an explicitly artificial social world, in the Human Nature argument with the Mencians, the defense, not of the crane's long legs, but of tumors and other exiguous growths, was hard to maintain over time.

---

[22]司殺者, the One in Charge of Killing, reminiscent of the deity 司命, the One in Charge of Fate [length of life], who is featured in two of the Nine Songs (see p177).

[23]For a fuller sample of the early Primitivist writings, see **#6:48-54.**

[24]"Nameless finger" 無名之指 for the fourth finger is a translation of the Sanskrit term anâmikâ (Zhu **Linguistic** 1-2).

And in the end, the Jwāngdž 8 group agreed. They recast their position:

> **7:42** (JZ 8:1, excerpt, c0273). Joined toes, extra fingers – these come from Nature, but are contrary to Virtue. Growths and tumors – these come from Form, but are contrary to Nature. Excessive practice in Benevolence and Righteousness may be [said to be] as fundamental as the Five Organs, but they are against the Way and Virtue . . .

Such was the sparring back and forth between the rival schools.

This passage from the Jwāngdž mixes magic and ordinary caution:

> **7:43** (JZ 17:1f, excerpt, c0270). A man of perfect virtue 德: fire cannot burn him, water cannot drown him, cold and heat cannot harm him, birds and beasts cannot injure him. Not that he makes light of these things, but that he distinguishes between safety and danger, is at peace with fortune or misfortune, and is careful about comings and goings – nothing can harm him.

Deep Reality. Here magic is rejected for something else. Lyèdž is distracted from his studies with his master Húdž by a shaman with magical powers, and winds up taking refuge in not making distinctions:

> **7:44** (JZ 7:5, excerpt, c0253). In Jv`ng there was a shaman named Jì Syén, who could foretell the life or death of men, the survival or extinction of states, fortune or disaster, long life or short, down to year, month, week and day, as though he were divine. When the people of Jv`ng saw him, they would run to get out of his way. Lyèdž went to see him and his mind was intoxicated. Coming back, he reported to Húdž, I used to think that the Master's way was the last word. But now there is another . . .
>
> Húdž said, I gave you the outline, but not the substance. You think you have gotten the Way? . . . Try bringing him, and showing me to him.
>
> Next day, Lyèdž brought him to see Húdž. When they had gone out, he said to Lyèdž, Alas, your master is dying; he cannot recover; he will not last a week. I saw something very strange, like wet ashes. Lyèdž went back, weeping and drenching his collar with his tears, and reported this to Húdž. Húdž said, Just now I appeared to him with the Pattern of Earth – still and silent, nothing moving, nothing standing up. He probably saw in me the Workings of Virtue Closed Off. Try coming again with him.
>
> Next day, he brought him again to see Húdž. When they had gone out, he said to Lyèdž, It is fortunate that your master has encountered me. He will get well; he is fully alive. I have seen signs of his revival. Lyèdž went in, and reported this to Húdž. Húdž said, Just now I showed him Heaven and Earth, without name or substance, but with the bodily mechanism working from the heels.[25] He has probably seen the Working of the Good. Try coming again with him.

---

[25] A special kind of breathing is said to come "from the heels."

Next day, he brought him again to see Húdž. When they had gone out, he said to Lyèdž, Your master is unstable; I cannot examine him. Let him become stable, and I will examine him again. Lyèdž went in, and reported to Húdž. Húdž said, I showed him the Great Void Without Distinctions. He probably saw the Working of the Balanced Breaths. Where swirling waves gather, there is an abyss. Where still waters gather, there is an abyss. Where running waters gather, there is an abyss. The abyss has nine names,[26] and these are three of them. Try coming again with him.

The next day he brought him again to see Húdž, but before he had taken his place [as a guest], he broke and ran. Húdž said, Pursue him. Lyèdž did pursue him, but could not catch up with him. He returned and reported to Húdž, saying, He is vanished, he is gone; I couldn't catch up with him. Húdž said, Just now I showed him the Ancestor Who Was Before Anything Existed. I appeared to him empty[27] and compliant, not knowing Who or What, at once indistinct and fluid. Therefore he fled.

After this, Lyèdž considered that he had not yet even begun to study. So he went back home, and for three years did not leave his house. He did the cooking for his wife; he fed the pigs as though he were feeding people. He did not prefer one thing over another; from "fine carving" he reverted to "plain material." He took his place like a mere clod of earth. Amid confusion, he was secure. And in this Oneness he ended his days.

So Lyèdž ends, not in study of another, but in isolation and self-concentration. He singlemindedly pursues nondiscrimination. The highest art is to use no art, but simply to "take one's place" among things.

Survival. Of comparable importance, in dangerous times, was the question of how not to get killed before one's time. Against the sword, as we have seen, magic was invoked, but more to the taste of the Jwāngdž people was avoidance through inconspicuousness, like a useless tree. Consider (says a tree criticized by a carpenter as useless) what happens to the *useful* trees . . .

> **7:45** (JZ 4:4b, excerpt, c0267) . . . As soon as their fruit is ripe, they are torn apart and abused. Their big limbs are torn off, their little limbs are pulled every whichway. Their usefulness makes their life bitter, and so they don't get to complete their Heaven-allotted years, but perish midway.

The Mencians agreed that an *allotted* lifespan is not a *guaranteed* lifespan:

> **7:46** (MC 7A2, c0269). Mencius said, There is nothing that is not fated, but one accepts only what is a proper fate. Thus those who understand Fate do not stand under a tottering wall. Those who die for their principles (道) have met a proper fate, but to die in fetters is not a proper fate.

Courage is appropriate to the gentleman, but not recklessness.

---

[26]Ywæn 淵 "abyss" is also the alternate personal name of Yén Hwéi.

[27]Again the quality "empty" (here syw̄ 虛), associated with Yén Hwéi in **#7:14**.

Government service imperiled one's chance of living out one's allotted span. Hence the Jwāngdž stories about leaving office to care for one's health:

7:47 (JZ 28:1, excerpt, c0248). Yáu wanted to hand over the world to Syŭ Yóu, but Syŭ Yóu would not accept it. He then tried to hand it over to Dž-jōu Jr̄-fŭ, but Dž-jōu Jr̄-fŭ said, To make me the Son of Heaven, that would be all right. But just now I have a painful disease, and I am on the point of putting it in order; I don't have time to order the world . . .

The archetypical Jwāngdž anti-service statement is also the shortest one:

7:48 (JZ 3:4, c0270). The swamp pheasant only gets a peck of food every ten paces, or a sip of water every hundred paces, but it does not want to be more lavishly provided for in a cage. Even if it were treated like a king, its spirit would not think well of it.

This is probably the central cry for freedom in all of Chinese literature.

The Useless Tree. It was not enough to opt out; one had to avoid *invitations* to office, since refusing invitations gave offense, and offense was risky. Some thus sought to keep from being noticed. Their parable was the Useless Tree:

7:49 (JZ 4:5a, c0268). Dž-chí of Nán-bwó was wandering near the Hill of Shāng, and there he saw a great tree, different from all the others; a thousand four-horse chariots could have sheltered in its shade. Dž-chí said, What manner of tree is this? It must be extraordinarily useful. But when he looked up at the small branches, they were too bent and twisted for roof beams or rafters, and when he looked down at the great trunk, it was too gnarled and knotty for coffins or caskets. He tasted a leaf, and his mouth was burned and sore; he sniffed it, and it was enough to make a man drunk for three days. Dž-chí said, After all, the tree is useless, and that is why it has grown so large.

Ah! The Spiritual Man for just this reason seeks to be useless too.

Lowliness is the only safety. The less you have, the less can be taken from you.

Methodological Moment. The book called Jwāngdž often mentions Jwāng Jōu 莊周, or Jwāngdž 莊子, "Master Jwāng." This does not mean that Jwāng Jōu wrote the book; on the contrary, it is not Warring States style for people to tell stories about themselves in the third person. Worse, some stories portray Jwāng Jōu as deluded or imperceptive. Not only did Jwāng Jōu not write these stories, neither did his friends or followers. But then what can we learn about him from these stories? Might he have written some of the nonstory material? We cannot reach an answer to that within the limits of this page and the next, . . . and so this Methodological Moment must be abandoned before it starts.[28]

---

[28]But data relevant to authorship will be along presently. **Methodological Moral:** Humanistic research needs acquaintance with the data, and acquaintance needs time.

What, for example, were Jwāng Jōu's ideas? We may start by looking at passages critical of him, which show him as *not* understanding some essential philosophical point:

7:50 (JZ 2:6, c0255). Once Jwāng Jōu was dreaming he was a butterfly, happily fluttering around as a butterfly, completely satisfied, and not knowing he was Jōu. Suddenly he awoke, and there he was: unmistakably Jōu. And he could not tell if he was Jōu dreaming he was a butterfly, or a butterfly dreaming he was Jōu. But between Jōu and a butterfly, there must be *some* distinction. This we call the Transformation of Things.

This is philosophically suggestive, but *in the story,* Jwāngdž is confused: his idea of himself does not include both his waking self and his dreaming self.

7:51 (JZ 20:8, c0256). Jwāng Jōu was wandering in Dyāu-líng Park, when he spied a magpie flying from the south; its wings were seven span broad, its eyes more than an inch around. It brushed against Jōu's forehead and settled in a chestnut grove. Jwāng Jōu said, What kind of bird is this? Its wings are huge but they don't carry it away; its eyes are big, but they don't see. He hitched up the skirt of his robe, strode forward, and took aim with his crossbow. Then he saw a cicada; it had found a nice bit of shade and had forgotten itself. A mantis stretched its arms to seize it; seeing a chance of gain, it had forgotten its form. The strange bird had come up and spied an opportunity; seeing the opportunity, it had forgotten its own reality. Jwāng Jōu was distressed and said, Alas! Things are so hostile, each making trouble for the next. He shouldered his crossbow, turned, and ran. The gamekeeper pursued him, cursing at him.

Jwāng Jōu got home, and for three months did not see anyone. Lìn Jyw̄ went up and asked him, Why has the Master not seen anyone for so long? Jwāng Jōu said, I guarded my form and forgot my self; I watched the turbid stream and lost the clear abyss. I heard from my master, "When you go to a place, follow its customs." Now, I wandered in Dyāu-líng and forgot my self; the strange magpie brushed against my forehead and wandered into the chestnut grove, forgetting *its* reality. The gamekeeper took me for a poacher. This is why I have not seen anyone.

He was confused between his small hunting agenda and his larger life. We may notice that in this story, as in few stories in the book, Jwāngdž has disciples.

Death. Next comes a more cosmic confusion:

7:52 (JZ 18:4, c0254). Jwāngdž went to Chǔ, and saw an empty skull. bleached but preserving its shape. He poked at it with his horsewhip, and asked, Did the Master in seeking life forget reason, and so come to this? Were you in charge of affairs in some doomed state, suffered execution, and so came to this? Did you do some evil deed, and ashamed to leave your father and mother, your wife and children, an ill reputation, come to this? Did you encounter freezing and starvation, and so come to this? Did the course of the seasons bring you to this?

At this point he ceased speaking. He pulled the skull over, and resting his head on it, he went to sleep.

In the middle of the night, the skull appeared to him in a dream, and said, You talk like some sophist. Everything you say reflects the cares of the living. The dead have none of these. Do you want to hear about the pleasures of the dead? Jwāngdž said, Yes. The skull said, The dead have no ruler above, and no subjects below. They also do not have the tasks of the four seasons, but have Heaven and Earth for their seasonal cycle. Not even the happiness of a King, facing south and ruling, could exceed it.

Jwāngdž did not believe him. He said, If I could have the Arbiter of Fate again give you life and form, make you bone and flesh, return you to your father and mother, your wife and children, your native village and your friends, would you want it? The skull opened its eyes and wrinkled its brow, and said, How could I ever cast away the happiness of a King facing south and once again take on the toils of human existence?

With his conventional view of life and death, Jwāngdž can understand only life.

But in this piece on death, someone else holds the conventional view:

7:53 (JZ 18:2, c0250). Jwāngdž's wife had died. Hwèidž went to mourn for her. Jwāngdž was just then sitting with his legs stretched out, beating on a bowl and singing. Hwèidž said, You lived with her; you raised children with her; you grew old in body along with her. It's bad enough that when she dies you don't weep for her. Isn't it a little too much to beat on a bowl and sing?

Jwāngdž replied, Not so. To be sure, when she had just died, how could I but feel distressed? But then I thought back to how at the beginning she had no life, and not only had no life but had no form, and not only had no form but had no spirit. Then there was a change, and she had spirit. The spirit changed, and she had form. The form changed, and she had life. Now she has changed again, and come to die. This is just like the seasonal progression of spring, summer, autumn, and winter. She has become weary, and for a moment has gone to rest in some great room. Were I to follow noisily after her with weeping, she herself would think I did not understand the ways of fate. Therefore I stopped.

Jwāngdž here sees life as part of something larger.

Methodological Recap. We have now seen Jwāngdž portrayed either as not understanding the larger picture, or as expounding it to someone else. When friends and enemies agree, it is possible that we have a workable result, and that this is the key Jwāngdž issue. We may then adopt it as a hypothesis that Jwāngdž's characteristic trait is *the larger view*, an understanding which he himself may have reached only after some time, or after previous confusion, or more likely, which others (his opponents in the text) held in a different form.

The large view is the basis of what we may call philosophical resignation. Death calls on people for whatever philosophical resignation they may possess. Some of the most touching passages in the Jwāngdž deal with just this theme. They do not all mention Jwāng Jōu, but they are compatible with the general tone of his thought, as far as that can now be isolated from the rest of the book. They may then belong to, or be consistent with, "his" part of the book.

Here is a gentle one:

> **7:54** (JZ 2:4, excerpt, c0245) . . . How do I know that loving life is not a delusion? How do I know that hating death is like losing one's way in youth and not knowing how to get back? Lady Lì was the daughter of the Border Warden of Aì. When Jìn first obtained her, she wept until the tears soaked her robe. But when she came to the King's place, shared the King's couch, and ate dainty foods, she came to regret that she had wept. How do I know that the dead do not regret having earlier longed for life?

And here is a more fantastic and lyrical one:

> **7:55** (JZ 6:3a, c0273). Dž-sž, Dž-yẃ, Dž-lí, and Dž-láı were talking together: Who can regard Nothing as the head, Life the back, and Death the rump; who understands that life and death, survival and extinction, are a single body? I will be his friend. The four looked at each other and laughed.[29] There was no discord in their hearts, and they became friends.
>
> Presently, Dž-yẃ fell ill. Dž-sž went to inquire about him. He said, Mighty indeed in the Creator; he is making me all crooked! My back sticks up like a hunchback, my five organs are on top, my jaw is hidden in my navel, my shoulders are higher than my neck, and my hair grows up toward the sky. His vital forces were all disordered, yet his heart was unconcerned. He dragged himself over to look at himself in the well, and said, Alas! the Creator is certainly making me all crooked!
>
> Dž-sž said, Do you hate it? Dž-yẃ said, No; what should I hate? In a little while, he will transform my left shoulder into a rooster, and with it I will be able to mark the hours of night. In a little while, he will transform my right shoulder into a crossbow, and with it I will be able to get an owl to roast. In a little while, he will transform my buttocks into wheels, and my spirit into a horse, and I will be able to ride around in it, how will I have any more need of a chariot?
>
> Getting is for a season, and losing is a matter of compliance. If one accepts the season, and abides in compliance, sorrow and joy have no place to enter in. This is what the ancients called being freed from bonds. One cannot free oneself: things have their knots; but things have never been able to defeat Heaven. So what should I hate?

Change is inevitable, emotions are futile, and the best course for the individual is to accept what cannot be otherwise. This too amounts to the large view.

---

[29]This is the laugh of philosophical recognition; it is often heard in Dàuist literature.

Hwèıdž. Jwāngdž is frequently paired with Hwèıdž, who was found by the authors of part of the text to be a suitable foil for the values they wanted to express through Jwāngdž. Hwèıdž or Hwèı Shī 惠施 was a real enough person. He seems to have served Ngwèı Syāng-wáng at the end of the 04c and into the early 03c. He was a student of rhetoric; several paradoxes are associated with him. One is called "hard and white" (the problem of nonexclusive attributes).[30] In Jwāngdž stories, Hwèıdž represents that artificial logic, or sometimes the common sense of the conventional man. Here is a story about large and small:

> **7:56** (JZ 1:6, excerpt, c0240). Hwèıdž said to Jwāngdž, The King of Ngwèı gave me some seeds of a great gourd. I planted them, and they grew a gourd big enough to hold five stone.[31] I filled it up, but it was so heavy I couldn't lift it. If I had split it to make dippers, they would have been too big to dip into anything. It's not that it wasn't fantastically big, but I figured that it was useless, and so I broke it up.
>
> Jwāngdž said, Your Excellency is certainly ineffective in using big things . . .[32] Now, you had a five-stone gourd. Why didn't you make it a great barge, and go floating around the rivers and lakes, instead of worrying that it was too big to dip into anything? Your Excellency still has a tangled mind.

And here is a story about other realms; in this case, other species. Hwèıdž takes a view of knowledge which is sometimes encountered in our own time:

> **7:57** (JZ 17:7, c0247). Jwāngdž and Hwèıdž were wandering above the weir on the Háu. Jwāngdž said, The minnows go wandering about at their ease – this is what fish like. Hwèıdž said, You are not a fish; how do you know what fish like? Jwāngdž said, You are not me; how do you know that I don't know what fish like? Hwèıdž said, I am not you, and I certainly don't know you. You are not a fish, and so the proof that you don't know what fish like is complete.
>
> Jwāngdž said, Let's go back to the beginning. You asked me *how* I knew what fish like, so you already knew *that* I knew it when you asked. As for *how* I knew it – I knew it by being here above the Háu.

This is a plea for intuition instead of intellection, and for the possibility of empathy and feeling between individuals. It can also be seen as an answer to **#7:50**, the butterfly story, where Jwāng Jōu *did not understand* the other realm. In this story, he does; it is now Hwèıdž who represents the less intuitive view.[33]

---

[30]This problem was discussed by the Mician logicians; see Graham **Disputers** 84.

[31]In weight of liquid; the dried gourd was used as a container.

[32]At this point Jwāngdž tells the story of the silk-washing formula; **#2:57**.

[33]The piece is very witty. Hwèıdž's question ("*How* do you know") implies that Jwāngdž *does* know, and merely inquires as to his *means* of knowing. Further, the adverb in the question is literally "*From where* do you know" 安知, and it is answered by another adverb of place from which, "*from being here on the Háu.*" See Brooks **Yēn**.

A reader might feel that this plea for emotion is inconsistent with Jwāngdž's suppression of his emotions at the time of his wife's death (#**7:53**). Somebody apparently noticed that, and added this piece to the text by way of explanation:

7:58 (JZ 5:6, c0247). Hwèìdž asked Jwāngdž, Can a man really be without emotions? Jwāngdž said, He can. Hwèìdž said, A man, and yet he has no emotions – how can one call him a man? Jwāngdž said, The Way gave him an appearance, Heaven gave him form, how can you not call him a man? Hwèìdž said, Given that we call him a man, how can he not have emotions?

　　Jwāngdž said, That is not what I mean by emotions. What I call having no emotions is when a man does not let his loving and hating do harm to him internally, but constantly follows what is natural and does not try to increase his life. Hwèìdž said, If he does not try to increase his life, how will he be able to maintain his self? Jwāngdž said, The Way gave him an appearance, Heaven gave him form, and he does not let his loving and hating do harm to him internally. But now you are treating your own spirit as external, you are wearying your essence. You lean on a tree and sing, you droop on your desk and doze. Heaven picked out your form, but you still sing of "hard and white."

It is Hwèìdž who is disconnected from his inner being, and clutters his mind up (#**7:56**) with logical quibbles. The way to handle your emotions is to go ahead and have them, but not to let them run around loose inside and cause damage.[34]

　　The famous sophist Gūngsūn Lúng 公孫龍, who is traditionally associated with logical problems such as the "white horse" or substance and attribute, appears in person in this next piece. He complains to Prince Móu of Ngwèi that for all his skill in the art of rhetoric and in Confucian philosophy, he is baffled by the words of Jwāngdž. Small wonder. In the course of answering him, Prince Móu tells this story:

7:59 (JZ 17:4, excerpt, c0244) Have you alone not heard of the frog in the collapsed well? He said to the Turtle of the Eastern Sea, "How happy I am! I hop around the well railing, or I go back and rest in a place where a tile has fallen out. When I go in the water, it supports me under my armpits and my chin; when I slide in the mud, it covers my feet and reaches my ankles. I look at the crabs and tadpoles, and none is my equal. To have charge of a whole pool of water; to command all the joys of a collapsed well: this is the ultimate! Why does not Your Excellency come some time and see?"

This invitation is accepted, with hilarious results:

---

[34]Jwāngdž in #**7:57** had defended the idea that we can know other entities; here, he defines how our emotions should be kept from interfering with what we do. We may observe that these would make useful guidelines for the modern historical investigator. A certain intellectual tact is inherent in some of the sayings attributed to "Jwāngdž."

The Turtle of the Eastern Sea's left foot was not yet in before his right thigh had become stuck. At that, he worked himself loose, withdrew, and told about the Sea: "A thousand leagues would not measure its size; a thousand fathoms would not compass its depth. In the time of Yw̌ there were floods nine years out of ten, but the waters never rose; in the time of Tāng there were droughts seven years in eight, but the distance between its shores did not grow less. Never to alter or shift, whether for an instant or an age; never to advance or recede, whether the inflow is great or small – this is the great delight of the Eastern Sea!"

When the frog in the collapsed well heard this, he was thunderstruck with surprise, bewildered and at a loss.[35]

The master metaphor for largeness occurs earlier in that chapter. It describes the Autumn Flood and the Sea, and refers in passing to the previous story:

7:60 (JZ 17:1a, excerpt, c0270). The time of the autumn floods had come. The hundred streams poured into the River. Its current swelled so much that, from one bank to the other, you could not tell a horse from an ox. At this the Lord of the River greatly delighted, thinking that the beauty of the world was all his. Following the current, he journeyed east until he came to the Northern Sea. Look as he would to eastward, he could see no end to the waters. The Lord of the River began to wag his head, and seeing how great the waters were, he looked afar off at Rwò, the God of Ocean, and said with a sigh, The vulgar saying has it, "He who is broadly learned in the Way thinks none equal to himself." That describes me. In the past, I heard men belittling the learning of Confucius and making light of the righteousness of Bwó-yí. At first I did not believe them, but now I have beheld your endlessness. If I hadn't come to your gate, I would have been in danger. I would forever have been laughed at by the Masters of the Great Method 大方之家.

Rwò of the Northern Sea said, With a frog in a well, you can't speak of the ocean; he is limited by his dwelling. With a summer insect, you can't speak of ice; he is confined to a season. With a pedantic scholar, you can't discuss the Way; he is bound by his doctrines. Now you have emerged from your banks and seen the Great Sea, so you realize your insignificance. You can now be told about the Great Principle 大理 . . .

The Inner Chapters of the Jwāngdž (JZ 1-7) are traditionally supposed to be the real Jwāng Jōu. And indeed, a number of Jwāngdž stories are to be found there. But for some readers, JZ 17 is the heart of the matter.

---

[35]The "frog in the well" is a common Indian metaphor for one who knows things only on a small scale, and is unaware of anything larger. Maitri Upanishad 1:4 "Be pleased to deliver me; in this cycle of existence I am like a frog in a waterless well." (Hume **Thirteen** 414). Giles **Chuang** 159 remarks that the image "is commonly used in Bengali colloquial;" compare Boyer **Get**, a modern Indian success manual

Methodological Moment. Of these two pieces, it might seem that the Frog story in JZ 17:4 is earlier, and that JZ 17:1, which takes for granted a familiarity with that story, is later. But this reasonable inference does not work. It was not the custom in this period for living persons to be named in stories, and 17:1 does not mention Jwāngdž, whereas 17:4 does. Then JZ 17:4 belongs to a later stratum than 17:1. If (as some suspect) Jwāngdž himself wrote 17:1, then the story must have been generally current in his time, and 17:4 simply retells it for its own purposes. Moral: Our first impression may sometimes need more work. In particular, we may sometimes need more material, to solve a given problem, than happens to be directly available in the text in question.

------·•••·------

Going With the Flow. However appealingly it is presented, the worldview that seems to have been most closely associated with Jwāng Jōu is essentially one of philosophical resignation in the face of higher power, whether that power is Heaven, the cycle of life and death, or the great ocean which takes to itself the smaller streams. It amounts to relinquishing any personal purpose. There is also a second strand in the book "Jwāngdž" which does not involve Jwāng Jōu. It recommends a more activist stance. The advice of these passages is to accept limitations on action, but not to give up altogether on what it is that one wants to *achieve* by action.

The idea of cautious ambition has parallels in the meditation literature, or (with the DDJ) in the statecraft literature which had earlier roots in meditation:

7:61 (GZ 36:15, excerpt, c0279).

> And so one must understand
>> the word that need not be not spoken 不言之言,
>> the deed that need not be done 無爲之事

7:62 (DDJ 73b, excerpt, c0270).

> The Way of Heaven:
>> not to contend, but to be good at winning,
>> not to speak, but to be good at getting answers . . .

7:63 (DDJ 76, excerpt, 0262).

> The strong and mighty will be put low,
> The soft and weak will be put high.

This is a philosophy of noncontention: not trying to dominate a situation, but to guide it from a position of weakness. It has a parallel in some Jwāngdž stories which counsel reticence, but also envision a purpose. The typical story of this type does not feature Jwāng Jōu, but rather Confucius, or various rulers and court officers. The element of mental concentration is often prominent, and is used to acquire the art of fitting in with the immediate situation. "Confucius," advising Yén Hwéi in **#5:94**, had told him to go along with the ruler's wishes, but obviously in the hope of later having a chance to influence him.

Some such purpose is usually visible in the typical Jwāngdž "skill story." One example, also featuring Confucius and Yén Hwéı (here, Yén Ywæn) is:

7:64 (JZ 19:4a, c0258). Yén Ywæn asked Jùng-ní, I once crossed over at Goblet Deep, and the ferryman handled the boat like a god. I asked him, Can boat handling be learned? He said, It can. A good swimmer will soon be able to do it. As for one who dives below the surface, he may never have seen a boat but will immediately manage it. I asked further of him, but he wouldn't tell me. May I venture to ask what he meant?

Jùng-ní said, "A good swimmer will soon be able to do it" – that means he has forgotten the water. "As for one who dives below the surface, he may never have seen a boat, but will immediately manage it" – that is because he sees the deep as dry land; he sees a boat overturning as a carriage being upset. Overturnings and upsettings might be occurring everywhere in front of him, but they could not enter his [mental] abode. Where could he go that he would not be at his ease?

He is at home in the medium, and thus remains unperturbed. So also:

7:65 (JZ 20:3, c0263). Běıgūng Shv̀ was going to collect taxes for Wèı Líng-gūng in order to make a set of bells. He made a platform outside the gate of the outer wall, and in three months the bells were completed, both upper and lower tiers. Prince Chìng-jı̀ gave him audience, and asked, What art do you employ? Běıgūng Shv̀ answered, In the midst of the Oneness, I would not dare employ anything. But Shv̀ has heard, "When you are done carving and polishing, go back to the simple." Dull, I am without understanding; placid; I am without uncertainty. Mysteriously, wonderfully, I bid farewell to what goes, and welcome what comes: what comes cannot be prevented, what goes cannot be stopped. I follow the violent, I go with the devious, I let them reach what end they will. And so from morning to evening I collect taxes and levies, without meeting the slightest resistance. How much less one who was on the Great Path!

This is indebted not only to the DDJ but to the Gwǎndž (#**7:21**). Even the chore of collecting taxes will benefit from a reticent, indeed, a compliant, approach. Would not a ruler benefit still more? That is the tacit question behind the story. In this next piece, that question is asked directly:

7:66 (JZ 7:3, excerpt, c0258). Tyēn Gv̄n wandered by Yīn Mountain. On the bank of the Lyáu River, he met a Nameless Man, and asked him, I beg to ask about ruling the world. The Nameless Man said, Begone! You are a low fellow! How inappropriate this question is! I am just about to accompany the Creator, and when *that* gets boring . . . How dare you disturb my mind with talk of putting the world in order?

He asked again. The Nameless Man said, Wander your mind in the simple, blend your breath with the vast, follow things as they naturally are, do not intrude the personal – and *then* the world will be in order.

That is, ruling is of its nature a mundane matter, of no interest to a higher being. But if one *will* rule, imitating the detachment of the higher being is best.

To "follow things as they are" is the theme of many of these "skill" stories. Here is the most famous of them:

7:67 (JZ 3:2, c0263). Cook Dīng was cutting an ox for Lord Wv́n-hwèi. The reach of his arm, the shift of his shoulder, the tread of his foot, the lean of his knee – so warily, so guidingly, he plied his knife so slidingly; not a note was out of tune. It could have been a "Mulberry Grove" dance; it would have suited a "Boar's Head" performance. Lord Wv́n-hwèi said, Excellent! Good indeed! Can skill really attain to such perfection?

Cook Dīng sheathed his knife and replied, What your servant loves is the Way; it goes beyond mere skill. When your servant first began cutting up oxen, everything he saw was an ox. After three years, he no longer saw a whole ox. And at the present time, your servant encounters the ox with his whole spirit, he does not observe it with his eyes at all. Where the senses reach their limit, the spirit carries on as it will, in accord with natural logic: along the large contours, through the large openings, following the line of least resistance.

The smallest bit of tendon I have never attempted; much less any solid bone. A good cook changes his knife yearly; he cuts. An ordinary cook changes his knife monthly; he hacks. Your servant's knife is going on for nineteen years, and it has cut up thousands of oxen, but the edge of the blade is as sharp as if it were fresh from the whetstone. At the joints there is always some space, and the edge of the blade has no thickness. If one inserts what has no thickness into what has some space, ever so carefully, there will always be enough room for the moving blade. It is for this reason that, after nineteen years, the edge of the blade is as sharp as if it were fresh from the whetstone.

Even so, when I come to a tight place, I see the difficulty. I proceed carefully. My gaze is fixed, my motions are slow, I move the knife ever so slightly – and then, all at once, it is cut through, like earth crumbling to the ground. I withdraw my knife and stand erect. I look all around me; I linger there until I am fully satisfied. And then I put my knife in good order, and store it away.

Lord Wv́n-hwèi said, Good! I have heard this Cook Dīng's words and I have learned from them how to care for my own life.

In Jwāngdž, the Indianate meditation tradition has been agreeably Sinicized. His doctrine of caution became the standard Dàuist message for later ages; the second philosophy of China's official class. In this view, the important thing is to avoid opposition, to achieve one's purpose without conflict.

Chí Versus Lǔ. Between these two centers of meditation text production, the DDJ in Lǔ is clearly the ancestor and senior member. Toward that ancestor, the texts coming out of the Gwǎndž meditation circle tend to be indebted, and sometimes even anthological. Even when the DDJ under Lǐ Jù's leadership dropped all mention of meditation, the Gwǎndž people continued, in their statecraft mode, to parallel the current DDJ offerings.

In GZ 38 (Báι Syīn 白心 or "Pure Heart"), the last Gwǎndž meditation text, the parallels continued, but the Báι Syīn had a Legalist tinge, already visible in GZ 36. Thus, in contrast to this comment from the DDJ:

> **7:68** (DDJ 77, excerpt, c0259). The Way of Heaven is to diminish those with excess to supply those with scarcity. The Way of Man is different; it takes from those with scarcity to augment those with excess.

we have this less sentimental idea from the Báι Syīn:

> **7:69** (GZ 38:2, excerpt, c0257) [The Sage] must follow change in making decisions; and understand the times in making allocations. When there is much, he may be generous; then there is little, he must be stringent. Things have their excess, but they also have their insufficiency.

The Báι Syīn was more enthusiastic about the recurrent Jwāngdž power theme of Going with the Flow. Here are two allusions to those stories:

> **7:70** (GZ 38:8, excerpt, c0254).
> They wrote in books what is wrong 惡,[36]
> spoke in words what is superficial 薄

> **7:71** (GZ 38:8, excerpt, c0254). What they could not express by name or word, or embody in form or color, was what they were unable to hand on. Of those who reach the ultimate, their teaching may or may not survive. Therefore it is said,
> Who crosses water in a boat is in harmony with the water 水,[37]
> Who acts rightly toward others is blessed by the spirits 鬼 . . .

When in 0255 Chǔ conquered half of Lǔ, the DDJ was ready with an assurance that after all, a reduced territory is better:

> **7:72** (DDJ 80, c0253). Make the country small 小國, and make its people few 寡民. Let there be mechanical contraptions but they are not used; let it be that the people regard death as a serious matter and do not serve afar. Though there be boats and carts, no one will ride them; though there be arms and armor, no one will array them. Let people again knot cords and use them [instead of writing]. Let them find their food sweet, their clothes fine, their dwellings comfortable, their customs good. Let neighboring villages be within view, and dogs and chickens be heard back and forth, yet the people grow old and die without ever going from one to another.

This is truly pathetic. To Lǔ, a state undergoing conquest and facing extinction, the DDJ has nothing to offer but a celebration of picturesque primitivism.

Counsels of reticence are paltry unless they promise later action. What gives point to all advice of this sort is the element of supernatural power within. Without that magic, the Gospel of Weakness loses most of its charm and force.

---

[36]See #5:106, above.
[37]See #7:64, above.

The Limits of Transcendence. In 0249, when Chŭ took the other half of Lŭ, and Syẃndž exercised his authority as governor of the area, not only the Dàu/Dv́ Jīng enterprise, but the Analects school, the Mician ethicists, and both Mencian groups, ceased to think and write. In the Jwāngdž groups which still remained active, we see a new assertiveness: no longer hiding from the world, but soaring above it. This piece was put at the head of the Jwāngdž text:

> 7:73 (JZ 1:1, excerpt, c0236). In the northern deep there is a fish whose name is the Kūn. The size of the Kūn is I know not how many thousand leagues. It transforms itself into a bird whose name is the Pv́ng. The wing span of the Pv́ng is I know not how many thousand leagues. When it launches into flight, its wings are like clouds draped across the heavens. This bird, when the ocean currents shift, sets out for the southern deep.

It makes a brave show, and no doubt about it. But it must be added, and be it noted to their credit that the Jwāngdž compilers *do* add it, that not everyone, whether in the story or out of it, really believes in this stuff. It continues:

> . . .The cicada and the dove laugh at this; they say, When we rise up and fly toward yonder green elm tree, sometimes we don't make it, but drop back to earth again. What is this about nine myriad leagues to the south?

Here, finally, is Lyèdž (a different Lyèdž than the one we met on page 195, but the Jwāngdž is a very diverse text), displaying his own supernatural powers:

> 7:74 (JZ 1:2, excerpt, c0236). Lyèdž traveled on the wind, perfectly content with himself, and only returned after a week and five days.

Those supernatural powers the author immediately qualifies:

> . . . As far as good fortune went, he had nothing to complain of. But though he was spared the trouble of walking, he still had to depend on *something*. Now, had he mounted the regularities of Heaven and Earth, driven the chariot of Six Breaths, and traveled to the Limitless, on what need he have depended? Therefore it is said, The highest man has no self, the divine man has no achievement, the sagely man has no fame.

No achievement indeed. The doubts of the little birds, and the limitations of Lyèdž the Magician, are ridiculed, but to replace them, we have only a highest man who has no powers of his own, and simply vanishes into the universe.

There is a yearning quality to these animal or human flights of fancy; a reaching beyond the possible into some higher realm where human limits do not apply, and worldly dangers no longer threaten. The imagery was powerful. But the Jwāngdž ends with no more substantial appeal than that of imagery.

At bottom, the meditationist attitude to the hazards of the time was not to dispute the ground with them, but to rise above it all. This has just one defect: it leaves the ground open to those who are prepared to take it over.

And with the ultimate triumph of those stronger spirits, the makers of war and the architects of Empire, we will conclude.

8. The Empire
(0221-0206)

Chín was respected for its military severity. Here, as poetically imagined, are three human sacrifices, waiting at the edge of the tomb of Chín Mù-gūng (r 0659-0621), the most renowned of the Spring and Autumn rulers of Chín:

8:1 (Shr̄ 131, Chín #6, early 04c).

131A   Crisscross fly the yellow birds;
        their nests at last they seek.
        Who did follow Mù the Prince?
        Dzǐgū's son, Yăm Zík,
        no one else but Yăm Zík –
        among a hundred men unique.
            He stood beside the pit
            and trembled as he looked at it;
            Azure Heaven there on high
            only our best will satisfy;
            Could he but be ransomed, ah,
            we'd let a hundred others die.

131B   Crisscross fly the yellow birds;
        and to their nests they throng.
        Who did follow Mù the Prince?
        Dzǐgū's son Jùng Hóng,
        No one else but Jùng Hóng –
        among a hundred, none more strong.
            He stood beside the pit
            and trembled as he looked at it;
            Azure Heaven there on high
            only our best will satisfy;
            Could he but be ransomed, ah,
            we'd let a hundred others die.

131C   Crisscross fly the yellow birds;
        and seek their nests anew.
        Who did follow Mù the Prince?
        Dzǐgū's son, Kām Hǔ,
        no one else but Kām Hǔ –
        a hundred men he could outdo.
            He stood beside the pit
            and trembled as he looked at it;
            Azure Heaven there on high
            only our best will satisfy;
            Could he but be ransomed, ah,
            we'd let a hundred others die.

This appalling ruthlessness was to be one of Chín's assets in the years ahead.

The Chín ruler Hwèi-wáng came to the throne in 0331, took the title King in 0324, and in 0316 annexed Shǔ, doubling the size of Chín. There followed Wǔ-wáng (0310) and Jāu-wáng (306), in whose long reign the *western* part of the Jōu enclave was conquered. In 0255. Syàu-wáng ruled for one year (0250). In 0249, Jwāng-wáng gave Lǔ Bù-wéi 呂不韋 command of the force which conquered the *eastern* part of Jōu, ending the Jōu Kingship, and leaving Chín to replace Jōu. Lǔ Bù-wéi was made a minister. The Lǔ-shr̄ Chūn/Chyōu, compiled under his patronage, was dated to "the 9th year of Chín" (0241), that is, the 9th year of the new dynasty as thus defined. Meanwhile, the next King, the future First Emperor,[1] had come to the throne in 0246.

Lǐ Sz̄ 李斯, the last and most important Chín political theorist, was born in Chǔ, and studied with Syẃndž. He went with Syẃndž to a conference in Jàu in 0250. Attached to the transcript of that conference is this conversation:

8:2 (SZ 15:3, excerpt, c0250). Lǐ Sz̄ asked master Sūn Chīng,[2] Chín for four generations has had only victories. Its troops are the strongest within the Four Seas, its might is felt among the Lords. They have not achieved this by benevolence and righteousness, but by managing affairs according to advantage [byèn 便]. Sūn Chīngdž said, This is not something you understand. What you call advantage is only a disadvantageous sort of advantage. What I call benevolence and righteousness are a highly advantageous sort of advantage. Benevolence and righteousness are how one perfects government. If government is perfected, the people will feel close to their superiors; they will delight in their ruler and think nothing of dying for him. Therefore it is said, Whatever concerns the army or its leadership are minor matters.

Chín for four generations has had only victories, but it has always been anxious lest the world should unite to oppose it. This one may call "the war-making of a decadent age;" there is no fundamental unification. So when Tāng deposed Jyé, it was not that he took advantage of the topography [of the battlefield] of Míng-tyáu; when Wǔ-wáng executed [the evil Shāng ruler] Jòu, it was not that he waited for the morning of the jyǎ/dž day [the first in the 60-day cycle] and only then conquered him; rather, both relied on their previous conduct and prior cultivation; these are what one may call "the warmaking of benevolence and righteousness."

Here was the crux. Can unity be imposed by force, within and without the state, or is it better elicited by a humane government of the Confucian type?

Shortly after this, Lǐ Sz̄ cast his personal vote for the imposed unity option, and went to seek his fortune in Chín.

---

[1]The terms "Empire" and "Emperor" are conventional but misleading. Chín was a large unified state like France, not a dominion of disparate peoples like Persia or Rome.

[2]There is a dialect factor in connection with Syẃndž; his surname Syẃn 荀 was pronounced Sūn 孫 – that is, without medial y – in the Chín/Hàn capital area.

At first, Lǐ Sz̄ served under Lǔ Bù-wéi, another alien in Chín service. Probably in the middle 0240's, a crisis arose for all outsiders:[3] it had been officially suggested that aliens serving in high office were politically unreliable, and should be expelled from the state. To this Lǐ Sz̄ replied in a memorial which was quoted from the Chín archives by the Shř Jì:

> **Shř Jì** 史記 (SJ, c0135-c090). A history of China to the reign of Hàn Wǔ-dì, begun by the Dàuist-trained Grand Astrologer Sz̄mǎ Tán, continued by his Confucian son Sz̄mǎ Chyén, and finished by Imperial command in late Hàn. It draws on diverse sources, from state papers to current legends, along with Tán's theory of Sinitic cultural unity. There are partial translations by Watson and Nienhauser.

8:3 (SJ 87, excerpts from Lǐ Sz̄'s memorial of c0242). Your subject has heard that the officials are debating whether to expel aliens. In my humble opinion, this would be a mistake. In the past, when Mù-gūng was looking for men, he chose Yóu Yẃ from the Rúng people in the west, obtained Bǎilǐ Syī from Wǎn in the east, welcomed Jyěn Shú from Sùng, and summoned Pí Bàu and Gūngsūn Jī from Jìn. These five were not natives of Chín, but Mù-gūng, by employing them, was able to annex twenty states and eventually to become hegemon over the Western Rúng.

Syàu-gūng, by putting in practice the laws of Shāng Yāng, reformed manners and altered customs, so that the population flourished, the state became rich and powerful, the people delighted in their duties, and the other feudal lords were amicable and submissive. He captured the armies of Chǔ and Ngwèi and gained 1000 leagues of territory, and the state to this day remains strong and well governed . . .

There are many objects not produced in Chín that are worthy to be deemed precious, and many gentlemen not native to Chín who are eager to render it loyal service. Now if His Highness expels aliens and thereby aids enemy states, if he depletes his population and thereby increases that of his opponents, he will empty his own state and plant resentment among the other states. If he hopes in this way to free Chín from danger, his hopes will be in vain.

One of Chín's advantages was its backwardness; its path forward was not cluttered with the leavings of obsolete cultures.[4] Lǐ Sz̄ is here arguing that the advantages of being backward should be consciously exploited. The catch is that a backward state needs a forward-looking leader to reach its full potential.

---

[3]The occasion may have been resentment of J̀ng Gwó 鄭國, a hydraulic expert from Hán who had built a drainage canal for Chín. Legend has grown around this and several relevant incidents, making the situation almost unavailable to serious history.

[4]It is often an advantage to be second. England led in many aspects of the Industrial Revolution, but was later overtaken by nations who had built on second generation technology. Trotsky (**History** 26f) calls this the Law of Combined Development.

Lŭ Bù-wéı's book, LSCC 1-12, was finished in 0241. He was disgraced in 0237 and committed suicide on his way to exile in 0235. Chín's success came not from this or any other book, but from steady application of military force. The final conquests were Hán (0230), Ngwèı (0225), Chŭ (0223), Jàu and Yēn (0222), and finally Chí in 0221. The classical period was at an end.

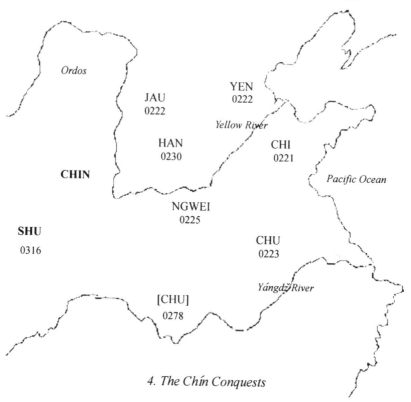

4. The Chín Conquests

The First Emperor

The Question of Feudalism. One might imagine that, on the morning after the last conquest, the Chín leadership would ask, How is all this territory to be governed? The answer had already been decided: central control. As states were conquered, they were governed by men like Official Syĭ (#**5:113**), who had been trained and appointed by Chín, and were responsible only to Chín.

At some point the archaizing party, perhaps a remnant of the Lŭ Bù-wéı group, did suggest refeudalizing:[5] parceling out the land to the ruler's family, and dividing Chín sovereignty itself on the Jōu model.

---

[5] According to **SJ 87**, the proposal was advanced by Chún'yŵ Ywè 淳于越, a man of Chí, who emphasized the security that would result from following ancient practice.

To this, the high legal official Lǐ Sz̄ replied:

8:4 (SJ 6, excerpt, c0221). The sons and younger brothers enfiefed by the Jōu Kings Wv́n and Wǔ were very numerous, but afterward they became estranged, attacking each other just as though they were enemies. The lords even invaded each other's territories, and put each other to death, and the Jōu rulers could neither restrain nor prevent them. Now, all within the Seas is subject to His Highness' divine and undivided rule. Let it all be made into administrative regions and districts, and let those who have earned merit be richly rewarded from revenues; this will be entirely adequate and easily instituted. But let the lands under Heaven have no divergent intentions: this is the way to secure peace. To set up feudal lords would not be suitable.

And the Emperor agreed, in these words:

The First Emperor said, That the world has suffered endlessly from war is because there were Lords and Kings. Thanks to the favor of the Ancestors, the world is now at last stable. To again establish separate states would be merely sowing weapons of war. And if we should then seek to pacify them, how could it but be difficult? The opinion of the Chamberlain 廷尉 is correct.

And so Chín organized its territories into 36 administrative regions (jyẁn 郡),[6] and no Kings at all.

The First Emperor did not see himself as reviving Jōu, but as making a new beginning. He scorned the Jōu title King, and reached back to the Shāng title Dì 帝, with its overtones of divinity. His preferred title, "The First Emperor" (Shǐ Hwáng-dì 始皇帝), openly proclaimed a departure from earlier precedent.

The First Emperor's successor was to be designated "The Second Emperor" (Àr-shǐ Hwáng-dì 二世皇帝), and so on for a myriad Emperors into the future. There would be no more dynastic transitions: Chín was there to stay.

Cosmic Cycles. The old Lw̌ Bù-wéi group ventured to dissent. They saw Chín as occupying a limited period within history: part of the Five Phases sequence. In the Lǎn, an addendum to the LSCC, they put it respectfully, comparing the First Emperor with several esteemed figures of antiquity:

8:5 (LSCC 13/2:1, excerpt, c0221). When an Emperor is about to arise, Heaven will first display omens among the people below. In the time of the Yellow Emperor, Heaven displayed great worms and crickets, and the Yellow Emperor said, The force [chì 氣][7] of Earth is dominant. Earth being dominant, for his color he honored yellow, and in his actions he imitated earth. Then in the time of Yw̌ . . .

---

[6]Plus the capital. The number of jyẁn later increased; Loewe **Biographical** 806f.

[7]The meanings of this word includes breath, vapor, ether, or other intangible force.

... Then in the time of King Wýn, Heaven displayed fire: a vermilion bird holding in its beak a cinnabar writing alighted on the Jōu ancestral shrine; and King Wýn said, the force of Fire is dominant. Fire being dominant, for his color he honored red, and in his actions he imitated fire.

What takes the place of Fire must be Water. Heaven has displayed the dominance of Water, so Water is dominant. Thus for a color, one should honor black, and in actions, imitate water. If the force of Water should arrive, but no one realizes it, its term will expire, and there will be a shift to Earth. What Heaven creates is the seasons, but it does not otherwise assist the farmers here below.

This makes the Emperor subordinate to a higher sequence of things.

The LSCC group also sought to diminish the influence of Legalism, a doctrine which thinks the worst of people, and may be deluded in doing so:

8:6 (LSCC 13/3:2, c0221). A man had lost his ax. He suspected his neighbor's son. Looking at his walk, it was that of an ax thief; his expression was that of an ax thief; his words were those of an ax thief – his whole movement and demeanor were nothing but those of an ax thief. Then while cleaning out a drain he found his ax. Next day when he again looked at his neighbor's son, his movement and demeanor were nothing like those of an ax thief. The neighbor's son had not changed; *he* had changed, and the change had no other reason than his own predilection.

The other person's evil nature may be only in one's own mind. And though Legalist harshness may work once, it may not be a good dynastic foundation:

8:7 (LSCC 14/4:2, excerpt, c0219). Of old, when Wýn-gūng of Jìn was about to do battle with the men of Chǔ at Chýngpú, he summoned his Uncle Fàn and asked, The Chǔ are many, we are few; what should I do? Uncle Fàn replied, Your servant has heard that a ruler who is involved in ritual never gets enough of the civil, and a ruler who is involved in battle never gets enough of deception. You should deceive them.

Wýn-gūng told Yūng Jì what Uncle Fàn had said. Yūng Jì said, If you dry up the marshes to catch fish, how could you not catch something? But next year there will be no fish. If you burn the grass to hunt, how could you not catch something? But next year there will be no game. Though the Way of Deception and Deceit would be effective in these circumstances, it cannot be used twice. It is not a farsighted method.

Wýn-gūng followed Uncle Fàn's advice and defeated Chǔ at Chýngpú. When he returned, he gave rewards, and put Yūng Jì ahead of the rest. His advisors left and right remonstrated, saying, The victory at Chýngpú was due to Uncle Fàn's strategy. Our lord followed his advice, yet in giving rewards he has put him last. Something is wrong! Wýn-gūng replied, Yūng Jì's advice would benefit a hundred generations. Uncle Fàn's advice would work only once. How could I put what would work only once ahead of what would benefit a hundred generations?

When Confucius heard of this, he said, To use deception in the face of difficulty is a fit way to repel an enemy. To return from battle and honor the worthy is a fit way to reward virtue. Though Wv́n-gūng did not end as he had begun, he was fit to be a Hegemon.

When rewards are large, people will want them. When people want rewards, they can be conditioned. If they are conditioned to be deceptive, then their success will be failure and their victory will be defeat . . .

Of course the safety of the state lay in employing the right kind of ministers:

8:8 (LSCC 13/5:3, excerpt, c0220). When the ruler is worthy and the age is orderly, worthy men occupy high positions . . . So in the present age, if one seeks for an officer who understands the Way, . . . what desire cannot be realized, what deed cannot be achieved?

Confucian ideas like just war did prove useful in portraying the unification process as a fully justified conquest. In 0219, the First Emperor visited the east. In a stone inscription set up on Mount Yì, his achievement is described thus:

8:9 (Chín Inscription #1, SJ 6, first half, 0219).[8]
        Long ago, in days of old,
        He came unto the Royal Throne.
        He smote the fractious and perverse,
        His awe was felt on every hand,
        Warlike and just, upright and firm.

[8]For these inscriptions, see Kern **Stele**.

His orders the generals received,
And in no very lengthy time
They had destroyed the Cruel Six.
In his six-and-twentieth year,
He offering makes to Those Above,
Resplendent in filiality.
And as he offers up his deed,
So there descends a special grace;
He tours in person the distant lands.
To Mount Yì he now ascends,
His ministers and retinue
All thinking how to make it long.

The Cruel Six were the states Chín had extinguished between 0230 and 0221. They were "cruel" in that "just war" theory *required* that they be cruel.

Law. The Chín laws continued in force, and were applied uniformly across the Empire. Weights and measures were standardized. The script was given its modern form, a simple style which had evolved for the use of clerks.

The Syūngnú 匈奴. Like other border states, Chín in the late 04c had tried to expand into the northern steppe lands. In the time of the First Emperor, the Syūngnú had become weaker than the peoples east and west of them. Chín planned to take the Ordos: the grazing lands lying within the northward loop of the Yellow River. The project looked dubious to many. How to suggest this?

Remonstrance. The Gwăndž people began by trying to establish an agreed institutional basis for dissent from policy, as essential to a wise sovereign:

> **8:10** (GZ 56, excerpt, c0216). Chí Hwán-gūng asked Gwăndž, I wish to possess and not lose; to gain and not relinquish; is there a Way to do this? He answered, Don't invent, don't innovate; when the time comes, follow it. Don't let your personal likes and dislikes harm the public good. Find out what the people dislike, and take those things as your own prohibitions . . . That the Yellow Emperor instituted the discussions in the Bright Terrace was so that the sovereign could view the worthy . . . These were the means by which the Sage Emperors and Wise Kings possessed and did not lose; gained and did not relinquish.
>
> Hwán-gūng said, I want to do as they did. What should I call it? He answered, Call it a Discussion of Complaints . . . Those who point out the faults of their superiors should be called Correction Officers . . . I request that Dūng-gwó Yá take this on. He is one who can contend in the presence of his ruler, in the interest of correct procedure.
>
> Hwán-gūng said, Good.

This amounts to the regular airing of grievances by the people, which had already been suggested in the late 04c (#**6:27**). To this it adds the idea that not everyone is qualified to oversee the complaint process in practice.

From another source there was criticism of the Ordos enterprise as such. For a literary model, the LSCC people also went back to the Dzwŏ Jwàn, in this case, to the account of an ill-fated long-distance campaign by Chín in 0628. The LSCC authors altered much in the DJ story, but the point was the same:[9]

8:11 (LSCC 16/4:2, excerpt, c0217). Of old, Chín Mù-gūng raised a host to attack Jv̀ng. Jyěn Shú remonstrated, saying, It should not be done. Your subject has heard that, when attacking the city of another state, one does not take the chariots further than a hundred leagues, or the men further than thirty leagues; their spirit being high and their strength at its peak, when they arrive, they can vanquish the enemy if they resist, or pursue them swiftly if they retreat. But now it is proposed to travel several thousand leagues, and in addition, to cross the territories of several other lords, in order to attack this state. Your servant does not understand how this can be done. Let the Sovereign reconsider his plan for it.

Mù-gūng did not listen. Jyěn Shú was seeing off the host outside the gate, and wept, saying, Alas, for the host! I see it depart, but I will not see it return. Jyěn Shú had sons named Shv̄n and Shr̀, who were to go with the host. Jyěn Shú told his sons, If Jìn ambushes the host, it will surely be at Yáu. If you do not die on the southern ridge, it will surely be on the northern ridge; it will be easy for me to recover your bodies . . .

Chín *was* defeated by Jìn, and its leaders were captured. In the prototype DJ story, Mù-gūng had apologized to his defeated army. The penance attributed to him in the LSCC version *exceeds* that prototype in an interesting way:

When Mù-gūng heard this, dressed in plain clothing [as in mourning] and from the tower of the ancestral shrine, he spoke to the multitude, saying, Heaven is not siding with Chín; it caused this Bereaved One not to heed the remonstrance of Jyěn Shú, and so brought on this disaster.

It was not that Mù-gūng wanted to be defeated at Yáu, but his wisdom was insufficient. When wisdom is insufficient, then one is untrusting, and when words [of others] are not trusted, the fact that the host would not return derives from this. Thus great is the damage caused by insufficiency.

This deals explicitly with the inadequacies of the ruler. Here, as with the above Gwǎndž tract (#**8:10**), the damage done is to the people, and it is to the people (not, as in the Dzwǒ Jwàn story, to the defeated host) that Mù-gūng is made to apologize. The incorporation of the people in the concept of the state, at least in the thinking of certain writers, had evidently come a long way.

---

[9]How do we know that they had this DJ story in mind? Well, we don't. There is no gimmick that solves questions like this for us. But experience with literary expression in the period (which was often indirect or allusive), and awareness of the political scene (which was urgent and dangerous), will tend to suggest it. **Methodological Reminder**: Humanistic research takes time (p197n). We need to know what these people knew, and how they wrote about it. Acquaintance with *what texts actually do* is part of the toolkit. It would be only a slight exaggeration to say that it *is* the toolkit.

Actual criticism remained difficult. Chín was both autocratic and absolutist. The ideal of such a system had been praised by the Gwǎndž theorists:

8:12 (GZ 45, excerpt, c0240). Of old, when Yáu governed the world, it was like clay in a mold for the potter to work; like metal in a furnace for the founder to cast. His people: he summoned them and they came; he dismissed them and they went. What he allowed them, they did; what he forbade them, they stopped. Yau's government was a fine understanding of orders of requirement and prohibition, and nothing else.

The consequence was that protest, whether from below or from within, had no institutional basis, and a daring critic, having protested, had no place to hide. It was a risky business. The LSCC people were at least willing to take the risk.

But the Syūngnú campaign *succeeded*. By 0215, general Mv́ng Tyén 蒙恬 had driven them off, occupied the Ordos, fortified it, and built a military road made level for heavy carts by "filling in valleys and leveling hills," to supply the new border outposts. The "Great Wall" (Cháng-chv́ng 長城, "Long Wall"), linked up several shorter defensive walls, earlier constructed by Chín and other northern states, into a single defensive perimeter, "a myriad leagues" long.[10] That wall defined the northern reach of Chín at its moment of greatest power.

It soon became prudent to celebrate this triumph rather than to oppose it. The LSCC did this by arguing that the wise ruler will *ignore* remonstrances. For their parable, they again chose a controversial long-distance campaign:

8:13 (LSCC 16/5:4, excerpt, c0214). When Ngwèi attacked Jūngshān, Ywè Yáng was general, and when he had conquered Jūngshān and returned to report to Wv́n-hóu, he had a look of satisfaction with his accomplishment. Wv́n-hóu sensed this, and told the secretary: "The documents submitted by the officials and the visitors: get them together and bring them here." The secretary got together two baskets and brought them to him. He made the general look at them, and all the documents were opposed to the policy of attacking Jūngshān. The general hastened back, faced north, bowed twice, and said, The success at Jūngshān was not due to your servant's prowess; it was the sovereign's achievement.

In those days, the advisors who were in opposition increased day by day. The impossibility of taking Jūngshān: How could it have required two baskets? One inch would have disposed of it. Wv́n-hóu was a worthy ruler, and yet things were like this; how much the more so in the case of a middling ruler? The problem for a middling ruler is that he cannot but do *something*, but he also cannot help but sympathize with the opposition.

---

[10]These walls are called "long" because unlike city walls, which encircle the city and return to their starting point, they are linear. They enclose nothing, but rather draw a line which marks a boundary, or at least a claimed boundary. For the "Great Wall" as it exists today, in a form far grander than the Chín prototype, see Waldron **Great**.

In any affair of permanent value, no feeling or expression or action but will be in support; how could there be any doubt or opposition among the officials? When they are unanimously in favor, there are no defeats. This is how Tāng and Wǔ achieved great things against Syà and Shāng, and how Gòujyèn was able to avenge his defeat. If the small and weak [rulers of the past] could be united in action and accomplish such things, how much more so with the great and strong?

For a modern reader, this piece and #8:11 may seem to cancel out. But the LSCC is not a unified theory; it is a minority view expressed under adverse and changing conditions. Each part made local sense when it was written.

The Chín Erudites not only produced policy comments; they also worked on their texts. The Jūng Yūng, which (#5:100) had influenced the Mencians, was extended, adding an anachronistic reference to Chín institutions. The Mencians had hated the blood-soaked Shū text called the Wǔ Chýng (#5:107); it and other Shū were now purged, yielding a repertoire of 29 approved Shū.[11]

The School Scene. How were these views and interpretations handed on? In part by individual teaching, but at least some of the time in a school setting. A Gwǎndž treatise seemingly written at about this period gives us a glimpse of what a day at such a school might have been like. Note the rigid decorum:

8:14 (GZ 59, excerpts, c0214).

> The master sets forth teaching, the disciples take it their model.
> Enthusiastic, respectful, receptive, they absorb what they receive.
> Seeing the good, they follow it; hearing the right, they accept it.
> They are gentle and filial, without pride or belligerence.
> They have no evil designs; their conduct is always correct.
> At home or outside they are always the same:
> They will invariably move toward those of virtue.
> Their expressions are proper; inwardly, they are exemplary.
> Rising early and retiring late, their attire is always proper.
> Learning at morn and practicing at eve, they are assiduous.
> Concentrating ceaselessly: such is the model student.
> The service of the younger is to retire late and rise early;
> In sweeping and rinsing, they maintain decorum . . .

(The omitted middle portion describes eating meals and cleaning the room).

---

[11]The Shū specialist Fú Shýng 伏勝 kept copies of the final 29 Shū, but concealed them in early Hàn, when his privileged position ended, and Confucian texts were still generally prohibited. The 0210 Chín ban on Confucian texts (see p221) was repealed in 0191; thereafter he openly taught his "modern script" Shū (so called because written in the new Chín script). Later schools of Shū interpretation all derive from Fú Shýng. Syẃndž's pupil Fóuchyōu Bwó 浮邱伯, though very old when Hàn became receptive to the Confucian classics, had a similar role in the dissemination of the Shr.

At the end of the text comes a section on the students training themselves, after the master has retired, in the technique of argument:

> When the master is about to retire, the students all rise.
> They offer pillow and mat, and ask where he will place his feet.
> (They ask this the first time; later on they do not).
> When the master has retired, each seeks out his friends.
> Cutting and polishing, each improves his arguments.
> When the daily routine is completed, it begins over again.
> These are the guidelines for students.

Parallels to some of these details may be found in the Indian Dharma Sûtras.[12]

Peace. With the Chín political unification, and the standardizing of chariot axles, among other things, people could go anywhere conveniently and safely. Travel flourished, opportunities for trade or favorable relocation multiplied, and unofficial doctrines spread. Graft and profiteering had always been a concern. The last of the Lord Shāng essays addresses these problems plus a new one: corruption in the system of military procurement for the armies on the frontier.

On salary inflation, parasitism, and consequent rural hardship:

> **8:15** (SJS 2:4, excerpt, c0214). If salaries are high and taxes many, the multitude who are supported will weigh heavily on those who are doing the farming. If those supported are reduced in status and put to work, the dissolute and idle population will have no way to eat, and if they have no way to eat, they will take up farming . . .

On grain speculation and consequent rural poverty:

> **8:16** (SJS 2:5, excerpt, c0214). Do not allow merchants to buy grain, nor farmers to sell grain. If farmers cannot sell their grain, then the lazy and idle will exert themselves and be energetic; if merchants cannot buy grain, they will have no particular joy over abundant years . . .

On waste and graft in military procurement for the frontier armies:

> **8:17** (SJS 2:15, excerpt, c0214). Let there be no women in the army markets, but order the merchants to have people gather armor and weapons, so that the army will be well furnished. Also let no one privately transport grain to the military markets . . .

> **8:18** (SJS 2:19, excerpt, c0214). Let those who forward grain not use rented carts or carry goods on the return trip. Carts, oxen, carriages, and wagons must all be according to the registry. If so, then the going will be swift and the coming will be rapid, and the traffic will not weigh heavily on the farmers . . .

---

[12]The oldest of these, the Âpastamba Dharma Sûtra, is somewhat earlier than this Gwǎndž chapter. For its rules for resident students, see Olivelle **Dharmasūtras** 9-16.

On how to limit travel:

> **8:19** (SJS 2:8, excerpt, c0214). Abolish inns. The false, the troublesome, the profiteers, and the dubious characters will not travel; the innkeepers will have nothing to eat, and will have to turn to farming . . .

On the specific danger that travel will spread the old high culture:

> **8:20** (SJS 2:14, excerpt, c0214). If ministers and nobles are learned and adept in disputation, let them not travel about or live in the various districts; then the rural people will have no way to hear intricacies or see ingenuities . . . clever farmers will have no ground for abandoning old ways, and stupid farmers will not become clever or fond of study . . .

Banning the Books. The spread of the old learning, with its pre-Chín and thus anti-Chín tendency, worried Lǐ Sź. In 0213, he submitted this memorial:

> **8:21** (SJ 87, excerpt, quoting Lǐ Sź's 0213 memorial). Of old, the world was in disorder and no one was able to unify it, hence the various lords arose. In their words they extolled the past to the detriment of the present, and elaborated empty expressions to the confusion of the truth. All valued what they had privately studied, in opposition to what their superiors had established. Now, His Majesty possesses all the world; he has separated white from black and has attained sole authority, yet private students join together in opposing the institutions of Legalist doctrine. I have heard that when an order is handed down, they discuss it in terms of their private views. At home, their hearts are opposed; in public, they argue along the byways. They gain reputation by opposing the ruler, achieve prominence with eccentric opinions, and foster sedition by leading the multitude astray. If this is not prohibited, the ruler's power will decline above, and factions will form below. The best course will be to prohibit it.
>
> Your subject requests / that all who possess literary documents, the Shī and Shū, or the sayings of the Hundred Schools, be made to dispose of them. / If within thirty days of this order, they have not disposed of them, they are to be branded and sent to labor on the walls. Writings not to be disposed of are those on medicine, divination, or forestry. Any who wish to study these subjects may take the officials as their teachers.

Methodological Moment. But a version of that memorial in a different chapter of the SJ substitutes, between the / marks above, the following:

> **8:22** (SJ 6, excerpt) . . . / that the archive officials should burn everything but the records of Chín, and, save for those in the possession of the court erudites, whoever in the world dares to keep the Shī and Shū, or the writings of the Hundred Schools, should gather them together for the officers to burn. Those who dare to discuss the Shī and Shū among themselves should be executed and their bodies publicly exposed; those who use the past to criticize the present should be executed together with their families. Any officials who know of violations but do not bring them forward shall be judged equally guilty / . . .

The difference is not minor; it is drastic. Which version is the original?

Embarrassingly enough, the long version leaves intact the short version's provision that violators shall be branded and sent to hard labor. But how do you kill someone and then send them to hard labor? Medically, it cannot be done. What we seem to have, then, is the archive text of Lǐ Sz̄'s memorial, included in SJ 87 by the eclectic Szmǎ Tán, plus a second, falsified version, demonizing Lǐ Sz̄ by making him recommend picturesque cruelties, which was interpolated in SJ 6 by Tán's son Szmǎ Chyēn, who, being Confucian-trained, hated Lǐ Sz̄. Chyēn's atrocity version has held the attention of readers down to the present. But close comparison of the two readily shows that it is not the original.

--------..•..--------

That same year, Lǐ Sz̄ was made Chancellor of the Left, and the period of Chín latitude toward Confucian ideas in the public sector was at an end.

The requirement to denounce criminals created a culture of betrayal even among the literate. Sensing betrayal became an important survival value:

8:23 (LSCC 18/3:1, excerpt, c0212). Once, by the sea, there lived a man who loved gulls. Whenever he was by the shore, he would go over to the gulls. The gulls would flock to him until they numbered in the hundreds, and still they would keep coming – before him and behind, to his left and to his right, everything would be gulls. All day long he played with them, and they would not leave him. His father told him, I hear the gulls come to you. Catch one and bring it here, so *I* can play with it. Next day, the man went to the shore, but not a single gull would come to him.

Filial Piety. Chín might be hostile to the diffusion of Confucian ideas or persuasions among the people (#**8:20, 8:21**), but it did recognize a widely accepted value which the Confucians had taken into their system: filial piety. Lack of filial respect was a crime in Chín law. A father could not himself put an unfilial son to death, but he could petition the authorities to do so:

8:24 (Shwèihǔdì #D85, c0220?). One who is exempt by age from labor service denounces another for unfilial behavior and asks that he be killed . . . He is to be promptly arrested and not allowed to escape.

8:25 (Shwèihǔdì #E18, c0220?). Denouncing a son. Commoner A of a certain village said in his denunciation: "My son, the commoner C of the said village, is unfilial; I ask that he be killed. This I venture to request."

Forthwith the Prefectural Officer E was ordered to go and arrest him. Prefectural Officer E's report: "With the prison bondservant X, I arrested C; we found him in the house of Y."

The Assistant N has interrogated C. His statement: "I am A's son. I have indeed been unfilial toward A." He has not been found guilty of any other crime.

How this confession was obtained we are not told. The concluding comment about the lack of a previous criminal record was normal procedure: second offenses were much more seriously regarded by Chín law than first ones.

LSCC now revisits the "Upright Gǔng" motif (#**3:46**), but this time, filial obligations are submerged, and only the law is to be obeyed:

8:26 (LSCC 19/2:5, c0211). In the time of Jāu-wáng of Jīng,[13] there was an officer named Shŕ Jŭ. In character, he was fair and upright, and without selfishness. The King made him a judge. Someone was murdered. Shŕ Jŭ set out to catch him, but it turned out to be his own father. He turned his carriage around and returned. Standing in the courtyard, he said, "The murderer is your subject's father. If I were to apply the law to my father, I would be unable to bear it, but to cast aside the laws of the state is impermissible. It is the duty of an officer." With this, he put axe and placard [naming his crime] on his back, and asked to die before the King. The King said, "To pursue but not overtake, how does that require a guilty finding? Resume your office." Shŕ Jŭ declined, saying, "One who does not feel a personal responsibility to his father cannot be called a filial son. One who serves his ruler by bending the law cannot be called a loyal subject. That the sovereign's command exculpates him is a mercy from on high, but to not dare put aside the law is the subject's duty." Without removing the axe and placard, he cut his throat in the King's courtyard.

When the law is violated, the violator must die. His father broke the law, but he could not bear [to execute him]; the King excused him, but he was not willing [to accept it] – Shŕ Jŭ's way of serving as a subject may be called both loyal and filial.

The disapproval of the "upright son" with which #**3:46** ended is lacking here. Law reigns alone, and filial duty is present only in name.[14]

The elimination of Confucian ideas generated this warning:

8:27 (LSCC 20/4:1, c0210). Things in the same category summon each other; things with the same spirit come together; sounds in tune will echo each other. Thus if you strike "C" then a "C" responds; strike "E" and an "E" emerges. With a dragon we summon rain, with a form we pursue the shadow that it makes. The causes of disaster or fortune are thought by many to be Fate, but how could they know? So when a state is in disorder, it is not merely in disorder, it also inevitably attracts bandits. If it were only disordered, it need not necessarily perish, but once it attracts bandits, there is no way it can survive.

This is the converse of the Mencian theory: an unprincipled government will attract unprincipled people ("bandits"). That prediction would soon be fulfilled.

---

[13]This is the older name of the state of Chǔ 楚. It is substituted for "Chǔ" since Chǔ was the personal name of the First Emperor, and could not be used in public writings.

[14]LSCC here sends a mixed message. LSCC 19/2:3 suggests that turning in one's relatives (a deed ascribed to a man from Chín) is despicable, and that principled refusal is noble. But the implacable character of the law is the moral of the next piece (19/2:4), and of this concluding item (19/2:5, #**8:26**). The last word of the LSCC text at this date is thus on the side of law, however monstrous a particular application of it may seem.

The Last Inscription. In 0210, the Emperor, accompanied by his new Chancellor Lǐ Sž, ascended Mount Gwèıjī. The inscription erected there makes no Confucian rhetorical gestures, but praises the Emperor in Legalist terms:

8:28 (Chín Inscription #7, SJ 6; first half, 0210).

> His Divine Majesty 皇帝, accomplished and outstanding
> Has subdued and unified all the cosmos,
> His virtue and kindness are forever.
>
> In his thirty-seventh year,
> He personally tours the world,
> Beholding all the distant regions.
>
> Then he ascends the Gwèıjī height,
> And observes the people's customs:
> The black-haired ones [common people] are all reverent.
>
> The many officials recite his deeds,
> Tracing the origin of his feats,
> Recalling his illustrious ways.
>
> The Sage of Chín beholds his state,
> He first fixed its terms and standards 刑名,
> He has showed forth the ancient code.
>
> He first made the laws and rules,
> Distinguished duties and offices,
> And thereby established constancy.
>
> The Six Kings were partial and perverse,
> Rapacious and uncontrolled,
> They led the many to make themselves strong.
>
> Cruel and harsh, without restraint,
> Proudly relying on their strength,
> They often resorted to armor and arms.
>
> They sent their agents secretly,
> Pursuing an Alliance plan,
> To realize their malign intent.
>
> Within, they made deceitful schemes,
> Without, they came to invade our land.
> Bringing disasters in their wake.
>
> With righteous might he punished them,
> Wiping out their cruelties,
> And their disturbances are no more.
>
> The Sage's virtue spreads far abroad,
> Within the Six Directions,
> His grace is endlessly bestowed.

The Emperor died on the way back from this expedition. With him were the Chancellor Lǐ Sž, the favored official Jàu Gāu, and the Emperor's youngest son Hú-hàı. The three conspired to suppress the Emperor's testament delegating the rulership to his eldest son Fú-sū, and instead to install Hú-hàı.

There followed a period of intense palace intrigue. The general Mv́ng Tyén was forced to commit suicide, and the Syūngnú promptly reoccupied the Ordos. The Chín dynasty began to unravel.

The Second Emperor

In this way did an inexperienced and, as it turned out, incompetent person become the Second Emperor of all-powerful Chín. Hú-hàı's first act was to force the suicide of the Heir Apparent and those who were loyal to him, thus beginning the dismantling of a harsh, but an undeniably effective, government. At first, Hú-hàı held things together. He revisited the sites where his father had earlier erected inscriptions, thus symbolically claiming the land as his own.

The First Emperor, in the first of those inscriptions (#**8:9**), had claimed to be filial. This should not be seen as the meek subordination of a humble person. A Confucian text of this period spells out the higher meaning of filiality . . .

Syàu Jīng 孝經 "The Classic of Filial Piety," an 18-chapter work whose core 6 chapters were composed in early Chín by Confucians holding rank as erudites; the last sections were added in Hàn. It features Dzv̄ngdž as the questioner of Confucius. Translated by Legge.

. . . as appropriate to rulers, and as itself conferring the virtues of rulership, including power over the people:

> **8:29** (Syàu Jīng 3, excerpt, c0220). In high position, yet not arrogant: he is lofty but not imperiled. Observing moderation and scrupulous of rule: he is full but not excessive. "Lofty but not imperiled" is how he long preserves his place of honor; "full but not excessive" is how he long preserves his wealth. If wealth and honor do not depart from him, only then can he secure the altars of soil and harvest, and produce harmony among the people. This is the filiality of the Lords . . .

And the piece concludes with the Shr̄ fragment quoted by Dzv̄ngdž in #**5:36**.

In quoting this and other passages from the Syàu Jīng, the erudites behind the Lw̌-shr̀ Chūn/Chyōu had made filial piety the root principle of the state:

> **8:30** (LSCC 14/1:1, excerpt, c0219). Those in charge of the world or ruling a state must put basics first and details last. What one calls basics are not ploughing and weeding, planting and harrowing – one attends to *people*. Attending to people is not enriching the poor or companioning the lonely, it is attending to the basic principle. And for attending to the basic principle, nothing is greater than filial piety . . .

Filial in character, yet colossally extravagant in execution, was the plan for the First Emperor's mausoleum: not so much a tomb as an underground realm. To execute the plan, myriads of workers were levied from all over the country. This produced widespread popular hardship, and led to protests.

One such protest appears in a parable in the final stratum of the LSCC.

Methodological Instant: Its protagonist is Hwèıdž (page 201). His image in the Jwāngdž is fictional, but did it have a basis? The LSCC story confirms two features of that image: his association with the state of Ngwèı, and his reputation as the most adroit persuader in Ngwèı. No story is definitive, but one text can sometimes clarify our opinion of the historical value of another text.

----------••••••----------

Rhetorically, it is notable for its adroit *reversal* of a filial piety argument:

8:31 (LSCC 21/1:2, excerpt, c0209). Ngwèı Hwèı-wáng had died, and the date for his burial had been set. But Heaven poured down snow, enough to reach to the eye of an ox. The officials remonstrated with the Heir Apparent, saying, The snow is very bad. If we proceed with the burial under these conditions, the people will suffer hardship, and we fear the funds will be insufficient. We request a postponement of the time and a change of the day. The Heir Apparent said, To be a man's son, and yet not to carry out the burial of the former King because of the hardships of the people and the inadequacy of funds, would be unrighteous. Do not speak of this again. None of the officials dared say anything, but they told the Syīshŏu,[15] and the Syīshŏu said, *I* have nothing to say to this; must it not rather be Master Hwèı? I ask that you inform Master Hwèı.

Master Hwèı said, Very well. He went in his chariot to see the Heir Apparent, and said, Is the date for the burial set? The Heir Apparent said, Yes. Master Hwèı said, Of old, when King Jìlì was buried at the foot of Mount Hwō, an underground spring ate away the burial mound, exposing the front of the coffin. King Wv́n said, Ah, the Former Sovereign must wish to see the officials and people once more, and so he had the spring reveal him. He called an assembly, and the people all viewed it. On the third day, he was reburied. This was King Wv́n's kind of righteousness.

Now, the day of burial has been fixed, but the snow is heavy . . . it is hard to walk. Can the Heir Apparent, merely because of a previously set day, not be ashamed to be hasty with the burial? I pray that he will change the day. The Former King must want to tarry a little, to care for the altars and give peace to the black-haired people, so he has made the snow be so heavy. To postpone the date and change the day, would have been King Wv́n's kind of righteousness. If you do not, people will think you are ashamed to model yourself on King Wv́n. The Heir Apparent said, Good. I will respectfully postpone the date, and pick another day for the burial.

Hwèıdž did not argue in vain. Not only did he cause the Heir Apparent of Ngwèı to delay burying his father, he expounded the Way of King Wv́n. How can one call it a small achievement?

---

[15]The untranslatable title of a high office in Ngwèı.

Work at the mausoleum went on. There were no human sacrifices, like those of Chín Mù-gūng long ago (#**8:1**); rather, thousands of life-size terracotta *statues* of warriors were buried as the Emperor's guards in the other world:

Those conscripted to do the actual excavation work were severely punished if they were late in arriving. That too drew a fable by way of protest:

8:32 (LSCC 21/1:3, c0209). Hán was walling Syīn-chvng. The schedule called for completion in 15 days. Dwàn Chyáu was in charge of the work. One district was two days late [with its section]. Dwàn Chyáu arrested the supervisor. The imprisoned man's son hastened to inform border guard Dž-gāu, saying, Only Your Excellency can save his servant's father from death; I pray that I may entrust this to him. Border guard Dž-gāu said, Very well. He went to see Dwàn Chyáu, and with his aid ascended to the top of the wall. Border guard Dž-gāu looked far to left and right, and said, A fine piece of work, this wall. You will certainly be highly rewarded. From antiquity until now, a work so great as this, and one accomplished without punishments or executions, there has surely never been.

Border Guard Dž-gāu left, and Dwàn Chyáu sent a man by night to release the imprisoned supervisor from his chains and set him free.

The usual mechanism of administrative self-correction, namely, remonstrance from the ranks, turned out to be too dangerous to be applied.

At first, the tactic was one of recommendation, and as usual, by means of a story illustrating the success of the recommended behavior. In this LSCC story, the leader of an attack on an enemy city, Jàu Jyèndž, gives orders to attack, but from a position of safety behind a screen. The soldiers do not advance, and he calls them weak. The official Jú Gwò disagrees: he points out that the soldiers merely reflect the quality of their leader.

8:33 (LSCC 23/1:4, excerpt, c0209) . . . When Wv́n-gūng had been on the throne two years, he trained them in courage, and by his third year the soldiers were daring. In the Battle of Chv́ng-pú he five times defeated the men of Jīng.[16] He surrounded Wèi, took Tsáu, and captured Shŕ-shẁ. He secured the Son of Heaven's position and made himself an honored name in the world. *He used these soldiers.* Thus it is the *ruler* that is incapable, how should the *soldiers* be weak?

Jyèndž then came out from behind his rhinoceros-hide screen, and stood within range of the arrows and stones. He beat the drum once, and the soldiers all scaled the wall; the battle ended in a great victory. Jyèndž said, Should I get a thousand armored chariots, it would not be worth as much as having heard the one remark of the messenger Jú Gwò.

This was perhaps not well received. The writers consoled themselves with a merely wry comment about another ruler, the one Mencius had served:

8:34 (LSCC 23/5:4, excerpt, c0209). King Sywæn of Chí liked archery, and loved to have people tell him he could draw a heavy bow. The bow he used had a pull of no more than three stone. He showed it to his retinue. They tried to draw it, but gave up without succeeding, and said, This can be no less than nine stone; if not the King, who could use it?

The truth about the King of Chí was that the bow he used was not above three stone, yet to the end of his life he imagined he was using a nine-stone bow. How pathetic! If not an upright officer, who will be able not to flatter the ruler? . . . The problem of the ruler of a disordered state consists in the fact that he regards a three-stone as a nine-stone.

The only solution to the problem of remonstrance in oppressive times was not to offer remonstrance, but to support the ruler in his delusions of competence. Thus was the problem of the self-deluded ruler literally shrugged off. So was the duty to do something about self-deluded or otherwise inadequate rulers.

With Chín in administrative disarray and incapable of putting itself right, with territory lost to the neighboring tribes and rebellions breaking out at home, the stage was set for the entry of another player.

Chŭ. Local rebellions needed a sponsor, a higher authenticating power. Chŭ was ready to play that part. Chŭ, with its non-Sinitic heritage, had always been discontent under Chín rule, and now, with Chín in disarray, it saw an opportunity to be the general sponsor, coordinator, and ultimate beneficiary, of the many spontaneous but local rebellions.[17]

---

[16]Chŭ, but here Jīng, observing the taboo on the name of the First Emperor's father.

[17]Most of the states were Sinitic, or had been culturally assimilated before they were conquered; Chŭ was the exception. We may contrast the Greek states, which had a common culture and language, but (Finley **Ancient**) were never unified as a single state.

Chǔ had reappeared as a kingdom under a new King, Hwái-wáng. Probably during his illness in 0207, a Chǔ poet revisited a non-Sinitic tradition known at an earlier Chǔ court (#6:42), and bade the King's soul return and rule:

8:35 (Chǔ Tsź, Dà Jàu, "The Great Summons," excerpts, c0207).

> Green spring follows the Withering; white sun shines, oh.
> The air of spring goes forth; All Creatures stir, oh.
> Dark and cold diminish; Soul, do not flee, oh!
> Let the soul return, and not go far away, oh!
>
> Let the soul come back,
> and go not east, go not west; go not south, go not north, oh!
> In the east is the great sea; its waves breaking ceaseless, oh.
> Pairs of dragons drift side by side, coiling up and down, oh.
> Mist and rain congeal; to brilliant white thickening, oh.
> Soul, go not eastward, to Tāng Valley impenetrable, oh.
>
> Soul, go not south!
> In the south is hot fire for a thousand leagues, and coiling serpents, oh.
> In mountain forests remote, tigers and leopards ready to spring, oh.
> Ngūngyūng and ghost-fox, and deadly python, oh.
> Soul, go not southward, where creatures will harm you, oh.
>
> Soul, go not west!
> In the west and the Flowing Sands, they go on endlessly, oh.
> The boar-head, the slant-eye, the scraggly-hair hanging down, oh.
> The long-claws, the jagged-fangs; loud and wild their laughter, oh.
> Soul, go not westward; where there are many harmful things, oh.
>
> Soul, go not north!
> In the north is Cold Mountain, its gaunt heights red, oh.
> Uncrossable Dài River, too deep to sound, oh.
> Sky white and thick; cold freezing everything, oh.
> Soul, go not there, to the northern end of the world, oh.

And after tempting the King's wandering soul with the pleasures of his palace, the poet ends by praising the world as it shall be under the King's rule:

> Filling the roads for a thousand leagues, they come like clouds, oh.
> The High Lords in their power, to judge the people like gods, oh.
> Caring for ill and lonely, that orphan and widow may live, oh.
> Soul, come back, and make a True Beginning, oh!
> Fields and cities apportioned, and people prosperous, oh.
> Fair favor extending to all, virtue reaching wide, oh.
> First awe, then peace; excellence brilliantly manifest, oh.
> Soul, come back! Let reward and penalty be fitting, oh.
> Your reputation, like the sun, brightening All Within the Seas, oh.
> Virtue equal to that of Heaven, the Myriad Folk orderly, oh.
> North to Yōu-líng, south to Jyāu-jǐr, oh.
> West to the Yáng-cháng Pass, east as far as the Sea, oh.
> Soul, come back! Promote worthy officers, oh!

Extend your rule, put an end to cruelty, oh!
Raise the best, suppress the worst, punish the wrongdoers, oh!
Be the upright and honest in power, as with Great Yw̌ of old, oh!
Let the heroes guide affairs, and their influence reach far, oh!
Soul, come back! For the sake of state and home, oh!
Mighty and awesome, Heaven's Power is manifest, oh.
In their dignity, the Three Princes ascend and descend, oh.
The Several Lords are present, the Nobles take their places, oh.
Early dawn has come; the targets are placed, oh.
Holding bow and grasping arrow, they show perfect courtesy, oh –
Soul, come back! Restore the ways of the Three Kings, oh!

And the highly Confucian final ceremonies end with a ritual archery contest.

Joining Chǔ. Chv́n Shv̀ 陳舍 was the first Chín rebel to turn to Chǔ. His movement had begun in 0209. It quickly expanded. Chv́n Shv̀'s formal name was Shv̀ng 勝 "Victory." He and his mate Wú Gwǎng 吳廣 made their move as members of a party of conscript laborers, sent to work on Chín fortifications. The party were delayed, and delay (see #**8:32**) meant death:

Chǔ/Hàn Chūn/Chyōu 楚漢春秋 (CHCC) "The Epic of Chǔ and Hàn." Attributed to Lù Jyǎ of early Hàn. Tells of the rivalry between Syàng Yw̌ and Lyóu Bāng and the perilous early years of Hàn. CHCC is the source for some of the most exciting parts of the Shř Jì. Lost in Táng, and now known only from quotations in Shř Jì commentaries.

8:36 (SJ 48, excerpt, late 02c). In the first year of the Second Emperor, in the seventh month, they sent out nine hundred men from the left [poor] side of town to garrison Yw̌-yáng. They camped on the way at Great Marsh County. Chv́n Shv̀ng and Wú Gwǎng were among those required to go; they were made camp chiefs. It happened that there was a great downpour, and the road became impassable. They realized that they had lost all hope of arriving by the assigned time, and for missing the assigned time, the law provided that they should all be beheaded. Chv́n Shv̀ng and Wú Gwǎng took counsel together, saying, "If we go on, we will die; if we undertake some great scheme, we will die. As long as we are going to die, may we not as well die in the hope of establishing a state?

This they did. Their enterprise, based on the city of Chv́n, was recognized by the revived Chǔ court. Several nearby towns murdered their Chín-appointed officials and joined Chv́n Shv̀. Following the lead of the Chǔ court, where old ways, including Confucian thought, were welcome, Chv́n Shv̀ added to his retinue Kǔng Fù, the son of Dž-shv̀n, the last head of the Analects school in Lǔ, thus affirming the older ideology. But then rival rebellions broke out, and in the resulting confusion, Chv́n Shv̀, the King, was murdered by his chariot driver. Kǔng Fù, aged 57, died with the rest of Chv́n Shv̀'s appointees.

Back at the Chín court, with all political action useless or dangerous, the literati at the Academy still felt they had to do something. Thus it happened that the last advice given to Chín by the successors of Lw̌ Bù-wéi, filling out the rest of the six-chapter plan of this part of the book, was merely informational.

Agriculture. From Spring and Autumn on, the power of the state had rested on the land, its conquest and cultivation. Chín's conquests had been completed, but it remained to make the most of those conquests. It is then not surprising that the last four sections of LSCC 26, the end of the work, incorporate, seemingly entire, an agricultural text in more or less poetic form, ascribed to the mythical Jōu ancestor Hòu Jì, the Lord of Millet. When in 0771 the Jōu were forced to leave their northwestern homeland, it was Chín which had inherited that strategically advantageous territory. Now Jōu (in the voice of Hòu Jì) again comes together with Chín, in a treatise whose concern for the proper season echoes the groundplan of the original 12 Jì chapters of the LSCC (#**3:82-84**). It concludes with an assurance that doing everything at the appropriste season makes for health and longevity:

> **8:37** (LSCC 26/6:8, c0206). So a planting done at the right season will thrive; a crop grown out of season will be scanty. With stems of the same length, the seasonable one will be heavier; its grains more numerous.
>
> When equal weights are hulled,
> > the seasonable one will yield more rice.
>
> When equal amounts are consumed,
> > the seasonable one will better sate hunger.
>
> So, with a crop planted at the right season,
>
> Its aroma will be fragrant,
> > its taste sweet,
> > > its energy strong.
>
> Eat it for a hundred days:
> > The ears and eyes will be percipient
> > and the mind will be sharp.
>
> The four limbs will be strengthened,
> > no noxious vapors will enter,
> > > and the body will receive nothing harmful.
>
> The Yellow Emperor said, If the Four Seasons are irregular, one need only adjust the Five Grains.

Man can compensate for the caprices of nature, and the state can be secure through understanding of its agricultural basis. This advice would be equally relevant to Chín, then in turmoil, or to anything that might succeed Chín.

Syàng Yw̌ 項羽. The successors were hard at work. Chv́n Shv̀ was killed by a subordinate in 0208, but other rebels appeared. A Chw̌ successor was made the King of Chw̌. As war weeded out the weak, the final contenders emerged: Lyóu Bāng 劉邦, a commoner from Lw̌ with uncommon organizational gifts, and Syàng Yw̌, a Chw̌ nobleman of unmatched martial prowess.

Chǔ recognized both as Kings. Lyóu Bāng, who at the end of 0207 had successfully entered the Chín capital area, claimed it as his territory, but Syàng Yǔ, on behalf of the Chǔ King, gave him the land of Hàn instead. Their rivalry soon developed into a war between Chǔ, represented by Syàng Yǔ, and Hàn, Lyóu Bāng's domain. The early Hàn romance Chǔ/Hàn Chūn/Chyōu, from which we have quoted above, told the dramatic tale of the end of Syàng Yǔ. This account has been famous down the years, in the original and as an opera. It is the kind of thing no book on the period can omit. Here is how it ends:

8:38 (SJ 7, excerpt, late 02c). King Syàng camped at Gāi-syà. His troops were few, his food was gone; the Hàn armies and the soldiers of the Lords had surrounded him several lines deep. In the night, from the Hàn camps on all four sides, he heard songs of Chǔ. King Syàng was startled, and said, "Has Hàn already gained all of Chǔ? How many Chǔ men they have!" King Syàng got up in the night and began to drink in his tent. He had a beautiful woman named Yǔ whom he always favored and took with him, and a fine horse named Dapple which he always rode. King Syàng now sang a sad air of heroic melancholy, and himself made verses for it:

My strength tore up the mountains, ah! The age I overtopped,
The times give no advantage, ah! and Dapple's hoofs are stopped.
Dapple's hoofs are stopped, ah; what more can I do?
Yǔ, ah! Yǔ, ah! how can I lose you too?

He sang it several times, and the beautiful woman echoed it. King Syàng's tears ran down in several streams, and his attendants to left and right all wept too. Not one of them could bear to raise his head to watch.

King Syàng then mounted his horse and rode forth. The stout officers and their mounted followers under his banner were eight hundred some men. While it was still night, they broke through the encirclement and galloped south. At dawn, the Hàn armies saw what had happened, and ordered cavalry commander Gwàn Yīng to pursue them with five thousand riders.

King Syàng crossed the Hwái; those who could keep up with him were only a hundred some men. When King Syàng reached Yīn-líng, he became confused and lost his way. He asked a farmer, but the farmer deceived him, saying "Go left." He went left, and stumbled into a marsh. For this reason, the Hàn pursuers caught up with him. King Syàng once more led his troops to the east, but by the time he reached Dūng-chvng, he had only twenty-eight riders left. The Hàn pursuing cavalry numbered several thousand.

King Syàng realized that he could not get away. He said to his riders, "It is eight years from the time when I first raised troops until today. I have fought more than seventy battles. All who opposed me I destroyed; all I attacked submitted. I was never defeated; in the end, as Hegemon, I possessed the world. Now at last I find myself hemmed in here. It is Heaven destroying me; it is no fault of mine in arms.

Today I am resolved to die, but I should like to make a sally for you gentlemen and win three victories – for you gentlemen, I shall break through the encirclement, behead a commander, and cut down a flag, so that you gentlemen will know that it is Heaven destroying me, and no fault of mine in battle." He then divided his riders into four companies, facing four ways, and the Hàn army surrounded them several ranks deep. King Syàng said to his riders, "I will now get one of their commanders for you." He ordered the riders facing in four directions to ride down, planning to form again in three companies east of the mountain. Then King Syàng gave a great shout and rode down, and the Hàn troops broke in confusion; he did in the end behead one Hàn commander. The Lord of Chr̀-chywǽn led the cavalry in pursuit of King Syàng. King Syàng glared and shouted at him, and the Lord of Chr̀-chywǽn's men and horses were startled and gave way for several leagues. His riders regrouped in three places; the Hàn army did not know which group King Syàng was in.

King Syàng now thought to cross the Wū River on the east. The Wū River station chief was waiting with a ferry boat. He said to King Syàng, "Though the land east of the river is small, its area is still a thousand leagues, with several tens of myriads of people; it too is worth ruling over. I beg the Great King to quickly cross. Only your servant has a boat; when the Hàn army arrives, it will have no way to cross." King Syàng laughed and said, "Heaven is destroying me; what use is there in crossing over? Moreover, years ago, with eight thousand youths from east of the river, I crossed over and headed west; now I return without one man of them. Even if the fathers and brothers east of the river pitied me and made me king, how could I face them? Even if they did not speak of it, would I not be ashamed in my heart?" He then said to the station chief, "I see Your Excellency is a worthy man. I have ridden this horse five years; in all who faced him there was not his equal; he once went a thousand leagues in a day. I cannot bear to kill him; I make Your Excellency a present of him."

He then had his riders dismount and go on foot, carrying short swords. When they joined battle, he alone killed several hundred of the Hàn army. King Syàng bore on his body more than ten wounds. He turned and saw the Hàn cavalry marshal Lw̌ Mǎ-túng, and said, "Are you not my old friend?" Mǎ-túng turned toward him, and gestured to Wáng Yì, saying, "This is King Syàng." King Syàng then said, "I hear that Hàn has put a price on my head: a thousand in gold, and a city of a myriad households. I will do you the favor." He then cut his own throat and died.

Wáng Yì took his head and others trampled on each other, contending for Kìng Syàng; several tens were killed in the ensuing scuffle. When it was all over, Rider of the Guard Yáng Syǐ, Cavalry Marshal Lw̌ Mǎ-túng, and Guardsmen Lw̌ Shv̀ng and Yáng Wǔ, had each gotten one limb. When the five put the body together, the pieces fitted.

And so they divided the prize territory into five fiefs.

Envoi

To the earlier Nine Songs (#6:67-68), the revived Chǔ court had added a tenth and eleventh Song, memorializing those who had fallen in the service of Chǔ and its imperial ambition. We quote them here in farewell to Syàng Yw̌:

8:39 (Chǔ Tsź, Nine Songs #10, c0207).

Those Who Died For the State

Spears of Wú we grasp, ah! armor of hide we wear,
Wheel-hubs clash below, ah! swords slash through the air;
Pennons hide the sun, ah! like clouds the foemen swarm –
Crisscross fall the arrows, ah! but on our captains storm.

Our lines are overwhelmed, ah! our ranks are put to flight,
A dead horse falls on the left, ah! and a wounded one on the right;
Axles twain are tangled, ah! turn the team around –
Seize the jaden drumsticks, ah! let the signal sound!

Heaven's times smile not ah! the gods are of angry mind,
The fearful slaughter done, ah! we leave the field behind.

They never shall return, ah! forever they are gone,
The level plain is distant, ah! the road runs on and on;
Swords yet girt about them, ah! their longbows firm they hold –
Head from body severed, ah! but still their hearts are bold.

Brave you were indeed, ah! and in battle skilled,
Valiant to the end, ah! your fearless blood you shed;
Though perished be your bodies, ah! your spirits still strike dread –
Your immortal souls, ah! are heroes among the dead.

The memorial service concluded with a solemn dance, accompanied by this address to the spirits of the fallen warriors:

8:40 (Chǔ Tsź, Nine Songs #11, c0207).

The Service To The Souls

The service ends, ah! in a flourish of drum.
The dancers' fronds, ah! are held at plumb.
The maidens' voices, ah! now softly hum.
The fragrant orchid, ah! the chrysanthemum –
Through endless ages, ah! of time to come.

And so our story ends as it began, in a showdown between Chǔ and the North. In that last contest, there perished the Last Warring State, the China That Was Not To Be, amid the ruins of the Empire That Was To Last Forever. And it did last forever, starting with its successor, the Hàn Dynasty. The heroic attempt of Syàng Yw̌ – to reinstate something along the old lines – had decisively failed.

What the Warring States had long labored to produce, and what they had destroyed themselves in the process of producing, now securely existed.

Apparatus

Major Events
Most dates are circa

0771   **Jōu** Yōu-wáng killed; effective end of Jōu Dynasty
0722   Beginning of Chūn/Chyōu chronicle of **Lǔ**
0656   **Chí** Hwán-gūng and allies make intrusion into Chǔ
0632   **Jìn** Wv́n-gūng and allies defeat Chǔ force in Wèi
0517   Exile of **Lǔ** Jāu-gūng (to a town on the Chí border)
0509   **Lǔ** Dìng-gūng succeeds; reigns from Lǔ capital
0479   Last year of Chūn/Chyōu. Confucius dies; sayings recorded in LY 4
0436   Dzv̌ngdž dies; his son Dzv̄ng Ywǽn succeeds as head of Analects school
0400   Kǔng family (Dž-sz̄) assumes leadership of Analects school; ritual focus
0390   Dzwǒ Jwàn begun in **Lǔ**. First Mician writing (MZ 17, against war)
0376   **Hán** extinguishes Jv̀ng and moves its capital to Jv̀ng
0365   **Ngwèi** moves its capital to Dà-lyáng
0360   Earliest Chí statecraft writings (GZ 1-3, 7)
0350   DDJ begun in Lǔ (mystical DDJ 14)
0343   **Chí** defeats Ngwèi at Battle of Mǎ-líng, in Ngwèi
0342   **Chí** ruler assumes title of King (Wáng 王)
0336   Lǎu Dān succeeds as leader of DDJ meditation school (DDJ 22, 10)
0327   Alexander completes conquest and Hellenization of Bactria
0322   First Chinese echo of a Greek literary motif (Upright Gūng, LY 13:18)
0320   Shr̄ repertoire is closed. Mencius sees **Ngwèi** [Lyáng] Hwèi-wáng
0316   Mencius achieves ministership in **Chí**
0315   **Yēn** ruler abdicates to his minister; civil chaos ensues. Chí invades Yēn
0314   **Chí** annexes pacified Yēn; Jàu and allies expel Chí and restore Yēn King
0313   Mencius departs; **Chí** King founds Jì-syà political theory establishment
0312   Dzwǒ Jwàn completed and presented to the **Chí** King
0286   **Chí** exterminates Sùng. Lǎu Dān dies (his last chapter is DDJ 66)
0285   Allies expel **Chí** from Sùng; Chí King dies in remote town
0284   Third DDJ master Lǐ Jù writes his first chapter (DDJ 67, against war)
0282   Earliest of the Jwāngdž writings (the primitivist JZ 8-10)
0278   **Chín** conquers Chǔ capital; Chǔ moves its capital eastward
0258   Sýwndž goes to **Chí** as the senior member of the revived Jì-syà
0255   **Chǔ** invades Lǔ and conquers half of it.
0254   Sýwndž becomes governor of **Chǔ**-occupied Lǔ
0249   **Chǔ** completes conquest of Lǔ; Chín extinguishes eastern Jōu remnant
0230   **Chín** extinguishes Hàn (0228 Jàu, 0225 Ngwèi, 0224 Chǔ, 0222 Yēn)
0221   **Chín** conquers Chí, the last remaining Warring State. Chín Empire
0213   Lǐ Sz̄ memorial against Confucian writings accepted
0210   **Chín** First Emperor dies
0209   **Chín** quickly collapses under Second Emperor; rebellions break out
0206   Nominal beginning of **Hàn**
0140   Accession of **Hàn** Wǔ-dì; end of Warring States theory debates

Outline of Text Chronology

Most texts are accretional, and have spans rather than single-year dates

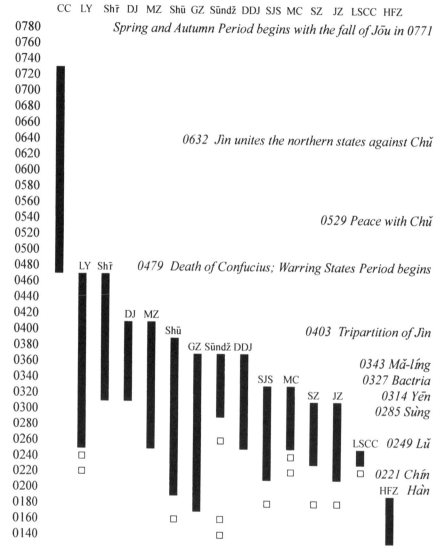

The "0720" line is the 20 years *beginning* with 0720. ■ denotes a continuation of an accretional text; □ is a later addition to a previously complete text. For text abbreviations, see p247. For events hinted at in the right margin, see Major Events, on the previous page. The chart ends with the accession of Hàn Wǔ-dì, whose reign is the effective end of the Hàn continuation of the Warring States theory debates. The winners were declared at this point, and advocacy-text production ceased.

Chinese Romanization Table

Common Alphabetic (CA) follows the formula "consonants as in English, vowels as in Italian," plus æ as in "cat," v [compare the linguist's ʌ] as in "gut," z as in "adz," and yw (after l or n, simply w) for "umlaut u." A lost initial ng- is restored to distinguish the states of Wèı 衛 and Ngwèı 魏, both now "Wèı." Tones are hīgh, rísing, lŏw, and fàlling. The other systems are Pinyin (PY) and Wade-Giles (WG).

CA	PY	WG	CA	PY	WG
a	a	a	chya	qia	ch'ia
ai	ai	ai	chyang	qiang	ch'iang
an	an	an	chyau	qiao	ch'iao
ang	ang	ang	chye	qie	ch'ieh
ar	er	erh	chyen	qian	ch'ien
au	ao	ao	chyou	qiu	ch'iu
			chyung	qiong	ch'iung
ba	ba	pa	chyw	qu	ch'ü
bai	bai	pai	chywæn	quan	ch'üan
ban	ban	pan	chywe	que	ch'üeh
bang	bang	pang	chywn	qun	ch'ün
bau	bao	pao			
bei	bei	pei	da	da	ta
bi	bi	pi	dai	dai	tai
bin	bin	pin	dan	dan	tan
bing	bing	ping	dang	dang	tang
bu	bu	pu	dau	dao	tao
bvn	ben	pen	dei	dei	tei
bvng	beng	peng	di	di	ti
bwo	bo	po	ding	ding	ting
byau	biao	piao	dou	dou	tou
bye	bie	pieh	du	du	tu
byen	bian	pien	dun	dun	tun
			dung	dong	tung
cha	cha	ch'a	dv	de	te
chai	chai	ch'ai	dvng	deng	teng
chan	chan	ch'an	dwan	duan	tuan
chang	chang	ch'ang	dwei	dui	tui
chau	chao	ch'ao	dwo	duo	to
chi	qi	ch'i	dyau	diao	tiao
chin	qin	ch'in	dye	die	tieh
ching	qing	ch'ing	dyen	dian	tien
chou	chou	ch'ou	dyou	diu	tiu
chr	chi	ch'ih	dz	zi	tzu
chu	chu	ch'u	dza	za	tsa
chun	chun	ch'un	dzai	zai	tsai
chung	chong	ch'ung	dzan	zan	tsan
chv	che	ch'e	dzang	zang	tsang
chvn	chen	ch'en	dzau	zao	tsao
chvng	cheng	ch'eng	dzei	zei	tsei
chwai	chuai	ch'uai	dzou	zou	tsou
chwan	chuan	ch'uan	dzu	zu	tsu
chwang	chuang	ch'uang	dzun	zun	tsun
chwei	chui	ch'ui	dzung	zong	tsung
chwo	chuo	ch'uo			

CA	PY	WG	CA	PY	WG
dzv	ze	tse	ja	zha	cha
dzvn	zen	tsen	jai	zhai	chai
dzvng	zeng	tseng	jan	zhan	chan
dzwan	zuan	tsuan	jang	zhang	chang
dzwei	zui	tsui	jau	zhao	chao
dzwo	zuo	tso	jei	zhei	chei
			ji	ji	chi
fa	fa	fa	jin	jin	chin
fan	fan	fan	jing	jing	ching
fang	fang	fang	jou	zhou	chou
fei	fei	fei	jr	zhi	chih
fou	fou	fou	ju	zhu	chu
fu	fu	fu	jun	zhun	chun
fvn	fen	fen	jung	zhong	chung
fvng	feng	feng	jv	zhe	che
fwo	fo	fo	jvn	zhen	chen
			jvng	zheng	cheng
gai	gai	kai	jwa	zhua	chua
gan	gan	kan	jwai	zhuai	chuai
gang	gang	kang	jwan	zhuan	chuan
gau	gao	kao	jwang	zhuang	chuang
gei	gei	kei	jwei	zhui	chui
gou	gou	kou	jwo	zhuo	cho
gu	gu	ku	jya	jia	chia
gun	gun	kun	jyang	jiang	chiang
gung	gong	kung	jyau	jiao	chiao
gv	ge	ke	jye	jie	chieh
gvn	gen	ken	jyen	jian	chien
gvng	geng	keng	jyou	jiu	chiu
gwa	gua	kua	jyung	jiong	chiung
gwai	guai	kuai	jyw	ju	chü
gwan	guan	kuan	jywæn	juan	chüan
gwang	guang	kuang	jywe	jue	chüeh
gwei	gui	kuei	jywn	jun	chün
gwo	guo	kuo			
			ka	ka	k'a
ha	ha	ha	kai	kai	k'ai
hai	hai	hai	kan	kan	k'an
han	han	han	kang	kang	k'ang
hang	hang	hang	kau	kao	k'ao
hau	hao	hao	kou	kou	k'ou
hei	hei	hei	ku	ku	k'u
hou	hou	hou	kun	kun	k'un
hu	hu	hu	kung	kong	k'ung
hun	hun	hun	kv	ke	k'e
hung	hong	hung	kvn	ken	k'en
hv	he	he	kvng	keng	k'eng
hvn	hen	hen	kwa	kua	k'ua
hvng	heng	heng	kwai	kuai	k'uai
hwa	hua	hua	kwan	kuan	k'uan
hwai	huai	huai	kwang	kuang	k'uang
hwan	huan	huan	kwei	kui	k'uei
hwang	huang	huang	kwo	kuo	k'uo
hwei	hui	hui			
hwo	huo	huo			

CA	PY	WG	CA	PY	WG
la	la	la	nu	nu	nu
lai	lai	lai	nun	nun	nun
lan	lan	lan	nung	nong	nung
lang	lang	lang	nv	ne	ne
lau	lao	lao	nvn	nen	nen
lei	lei	lei	nvng	neng	neng
li	li	li	nw	nyu	nü
lin	lin	lin	nwan	nuan	nuan
ling	ling	ling	nwo	nuo	no
lou	lou	lou	nyang	niang	niang
lu	lu	lu	nyau	niao	niao
lun	lun	lun	nye	nie	nieh
lung	long	lung	nyen	nian	nien
lv	le	le	nyou	niu	niu
lvng	leng	leng	nywe	nüe	nüeh
lw	lyu	lü	ou	ou	ou
lwan	luan	luan			
lwo	luo	lo	pa	pa	p'a
lya	lia	lia	pai	pai	p'ai
lyang	liang	liang	pan	pan	p'an
lyau	liao	liao	pang	pang	p'ang
lye	lie	lieh	pau	pao	p'ao
lyen	lian	lien	pei	pei	p'ei
lyou	liu	liu	pi	pi	p'i
lywe	lüe	lüeh	pin	pin	p'in
			ping	ping	p'ing
ma	ma	ma	pou	pou	p'ou
mai	mai	mai	pu	pu	p'u
man	man	man	pvn	pen	p'en
mang	mang	mang	pvng	peng	p'eng
mau	mao	mao	pwo	po	p'o
mei	mei	mei	pyau	piao	p'iao
mi	mi	mi	pye	pie	p'ieh
min	min	min	pyen	pian	p'ien
ming	ming	ming	r	ri	jih
mou	mou	mou	ran	ran	jan
mu	mu	mu	rang	rang	jang
mvn	men	men	rau	rao	jao
mvng	meng	meng	rou	rou	jou
mwo	mo	mo	ru	ru	ju
myau	miao	miao	run	run	jun
mye	mie	mieh	rung	rong	jung
myen	mian	mien	rv	re	je
myou	miu	miu	rvn	ren	jen
			rvng	reng	jeng
na	na	na	rwa	rua	jua
nai	nai	nai	rwan	ruan	juan
nan	nan	nan	rwei	rui	jui
nang	nang	nang	rwo	ruo	jo
nau	nao	nao	sa	sa	sa
nei	nei	nei	sai	sai	sai
ni	ni	ni	san	san	san
nin	nin	nin	sang	sang	sang
ning	ning	ning	sau	sao	sao
nou	nou	nou			

CA	PY	WG	CA	PY	WG
sha	sha	sha	tsa	ca	ts'a
shai	shai	shai	tsai	cai	ts'ai
shan	shan	shan	tsan	can	ts'an
shang	shang	shang	tsang	cang	ts'ang
shau	shao	shao	tsau	cao	ts'ao
shei	shei	shei	tsou	cou	ts'ou
shou	shou	shou	tsu	cu	ts'u
shr	shi	shih	tsun	cun	ts'un
shu	shu	shu	tsung	cong	ts'ung
shun	shun	shun	tsv	ce	ts'e
shv	she	she	tsvn	cen	ts'en
shvn	shen	shen	tsvng	ceng	ts'eng
shvng	sheng	sheng	tswan	cuan	ts'uan
shwa	shua	shua	tswei	cui	ts'ui
shwai	shuai	shuai	tswo	cuo	ts'o
shwan	shuan	shuan	tsz	ci	tz'u
shwang	shuang	shuang	tu	tu	t'u
shwei	shui	shui	tun	tun	t'un
shwo	shuo	shuo	tung	tong	t'ung
sou	sou	sou	tv	te	t'e
su	su	su	tvng	teng	t'eng
sun	sun	sun	twan	tuan	t'uan
sung	song	sung	twei	tui	t'ui
sv	se	se	two	tuo	t'o
svn	sen	sen	tyau	tiao	t'iao
svng	seng	seng	tye	tie	t'ieh
swan	suan	suan	tyen	tian	t'ien
swei	sui	sui	v	e	e
swo	suo	so	vn	en	en
sya	xia	hsia	vng	eng	eng
syang	xiang	hsiang	wa	wa	wa
syau	xiao	hsiao	wai	wai	wai
sye	xie	hsieh	wan	wan	wan
syen	xian	hsien	wang	wang	wang
syi	xi	hsi	wei	wei	wei
syin	xin	hsin	wo	wo	wo
sying	xing	hsing	wu	wu	wu
syou	xiu	hsiu	wvn	wen	wen
syung	xiong	hsiung	wvng	weng	weng
syw	xu	hsü	ya	ya	ya
sywæn	xuan	hsüan	yang	yang	yang
sywe	xue	hsüeh	yau	yao	yao
sywn	xun	hsün	ye	ye	yeh
sz	si	ssu	yen	yan	yen
ta	ta	t'a	yi	yi	i
tai	tai	t'ai	yin	yin	yin
tan	tan	t'an	ying	ying	ying
tang	tang	t'ang	you	you	yu
tau	tao	t'ao	yung	yong	yung
ti	ti	t'i	yw	yu	yü
ting	ting	t'ing	ywæn	yuan	yüan
tou	tou	t'ou	ywe	yue	yüeh
			ywn	yun	yün

Works Cited

In addition to references which were cited in footnotes or in text boxes, we have silently included some works that may be useful as general collateral reading.

Short citations (Surname **Title**) are here expanded to Full Name (in the order of the language in question) **Title** Publisher Date: the minimum needed for library retrieval; X University Press is usually abbreviated as X. Bracketed abbreviations, such as [JZ], identify a title as containing a substantial or complete translation of that text.

Art of the Houma Foundry. Princeton 1996

Artistic Style of Cultural Relics From the Tomb of Zenghouyi. Hubei Fine Arts 1992

Christopher I Beckwith. Empires of the Silk Road. Princeton 2009

Robert Bagley (ed). Ancient Sichuan. Princeton 2001

Johan Bjorksten. Learn to Write Chinese Characters. Yale 1994

Derk Bodde. Henry A Wallace and the Ever-Normal Granary. Far Eastern Quarterly v5 #4 (Aug 1946) 411-426

Chuck Boyer. Get Your Frog Out of the Well. Wiley India 2008

A Taeko Brooks. Distancing Jí 及 in the Chūn/Chyōu. WSP v1 (2010) 27-39

A Taeko Brooks. Enfiefment Renewal in Lǔ. WSP v1 (2010) 214-215

A Taeko Brooks. Evolution of the Bà 霸 "Hegemon" Theory. WSP v1 (2010) 220-226

A Taeko Brooks. Heaven, Li, and the Formation of the Zuozhuan. Oriens Extremus v44 (2003/2004) 51-100

A Taeko Brooks. The League of the North. WSP v1 (2010) 204-213

A Taeko Brooks. The Lǔ Lore Tradition. WSP v1 (2010) 40-42

A Taeko Brooks. Military Capacity in Spring and Autumn. WSP v1 (2010) 183-188

A Taeko Brooks. Re-Dating the Sources. WSP v1 (2010) 9-14

A Taeko Brooks and E Bruce Brooks. Defeat in the Chūn/Chyōu. WSP v1 (2010) 189-198

E Bruce Brooks. Alexandrian Motifs in Chinese Texts. Sino-Platonic Papers #96 (1999)

E Bruce Brooks. Interrogative Yēn 焉 and Ān 安 in Jwāngdž. WSP v1 (2010) 52-54

E Bruce Brooks. Numbers and Losses at Chv́ng-pú. WSP v1 (2010) 199-200

E Bruce Brooks. Political Geography of the Shī̄. WSP v1 (2010) 238-241

E Bruce Brooks. Template Songs of Chv́n 陳. WSP v1 (2010) 79-83

E Bruce Brooks. Textual Evidence for 04c Sino-Bactrian Contact, in Mair **Bronze** 2/716-726

E Bruce Brooks and A Taeko Brooks. The Nature and Historical Context of the Mencius, in Chan **Mencius** 242-281

E Bruce Brooks and A Taeko Brooks. The Original Analects [LY]. Columbia 1998

E Bruce Brooks and John V Lombardi. Peace in Multi-State Systems. WSP v1 (2010) 245-249

Alan K L Chan (ed). Mencius: Contexts and Interpretations. Hawaii 2002

Wing-tsit Chan. The Way of Lao Tzu. Bobbs-Merrill 1963

Winston S Churchill. The Gathering Storm. Houghton 1948

Winston S Churchill. Their Finest Hour. Houghton 1949

Raymond Cohen et al (ed). Amarna Diplomacy. Johns Hopkins 2000

Constance A Cook. Death in Ancient China [Bāushān]. Brill 2006
Constance A Cook et al (ed). Defining Chu. Hawaii 1999
Rushton Coulborn (ed). Feudalism in History. Princeton 1956
Herrlee G Creel. The Origins of Statecraft in China. v1 Chicago 1970
Herrlee G Creel. Shen Pu-hai [Shv̄n Bù-hàı]. Chicago 1974
J I Crump. Chan-kuo Ts'e [JGT]. 2ed Michigan 1996
Carine Defoort. Can Words Produce Order? Cultural Dynamics v12 #1 (2000) 85-110
Darrel P Doty. The Bronze Inscriptions of Ch'i. UMI 1982
Robert Drews. The Coming of the Greeks. Princeton 1988
Robert Drews. The End of the Bronze Age. Princeton 1993
J J L Duyvendak. The Book of Lord Shang [SJS]. 1928; Chicago 1963
Benjamin A Elman. From Philosophy to Philology. 2ed Asia-Pacific Institute 2001
Robert Eno. Sources for the Analects 8 Layers. WSP v1 (2010) 93-99
Europe Studies China. Han-Shan Tang 1995
D Ellis Evans (ed). Proceedings of the Seventh International Congress of Celtic Studies.
    Oxbow 1986
Lothar von Falkenhausen. The Waning of the Bronze Age, in Loewe **History** 450-544
M I Finley. The Ancient Greeks and Their Nation, in Finley **Use** 120-133
M I Finley. Aspects of Antiquity. Viking 1968
M I Finley. The Emperor Diocletian, in Finley **Aspects** 143-152
M I Finley. The Use and Abuse of History. Viking 1975
Thomas W Gallant. Risk and Survival in Ancient Greece. Stanford 1991
Herbert A Giles. Chuang Tzu. Allen & Unwin 2ed 1926
Lionel Giles. Sun Tzu on the Art of War. Luzac 1910
A C Graham. Disputers of the Tao. Open Court 1989
A C Graham. Later Mohist Logic, Ethics and Science. SOAS 1978
A C Graham. The Nung-chia "School of the Tillers." BSOAS v42 #1 (1971) 66-100
David Crockett Graham. Songs and Stories of the Ch'uan Miao. Smithsonian 1954
Marcel Granet. Festivals and Songs of Ancient China. 1919; Dutton (tr Edwards) 1932
André G Haudricourt and David Strecker. Hmong-Mien (Miao-Yao) Loans in Chinese.
    TP 2ser v77 #4/5 (1991) 335-341
David Hawkes. Ch'u Tz'u [CT]. Oxford 1959
A F P Hulsewé. Remnants of Ch'in Law [Shwèıhǔdì]. Brill 1985
Robert Ernest Hume. The Thirteen Principal Upanishads. Oxford 2ed 1931
Ian Johnston. The Mozi [MZ]. Chinese University Press 2010
Bernhard Karlgren. The Book of Documents [Shū]. BMFEA v22 (1950) 1-81
David N Keightley. The Ancestral Landscape. Institute of East Asian Studies 2000
David N Keightley. The Shang, in Loewe **History** 232-291
David N Keightley. Sources of Shang History. California 1978
Martin Kern. The Stele Inscriptions of Ch'in Shih-huang. AOS 2000
John Knoblock. Xunzi [SZ]. Stanford v1 1988, v2 1990, v3 1994
John Knoblock and Jeffrey Riegel. The Annals of Lü Buwei [LSCC]. Stanford 2000
D C Lau. Mencius [MC]. Penguin 1970

James Legge. The Ch'un Ts'ew [CC, DJ]. Oxford 1872; Hong Kong 1960

James Legge. Confucius [LY, JY]. 2ed Oxford 1893; Dover 1971

James Legge. Hsiao King [Syàu Jīng], in Sacred Books of the East, v3 Oxford 1879

James Legge. The She King [Shŕ]. Oxford 1871; Hong Kong 1960

James Legge. The Shoo King [Shū]. Oxford 1875; Hong Kong 1960

James Legge. The Works of Mencius [MC]. 2ed Oxford 1895; Dover 1970

Howard S Levy. Yellow Turban Religion and Rebellion at the End of Han. JOAS v76 #4 (1956) 214-227

Li Xueqin. Eastern Zhou and Qin Civilizations. Yale 1985

W K Liao. Han Fei Tzu. Probsthain 1939 (v1), 1959 (v2)

Walter Liebenthal. Lord Ātman in the Lao-tzu. Monumenta Serica v27 (1968) 374-380

Li Liu and Xingcan Chen. State Formation in Early China. Duckworth 2003

James J Y Liu. The Chinese Knight Errant. Chicago 1967

Michael Loewe. A Biographical Dictionary of the Qin . . . Brill 2000

Michael Loewe et al (ed). The Cambridge History of Ancient China. Cambridge 1999

Michael Loewe et al (ed). Early Chinese Texts. Society for the Study of Early China 1993

Alexander Lubotsky. Tocharian Loan Words in Old Chinese, in Mair **Bronze** 1/379-390

Luo Chia-li. Coastal Culture and Religion in Early China. UMI 1999

Victor H Mair (ed). The Bronze Age and Early Iron Age Peoples of Eastern Central Asia. 2v Institute for the Study of Man 1998

Henri Maspero. China in Antiquity. 1927, rev 1965; Massachusetts (tr Kierman) 1978

Yi-pao Mei. Ethical and Political Works of Mo Tzu [MZ]. Probsthain 1929

Frederick W Mote. Intellectual Foundations of China. 1971; 2ed McGraw 1989

William Nienhauser et al. The Grand Scribe's Records [SJ]. Indiana 1994-

Patrick Olivelle. Dharmasūtras. Oxford 1999

Patrick Olivelle. Upanisads. Oxford 1996

Ke Peng. Coinage and Commercial Development in Eastern Chou China. UMI 2000

Stuart Piggott. Horse and Chariot: The Price of Prestige, in Evans **Proceedings** 25-30

Henri Pirenne. A History of Europe. 1936; Doubleday (tr Miall) 1958

Timoteus Pokora. The Canon of Laws by Li K'uei – a Double Falsification? Archiv Orientálni v27 (1959) 96-121

Timoteus Pokora. Pre-Han Literature, in Leslie **Essays** 23-35

S Robert Ramsey. The Languages of China. Princeton 1987

Robert L Reynolds. Europe Emerges. Wisconsin 1961

Allyn Rickett. Guanzi [GZ]. Princeton v1 1985 (CCT rev 2001), v2 1998

Martha T Roth. Law Collections from Mesopotamia and Asia Minor. SBL 1997

Steven F Sage. Ancient Sichuan and the Unification of China. SUNY 1992

G B Sansom. Japan: A Short Cultural History. Appleton 2ed 1943

Ralph W Sawyer. The Seven Military Classics of Ancient China. Westview 1993

Axel Schuessler. ABC Etymological Dictionary of Old Chinese. Hawaii 2007

Edward L Shaughnessy (ed). New Sources for Early Chinese History. SSEC 1997

Edward L Shaughnessy (ed). Sources of Western Zhou History. California 1991

Shwèihŭdì: 雲夢睡虎地秦墓. 文物 1981

Laura A Skosey. Legal System and Legal Tradition of the Western Chou. UMI 1996

Jenny F So (ed). Music in the Age of Confucius. Smithsonian 2000
Jenny F So (ed). Traders and Raiders. Smithsonian 1995
John Steele. The I-li [YL]. Probsthain 1917
Carl Stephenson. Mediaeval Feudalism. Cornell 1942
Joseph R Strayer. On the Medieval Origins of the Modern State. Princeton 1970
Joseph R Strayer et al. The Idea of Feudalism, in Coulborn **Feudalism** 3-11
Nancy Lee Swann. Food and Money in Ancient China. Priceton 1950
Patricia V Symonds. Calling in the Soul. Washington 2004
Paul Mulligan Thompson. The Shen Tzu Fragments [Shv̀n Dàu]. UMI 1971
Robert L Thorp. China in the Early Bronze Age. Pennsylvania 2006
Leon Trotsky. The History of the Russian Revolution. Simon (tr Eastman) 1932
Donald B Wagner. Iron and Steel in Ancient China. Brill 1993
Arthur Waldron. The Great Wall of China. Cambridge 1990
Arthur Waley. The Analects of Confucius. Allen & Unwin 1938
Arthur Waley. The Book of Songs [Shī]. 1937; Grove (ed Allan) 1996
Arthur Waley. The Nine Songs [CT]. Allen & Unwin 1935
Arthur Waley. The Way and Its Power [DDJ]. Allen & Unwin 1934; Grove 1958
Burton Watson. The Complete Works of Chuangtzu [JZ]. Columbia 1968
Burton Watson. Records of the Grand Historian [SJ]. Columbia 3v 1993
Eugen Weber. Peasants Into Frenchmen. Stanford 1976
Susan R Weld. Chu Law in Action [Bāushān], in Cook **Defining** (1999) 77-97
Susan R Weld. The Covenant Texts from Houma, in Shaughnessy **New** 125-160
Raymond Westbrook. International Law in the Amarna Age, in Cohen **Amarna** 28-41
Richard Wilhelm. The I Ching. 2v Pantheon (tr Baynes) 1950
E C Young. A Journey from Yün-nan to Assam. Geographical Journal v30 #2
    (August 1907) 152-[196]
Zhu Qingzhi. Some Linguistic Evidence for Early Chinese Exchange Between India and
    China. Sino-Platonic Papers #66 (1995)

Passages Translated

The reference code **4:75** means Emergence Chapter 4, example #75.

Analects (p40)
1:1. **5:78**
1:13. **5:79**
2:3. **3:58**
2:12. **5:59**
2:23. **5:76**
3:1. **3:9**
3:2. **3:10**
3:4. **4:35**
3:5. **4:36**
3:6. **4:37**
4:1. **5:7**
4:2. **5:8**
4:3. **5:9**
4:4. **5:10**
4:5. **2:2, 5:11**
4:6. **5:12**
4:7. **5:13**
4:8. **5:14**
4:9. **5:15**
4:10. **5:16**
4:11. **3:2, 5:17**
4:12. **5:18**
4:13. **3:5, 5:19**
4:14. **5:20**
4:15. **5:23, 5:75**
4:16. **5:21**
4:17. **5:22**
5:1. **3:3, 5:5**
5:2. **3:4, 5:6**
5:3. **5:24**
5:9. **7:3**
5:12. **5:25**
5:18. **5:2**
5:19a. **5:3**
5:19b. **5:4**
6:3. **6:1**
6:4. **2:3**
6:5. **2:4, 6:10**
6:6. **5:26**
6:7. **7:2**
6:11. **7:1**
6:22. **6:11**

7:1. **5:32**
7:5. **5:34**
7:7. **5:27**
7:8. **5:28**
7:11. **4:19n**
7:16. **5:29**
7:17. **5:31, 7:6**
7:20. **5:33**
7:22. **5:30**
7:23. **5:35**
7:24. **7:7**
7:29. **7:5**
7:35. **7:8**
8:3. **5:36, 7:17**
8:5. **7:4**
9:3. **2:5**
9:5. **5:37**
9:11. **7:9**
9:12. **7:10**
9:13. **2:9**
9:15. **3:7**
9:17. **5:38**
9:23. **5:39**
9:24. **5:40**
9:30. **5:41**
10:2. **5:43**
10:3. **5:44**
10:7b. **2:14, 6:12**
10:8. **2:15, 6:13**
10:13. **5:45**
10:14. **5:46**
10:18. **5:47**
11:14. **2:16**
11:18a. **7:14**
12:1. **7:19**
12:2. **5:70**
12:5. **5:68**
12:7. **2:17, 3:57**
12:9. **2:18**
12:13. **3:59**
12:18. **3:30**
12:19. **3:60**
12:20. **3:45**
12:22. **5:69**

13:2. **5:57**
13:4. **2:29**
13:5. **5:71**
13:11. **3:61**
13:16. **2:30**
13:18. **3:46**
13:20. **2:21**
14:17. **4:34**
14:19. **3:36**
15:1. **5:77**
15:3. **5:74**
15:6. **5:72**
15:31. **7:22**
17:2a. **6:65**
17:2b. **6:66**
17:15. **6:2**
17:19. **6:45**
18:5. **5:92**
18:6. **5:93**

Bāushān Texts (p82)
  3:62-66

Brhad Âranyaka (p184)
3:7. **7:29**
3:9. **7:11**
4:4. **7:12**

Bronze Inscription (p18)
  1:1

Chí Inscription (p68)
  3:8

Chín Inscriptions (p215)
#1. **8:9**
#7. **8:28**

Chǔ/Hàn Chūn/Chyōu (p230)
SJ 7. **8:38**
SJ 48. **8:36**

Chǔ Tsź (p170)
  Nine Songs
    1. **6:67**
    8. **6:68**
    10. **8:39**
    11. **8:40**
  Dà Jàu. **8:35**
  Jàu Hún. **6:42**

Subject Index

In addition to subjects and key terms, this Index includes some mnemonic phrases (such as Frog in the Well) for the more prominent of the translated passages.